PRAISE FOR *I AM YOURS*

"Tender, fierce, compassionate, and wise, Reema Zaman's *I Am Yours* is a moving story about how one woman found her voice—and her power. I was enthralled by this beautiful book from the first page to the last."

—**CHERYL STRAYED**, author of the #1 *New York Times* bestselling memoir *Wild* and NYT bestsellers *Tiny Beautiful Things* and *Brave Enough*

"Zaman's voice is a fire—full-throated, wide-open, and roaring."

—***FOREWORD REVIEWS***, starred review

"This story is a phenomenal triumph of one woman's body and voice rising up and through a culture that would quiet her."

—**LIDIA YUKNAVITCH**, NYT bestselling author of *The Book of Joan*

"An eloquently searching and intelligent memoir."

—***KIRKUS REVIEWS***

"Astonishing—as light as a healing wand, and as deep as honesty can go. Reema Zaman has the voice and wisdom of a leader."

—**RENE DENFELD**, international bestselling author of *The Child Finder*

"Reema Zaman's precision and ability to capture the nuances of emotional abuse and how we process and carry trauma is remarkable."

—**ERIN KHAR**, author of *Heroine* and Managing Editor of Ravishly.com

"An important, incandescent tale about what it means to be female in this world."

—**KAREN KARBO**, international bestselling author of *The Gospel According to Coco Chanel*

"Zaman finds her voice through the journey of her obstacles, which galvanizes us to overcome our own . . . A born leader."

—**TRISHA SAKHUJA-WALIA**, CEO of BrownGirlMagazine.com

"You don't want to rescue this writer. You don't hope that somebody (or even love) 'saves' her. You feel empowered and awed by her strength; in full respect, all you want to do is wish her the limelight."

—**CHAYA BHUVANESWAR**, author of *White Dancing Elephants*

". . . a nightstand book lit from within by the audacity to cherish the Self, independent and whole."

—**JENNY FORRESTER**, author of *Narrow River, Wide Sky*

"I finished this story feeling as though my own heart had become softer, more open, and full of possibility."

—**KELLY SUNDBERG**, author of *Goodbye, Sweet Girl: A Story of Domestic Violence and Survival*

"A healing book that lifts you up . . . What a gift."

—**TERESE MAILHOT**,
NYT bestselling author of *Heart Berries*

"Reema Zaman empowers herself and others to heal from adversity and reclaim their own voice and bodies for themselves."

—**NADYA OKAMOTO**, author of *Period Power: A Manifesto for the Menstrual Movement*
and founder of PERIOD

"In her writing as in her life, Reema Zaman is a force to be reckoned with, a fierce and brave advocate of women everywhere."

—**ETAF RUM**, author of *A Woman Is No Man*

"This is a book girls and young women everywhere need and deserve."

—**GIRLS INC. OF THE PACIFIC NORTHWEST**

A Shared Memoir

I Am Yours

Reema Zaman

IDAHO

Amberjack Publishing
1472 E. Iron Eagle Drive
Eagle, ID 83616
amberjackpublishing.com

Library of Congress Cataloging-in-Publication Data
Names: Zaman, Reema, 1983- author.
Title: I am yours : a memoir / Reema Zaman.
Description: Eagle, ID : Amberjack Publishing, [2019] | Includes bibliographical references and index.
Identifiers: LCCN 2018037184 (print) | LCCN 2018050790 (ebook) | ISBN 9781948705226 (ebook) | ISBN 9781948705110 (hardcover :alk. paper)
Subjects: LCSH: Zaman, Reema. | Essayists—United States—Biography.
Classification: LCC CT275.Z34 (ebook) | LCC CT275.Z34 A3 2019 (print) | DDC
920—dc23
LC record available at https://lccn.loc.gov/2018037184

Hardcover ISBN: 978-1-948705-11-0

eBook ISBN: 978-1-948705-22-6

For Nana Bhai, who wrote my truth into being.

For you, who too has lived long years of silence. Who too has endured heartbreak, abandonment, trauma, and cruelty. Who too yearns to feel seen, heard, understood, and loved. Who too believes that humankind, we can and must do better. The love begins with us. You and I, ultimately, are the voices to alleviate the darkness. I wrote this for you. I am yours.

I am woman.
Hand me pain and I will turn it into poetry
Wound, and watch as I morph into wisdom
Every stone I will take as my opportunity to climb
Adversity is but an anniversary for my next, new talent.
I am woman.
Hurt me, and I will find a way to love you, nonetheless
For I have the power to do so.
I will love, but rest assured,
I will leave, and love from afar.
You will never know love, forgiveness, or loss
like mine.
I am woman.
Give me straw and earth;
Witness as I midwife mundanity into magic
For in my limbs I hold inherited spells
from my mother, her mother, and hers.
In my blood pulses the anthem they have taught me to sing
In my womb glows the power to birth change
In my mouth live both honey and swords
In my hands shimmers revolution.
I am woman.
I stand as one, but I exist as thousands.
Ever tied to my sisters, mothers, daughters.
Who we are. What we are. How we are.
Magnificent.
I am woman. Every day, ours.

Author's Note

Memoir is art. Every person understands, remembers, and feels truth differently. This memoir contains the truth as I feel it. I have written this book to the best of my ability, clarity of memory, integrity, humility, and compassion of spirit. In some sections, certain elements of time have been compressed in honor of narrative cohesion. With some characters, certain identifying qualities have been changed in order to preserve their privacy. These creative devices have neither touched the veracity nor tampered with the meaning of the specific and larger story.

I began writing *I Am Yours* in 2013. It sprang from my need to mend my past. Then, as the pages evolved, I realized I had entered into a larger dialogue—a shared experience of connected and collective healing, hope, and triumph. A reckoning of self, story, and society.

This book was written as a love letter and a call to action. A shared memoir.

It is time.

ACT 1

BEGIN

BEGIN

✦

Dear love,

I am 30. I sit somewhere between formed and forming. Thankfully, you are here with me. Three decades, and still you haven't left. You and I, two misfit kids who met in the loud silence, back when we were barely knee-high. Here in our own space, we speak in words only we know.

Together we haunt this house, pulling my anger room to room. It lumbers behind us like an enormous, devoted, shaggy pet. I tug it by its dirty, frayed rope, one end tied around its neck, the other around my wrist. You can see the rope rubbing raw the flesh, but neither one of us can undo the knots. At night we sleep curled on the same bed, my head on anger's warm belly, my two breaths for its one. You sit by the window, guarding until fatigue pulls you in too.

"What are you angry about?" Momma arranges her syllables carefully. "For it not working out? It was your dream, I know. But you didn't fail. Or, is it—do you miss him? Or, is it your—?"

"No, Momma. It's not one thing or person."

"Then what?"

"It's . . ." The words fall into line without me. "It's all the things that happened and all the things I have allowed. For thirty years."

Momma's face surrenders color, the tendons tense in her neck, and I silently berate myself for causing her pain.

"How are we going to . . ." Momma doesn't know how to finish her sentence.

"I don't know. I'm sorry. I just . . . I want to be."

"Be what?"

"Just *this*. I want to sit and—"

How can I explain that I simply wish to sit and speak in the stillness with you? Long ago I stopped trying to explain you to anyone. My loved ones have collected fistfuls of reasons to question my sanity. I don't need to add to the pile. Thus, you and I do what we always have. We tuck ourselves into a room and try to make sense of our pieces. For long minutes I sit staring at my hands or at my reflection, asking, *How have I become the person I am? How can I feel better?*

Even in my present state, I know anger is a side effect of pain. And I know that when one is hurt, one needs love.

From the spot where my spine meets my brain comes a clear answer and stern order: Write. Record these words. Draw forth and transcribe the lines of you and me until we forge the love I so desperately need.

Beginning where?

Ever practical, you reply, *At the beginning.*

I AM TWO DAYS shy of being born. I'm trying to be good, to let the day end before I begin the task of arriving. Momma walks the hallway back and forth like a dutiful pendulum. She is 22. Dhaka University feels deserted but hums with fierce concentration. It is exam season.

Her giant belly leads and dictates her sway. She is attached to it more than it to her, being pulled like a child tethered to an adult. She walks to alleviate the searing pain in her back and the swelling in her feet. Once the swelling ebbs, she returns to the classroom for a few blessed minutes before I force her to resume walking.

She performs this pattern for the three hours allotted to the exam. When she leans forward to write, I kick furiously, determined to arrive, begin ... and break. Momma is ... h literature. The exam ... omma is a remarkable ... ese two qualities have ... lthough she has been ... wo households—first ... l verbal exam, Mom- ... d plays and sonnets. ... h as I kick like a flag ... he graduates second

... y, a surprise for ev- ... rned with an occu- ... re mortified by the ... of her: an ambling embodiment of quashed possibility. She had been preparing for a career in teaching and writing. Now I, my unborn self, ensure her hopes remain muted, indefinitely.

“Why?” her professors ask, aghast. They know my grandfather, my nana bhai, is a civil servant and writer. “Your family is progressive. We thought your parents were different.”

“Well, my husband is highly educated,” Momma says. “And you know his family.”

They nod. Of course. Papa’s family is Zamindar, generations deep, one of the two political clans that volley power in Bangladesh. His cousin is the prime minister.

“He didn’t ask for a dowry,” says Momma. “My parents don’t have much. They didn’t think another offer of this nature would come our way. Declining was an impossibility.”

The contractions start the day after her final exams. Momma and I, we already have an understanding. But although I waited for the school year to finish, I take forty-eight hours of pain to arrive. Everyone cries, sweats, and huddles. On November 20th, 1983, at 2:15 p.m., I am born, serenaded by the hum of mosquitoes the size of a child's fingernail, under a single ceiling fan offering little relief from the heat. My cot is white, the paint peeling in petal-shaped pieces, a line of rust spreading along it like a meandering vein. At 7 pounds, 8 ounces, I am a compact baby with long limbs. My eyes are dark blue initially before they deepen to brown. Papa hasn't a car. To drive home, we borrow Nana Bhai's. Ferociously protective, terrified of germs, and suspicious of others' abilities, Papa prohibits everyone but Momma and my grandparents from touching me. He says, "Right now, the child is perfect."

As I grow, whenever Momma, Papa, and I go to doctor's appointments, we travel by rickshaw. One time, Momma's sari gets caught in the wheels. Thankfully, it's made of cotton and Momma is a mother. She tears her sari while holding me in her other arm before the wheels can suck us under. We start to fall. She jumps. We land on her left side. That wrist will forever click, sounding like a child cracking her knuckles. But we are otherwise unharmed.

Were her sari made of silk, this book would not be.

I AM 30. Try as I might, I cannot still the stenographer in my mind. The scenes arrive fully formed, sodden with color, scent, sound, taste, and texture, each memory heavy as a hunk of bread used to soak the final flavors of a meal. They need but the lightest contact with the page to transfer from past to present.

I feel everything still. All the moments you and I have soldiered through, they live potently, the past pulsing with equal, solid urgency as the present. The blunt hardness of tailbone hitting wood. The butterscotch of his voice threaded thickly with the acrid scent of tequila, his favorite. The gaping maw of hunger, how it sits inside me like a hole that is tangible. You keep repeating, *Let the memories be. Write them here.*

I am writing a book. But I haven't harbored a lifelong dream of writing a book. What I have longed for is a book I could read whose world mirrored mine. Reading it would feel like coming home. "Home" has been such an elusive shadow, one that dances over the walls, slipping out of sight as often as it slips in. Ever since I was a child, I have looked for this imaginary book. I was convinced it would be my direct, unhurried line of love. A balm for my every ache. A friend for my every flaw. A tonic for my anger. But it never arrived. Thus, now, I am trying to give myself that book.

I am 30 and I sit in my younger sister's bedroom, in a house foreign to me. I didn't grow up here, but my face can be found in photos walling the rooms of this house. Peering at my child self, I'm still shocked that I look any different when I turn my gaze toward a mirror. In every frame, the eyes remain the same. They stare into the lens, daring the world to break contact. In every photo, little gold hearts glint on my tiny ears. I remember the tantrum I threw to acquire them, a month before my second birthday. My only tantrum. I begged Momma to pierce my ears, promising I wouldn't cry.

I didn't. You and I, my love, we are our will. Should we want something, we attach ourselves to it with the surprising stubbornness of a baby gripping an adult's thumb.

"Reema! Dinner!"

"Alright, Momma," I reply, hardly loud enough for me to hear, let alone her, amidst the din downstairs of contrasting voices threaded in happy disharmony. I search myself for hunger only to realize I haven't the kind that can be sated with a meal. Still, I should join them.

Momma says from the time I switched to solid food, it was brutal trying to get me to eat. She finally found a way. She would stand me on a windowsill, point to the trees and sky outside. I'd talk to the birds, neighbors, you. Between sentences, Momma would sneak me a bite.

I rise to go toward her voice. Blood rushes then leaves my mind. Clutched in the cold vertigo, I think for the infinite time, Thank goodness you are here. My love, the fact that you are confirms I am too, however weary my tread as I walk the steps to my waiting family. I wrap myself tightly in you.

I AM 3. I know some things, but I don't know many. I know crayons don't taste like their names. A name is a word, and a word is different from a promise. I know I don't like loud. At home it is happy and quiet and then loud. Loud makes my head hurt. It is happy, quiet, loud, and then quiet again. Sometimes it is so quiet, it is loud. That hurts too.

We live in Oahu now. We moved from Dhaka last year. Papa goes to university, and Momma has a baby in her belly.

Momma is crying again. She is trying to hide, but I am too good at seeing. I am small so I can see from everywhere. There are many places to hug her because I always fit. There are many ways to love Momma. Hugs, drawings, staying asleep until 7 a.m. and going to bed at 7 p.m. There are many ways to love me because I still need help with things like tying shoelaces and making the slanted leg on the letter *R*. Momma takes care of all that to let me know she sees me.

I ask Momma who God is. She says, "The one who made all things and takes care of all of us." This makes me laugh. I don't know why Momma has two names. God and her real name, Momma. How silly. When she cries, her face folds like paper and she looks like me. She always looks like me and I look like her, but when she cries, she stops looking like Momma and looks like a baby.

Momma, Papa, and I sleep on a big mattress on the floor. I like jumping on it when Momma throws up a clean, new sheet, making a bubble for me to pop. Sometimes, you sleep here too. You share my pillow. But mostly, you sit by me. You sit through the night, and that's how I first found you. There was a noise, I woke up, and you were there. Sitting. Watching. You spoke:

I am here. I love you. I am yours.

We have one mirror on the back of the door in our bedroom. When I look into my face, you are there too. In the mirror, I sometimes make Momma's face. I put her on like makeup. Her smiling face, laughing face, crying face. I tell my face, *Go this way, jump, crouch, hide,* and it does. This is our favorite game, yours and mine. Our other favorite is singing. I know many words, but there are so many new ones every day. We put them in a song because then they will never leave. We didn't do this before and then, in tomorrow's morning, we couldn't find yesterday's words. But now we know the trick. A song makes the words sticky. Tomorrow, the words will still be here like when I peel a sticker off my arm and, the next day, find fuzzy things on the spot.

Momma's teaching me how to read and write because sometimes I have too many thoughts, flying like hummingbirds in my head. Sometimes they grow and move so quickly that they hurt. She says if I write them down I'll be okay. She teaches me all the words I want to know. We stand at our window. I point. Momma says, "Hum-ming-bird. Hi-bis-cus."

I ask Momma questions, all the time.

"Hey, Momma." I pull on the tail of her salwar kameez. "Hey, Momma, Momma, Momma. Where does water come from? Why is sweet sweet and spicy spicy? Why does it hurt when I fall? Where does pain go when I stop hurting? Is it like love and we hold it inside, waiting to feel it the next time we fall?"

She always tries to answer my questions. She talks and talks until I'm happy. I talk and talk, too, because there are so many days all the time.

This is something we learned the other day: there are *more* days. I was reading a book. I finished it. I got so sad then scared because I thought, *If books can finish, can we? Will Momma finish?* I try never to cry but I had to.

"Momma, when do we finish? When does tomorrow finish?"

"Finish what, jaan?" *My soul*, in Bengali. "Every day ends at 12, midnight."

I make a scrunched face. She didn't understand.

"When does tomorrow stop coming? When's the last one?"

She smiles. "Tomorrow will come, always. There is always a new one. And you will always be mine and I'll always be yours. That will never change or end."

I climb onto Momma. She takes me in like a deep breath. We sit as one body in our chair. I put my head on her to hear her heart. She kisses my head. I'm so happy I giggle and kiss back. That makes Momma happy, and this is my biggest favorite. I love making Momma happy. We're happy, Momma, me, and you. We love things a lot until it gets loud.

Papa tries to talk, too, but he doesn't know all the things Momma does. That's okay. Momma says that's not his job. Sometimes, I tell Papa things and he small-smiles. Small-smile is different than big-smile, laugh-smile, and happy-smile.

Sometimes he doesn't have small-smile, and he looks very sad and worried. I love him so much I get sad and worried too. Then I do a dance or a song, a giggle, jump, and clap, and then he big-smiles and laughs, and I'm so happy I'll pop like a bedsheet bubble. But I have to be careful not to do the wrong dance or sound. The other day, I twirled and my dress started flying, and everyone could see my underwear. Papa said, "Chi, chi, chi!" *Shame, shame, shame!* Bad Reema. I made the loud happen.

I try to make Papa's faces in the mirror. He has small-smile face, sad face, angry face, and big-angry face. His face changes quickly, so that is fun for me to practice. Like jumping but only with my mouth, eyes, and nose. There's a TV show I watch with Momma, with many people sitting down to play music with violins, trumpets, and drums, in a huge room with many lights. The music has no words. The sound is too beautiful to hold anything more. I make the music from the

TV when I stand in front of the mirror. I move my hands like the man standing in front of the sitting people, and I jump my face from sad to angry to big-angry, fast, fast, fast like the violins. Louder and louder and louder. *Papa, Papa, Papa, please look at me.*

One day I ask, "Momma, why do you cry?"

She makes a sound like the air has cut her. She turns away. She doesn't answer me. But Momma always does. Every question. Now she's not even looking at me. She's looking at the door. She looks sadder than any face I've seen or know how to make. I need to make her happy again.

I AM 4. I have a brother now. He is my most favorite thing. He is three years, nine months, and five days younger than me. And like me, he was born nine days earlier than the doctor said he would be. That's because my brother knows there's so much to do. He hasn't stopped moving since he arrived. He crawls, jumps, falls, everywhere. Momma has to run after him all the time. It's good that I'm good. She runs after him, and you and I play for hours, happy.

Momma now takes care of many babies in our apartment, not just my brother, from upstairs and down the street. I'm her sidekick. I know the difference between the sound of a baby crying for a hug, a bottle, a diaper change, or a nap.

Momma loves the babies. No one loves the way she does. She loves so big. She loves me, Papa, my brother, our neighbors, the Korean family whose mama teaches me piano—anyone and everyone, really.

I love everything except for school. That's kind of a lie. I love it, but I also don't. I love my books and my crayons with names like cinnamon, cotton candy, burnt sienna, and daffodil. But I hate being there. You come with me, but I hate any time I'm away from Momma. I beg my teacher to let me come home. Momma cuts fruit, cheese, and veggies into squares and hearts and puts them onto toothpicks for me, to make them pretty so I'll eat. I take them out of my pink

Tupperware and stand them like flowers. But I can't eat. I miss her too much. I want to be tightly gift wrapped in Momma. Even if someone tried with their sharpest fingernail, they wouldn't find the Scotch Tape lines to tear us apart.

At school I draw Momma a picture of her face. She's wearing a necklace of pink jewels. "Crimson rose" from my box of one hundred colors. They smell old and feel sticky but are still beautiful. On her picture I write "I love my Momma because she loves me and takes care of me." Those are two different things.

I put the picture up to my face to see if the colors smell different now that they're the shape of Momma. No. They don't smell like honey and flowers. They smell stale. So many things aren't what I hope they'll be.

I draw you too. I draw you and me. I cannot tell what you look like, so I draw how you feel. Like light. The best I can do is "buttercup yellow" in a big circle next to me.

I draw when it is loud. I draw also when I have a cold and fever. Cold and fever make my fingers and toes white. I put my hands in my mouth to make them warm, as far as they can go, up to the top knuckles. They only turn my mouth cold. I press my hands under my armpits. I fold them between my legs. It doesn't work. I cough. It hurts, and my mouth tastes like a coin.

"Why is the child coughing?" Papa is angry.

"She has a cold." Momma's voice is slow, quiet, like a lake.

"Stop it." Papa uses his hard voice. It sounds like the ground.

I order my throat to stop. The cough pushes against it, making it burn, and my eyes, wet. The place where my heart lives starts hurting. The hummingbirds fly faster. But I don't cough.

Love is love but it sits inside people differently. In Momma, love makes her soft. In Papa, love makes him hard, makes him say, Why are you coughing, stop.

It is love.

Sometimes he tells Momma, "We are lucky. We are fortunate."

Momma has a special trick. She knows how to cry without making a sound. It's like magic. Her face doesn't move.

"You should be happy," he says.

"I am," she says, over and over. "Thank you," she says, over and over.

We are happy. Momma. Me. You. We are always smiling.

I AM STILL 4. Growing up takes a long time.

"Today's our day, amanjee," Papa says. Amanjee means *little mother*. He's skipping university, and I'm skipping kindergarten. We go to McDonald's, then the playground. We play on the swings and monkey bars and he takes so many photos of me. I look like a vampire because the dentist took out my top front teeth. I've only the pointy ones. We lie on the grass and look for angels in the clouds. My skin turns warm, then hot, from the sun. I won't burn because I'm already the color of honey. When I become browner, it means I'm stronger, full of more light than before. I know Momma says there are always more tomorrows, but I already know. Today is the happiest day of my life.

I have three best friends now. You, Momma, and my brother. He is 2. We can talk about everything except for the things he isn't supposed to know. He's learning words fast because I never stop talking. His hair is softer than a feather and smells like milk, baby powder, and Johnson & Johnson's No-More-Tears Shampoo. It's gold in a bottle. His head is my favorite smell in the world, even better than Momma's head. All of us sleep on one big bed, not a mattress anymore, an actual bed. Every night I go to sleep smelling his head and listening to Momma sing.

My brother has dimples right under each cheek, not on the sides of his face but closer to his nose, above his smile. He drools all the time. When he's asleep, when he's awake, when he's laughing, when he's crying, eating, playing, running, jumping. I don't care. I love him more because he drools. I will love him always and forever. He's my baby. I get to take care of him and wipe his face. I'm like Johnson & Johnson shampoo except my name is No-More-Drool.

We watch *Sesame Street*, eating cinnamon Teddy Grahams and drinking apple juice. The cinnamon is sandy on my tongue. My brother eats three bears. He doesn't eat the last one. I finish my four.

"Can I eat yours?" He drools, smiles, and nods.

Some of the drool falls off in a string and drops onto his tummy, which always pokes out from under his T-shirt. We giggle. I reach for the last bear. I bite off the right arm, then the left. Momma checks on us.

"Reema! You don't take your brother's food! That's not nice! That's selfish." Her voice is loud but not angry. She sits beside me on the carpet. "No, no, jaan. We don't take things from one another."

"But Momma, he said yes! I asked him."

She smiles, frowns a little. "Really?"

I nod many, many times. My head will come off like my Barbie's.

"Yes, Momma. Honest. He did."

I cry. I don't like seeing Momma sad, especially with me. This is the worst moment of my life. I will cry and die forever.

"I believe you." She kisses my head, pulls me onto her lap. She pulls my brother in too. We sit three as one, under our blanket of crumbs, kisses, and drool.

"Momma, why am I a selfish? What does it look like?"

"Selfish isn't a fish, jaan. It isn't a thing you can see. It's something you feel. Meanness inside a person that makes them unkind toward another person. You do the mean thing because you're thinking about yourself and don't care that you're hurting someone else. But the other person feels very sad."

"Momma, I never want to make sad people."

"I know, babu." Babu means *baby*. "You're only kind. You'll make happy people."

She rocks us like a chair. Momma gets us more juice and two more bears each. One of my brother's bears is missing an arm. I swap it with one of mine. The other I offer to Momma, but like always she says, "No, thank you." She eats very little because eating makes a person fat. My brother makes paste out of his bears and wears it like lipstick. This makes us laugh so he laughs too. He starts to hiccup from laughing so much. Laughing is my favorite thing he does. Sometimes I poke his belly to make a giggle pop out and his dimples pop in. Sometimes he hiccups so hard he tumbles over to his side, then laughs and hiccups more. Oh, his laugh is the best thing ever. If life has only one poem, I want it to be this.

That night I have the first dream I actually remember. In my dream I am on *Sesame Street* as Ernie and Bert's guest friend for the day. The letter of the day is *L*. We bake lemon cookies and talk about love. They ask for my thoughts.

"If you give someone the bigger half of your cookie, you know you love them. Now, they know it too."

Ernie and Bert nod.

I wake up. I'm between Momma and my brother. You're sitting by the window. On the other side of my brother is Papa. He's snoring. The garbage truck beeps its special beep outside. My brother wakes up, jumps out of bed, shouting, "Dump tuck, dump tuck!" His favorite word and favorite sound. Momma and Papa wake up. We laugh and point outside for my brother, because he's pointing and he likes when we do it too. He loves, so we love. Love, like a song, is sticky like that.

On the bus, my brother and I share a seat. On the carpet, he has Kermie, I have Miss Piggy. Outside, he has a puddle he sits in to collect worms after it rains, and there I am like Johnson & Johnson.

MOMMA SAYS WHEN I feel things, I feel them big. When I'm happy, it's all people see. When I'm quiet, it's all people hear. "You're a very serious girl, aren't you?" Momma says, watching. I tell her, "I'm just thinking."

When I get angry, it's all people feel. It always happens for the same reason: if a person hurts someone I love, I will hurt them back. One time, we were playing outside and one kid knocked my brother down. I sat on that kid and screamed in his face, one long note.

My hands and feet are always cold, but like my head, my heart is hot. My heart doesn't feel like it's filled with hummingbirds—it *is* one. I put my hand over my brother's heart. His beats so quickly too. When Papa is asleep, I place my hand carefully on his chest. His heart is slower.

Momma and Papa invite two friends to our house, a man and a woman. Papa and the man play cards at the dining room table. They play for a long time, laughing, talking. Suddenly, the man slams his cards on the table, laughs, and hits Papa on the arm. I feel hot. My brother and I are playing on the floor. I jump onto the man. I hit him and hit him and hit him on his stomach, on his chest, on his shoulders.

"You will not hurt my Papa!"

Papa pulls me off the man, who is too surprised to say or do anything. I cry in Papa's lap, hiding.

"Shh, shhh, amanjee," he says. "It's okay. He didn't hurt me. We were just joking around."

The man rubs his shoulder. "She sure loves her Papa," he says.

Papa rocks me until I calm down.

FEEL

FEEL

✦

I AM FINALLY 5.

"Reema, come line up!" My kindergarten teacher waves her hand. I hurry my work. I scoop the beetles, cupping them carefully. My arm travels up and down the crack where the beetles live, on the edge of the playground. My OshKosh B'gosh overalls have a lot of pockets. Perfect to carry beetles home. If they stay here, the other kids kill them for fun.

"Reema!"

I run over. I go to Queen Ka'ahumanu Elementary School. Most of the other girls are higher than my head. They are so pretty. They have long hair, gold like my Barbie. Their hair is straight. My Barbie's is curly because her box says she's a rock star. Momma says it's because this is the '80s. I don't know what that means.

I am not pretty. I'm the only one that looks like me. Which is how it is for everyone but especially if you're me. The other girls are Hawaiian, with caramel skin, brown eyes, dark black hair, or they're white, with creamy skin, blue eyes, gold hair. Every girl makes friends with those who look like her.

This is why I'm not allowed to be friends with the goldilocked girls. That's what they said. It's all right. I have you. They all take ballet together after school. I wish so much I could take ballet, but I don't think we have the money. Also, I don't think ballet is for Bangladeshi girls. One time, for show-and-tell, four of the girls brought in matching toys: ballerinas that live inside little pink music boxes. Each box opens like a present, a beautiful song that sounds like rain starts playing, and the ballerina spins. Slowly. I don't have one. I make one in my mind.

At naptime, everyone sets their mats near their friends, like island clusters. My island doesn't have a place. I move.

Today, my mat is next to the prettiest goldilocked girl. Her face is the kind of special that makes me look and want and always remember. Her arms and legs are long and thin. I'm round, small, brown. A pebble. Not something to remember. When I look at her, I feel lonely and little, like the extra button sewn on the inside of a shirt or pocket. Momma says it's there in case the other ones go on to bigger, brighter things. Then this hidden button gets to be a button. Until then, it hopes. Sometimes, when I feel shy or scared, from not knowing the correct English word or joke, I touch the button on the inside of my pocket.

I smile at the goldilocked girl. She smiles back, and my heart becomes a blur.

"You're pretty," I whisper.

She sticks out her tongue. It's the pinkest tongue I've ever seen. I want to pinch it, bite it, make it mine. She giggles. Her friends giggle. She looks away.

It's fine. Meanness doesn't hurt my feelings. But it's wrong. Later, when the girls are playing dress-up in the Cinderella castle, I go to her cubby and steal the crystal pendant she brought in for today's show-and-tell. Her papa gave it to her for her birthday. I hide it in my backpack, in the pocket that is the safe one.

I go to the reading nook to read *Corduroy*, one of my favorite books. It's about a bear who needs to find his missing button before he can have a home. He needs to be perfect. I cry every time I read it; I don't know why.

That night, Momma does laundry. She finds my overalls. And the beetles. Her eyebrows vanish into her bangs.

"You wanted to save them, again?" She stretches each word the way you wish you could a Sunday so Monday wouldn't come as quickly.

I nod.

Momma smiles. Then her face gets crinkly. "Have you made friends yet?"

"I *have* a friend."

She's going to say something but stops. I don't use your name because I don't know it.

I wait three days. I sneak the crystal back into Goldilocked Girl's cubby. I know I scared her. I feel bad. But not too bad.

It's Saturday now. We go to the store. Papa always says, "Buy a new toy." I look. I feel silly.

"I don't need anything else, Papa."

I have Miss Piggy. I have Love-a-Lot, my Care Bear. I have my magic wand. It's made of glass that's actually plastic. Don't tell anyone. There's magic inside. It makes the glitter move up and down like a lazy dream. Best of all, I have you. I cannot see you or touch you but I know you are always here, the way I know the sun can be found behind any storm cloud. Waiting to warm me.

In the car home, Papa says we are moving. Faraway to the other side of the Earth, to Bangkok. Please come with us. I will find you a window to sit by. We are moving because Papa got a job with the United Nations. Papa is a new word I've learned: an economist. United Nations sounds like a place where many small countries come together to make a big country, but it's actually like a club. Or, a big company. They meet, talk, and find ways to make the world a better place. That's what Papa told me.

Momma packs half our things to take, half to give to Goodwill.

Papa takes the wrong pile to the store.

I have never seen Momma angry before. I cry. I'm so sad Momma is angry, I forget to miss my toys.

"Momma, it's okay."

She sighs. "I know, Reemani." That's her special name for me. "As long as we have each other, we have so much. We can send a little of this to others. Somewhere, a little girl is so happy because you shared. She'll take good care of Love-a-Lot. Let's send her a hug as a thank-you."

We hug. Momma, my brother, and I, we sit as one body in our chair until we feel our hearts tick together. I make a goodbye card for Goldilocked Girl. It says, "Thank you. Best of Luck." That's what adults say to one another.

Papa flies to Bangkok. Momma, my brother, you, me, we fly to Dhaka. We'll live with Nana Bhai and Naan, my grandpa and grandma, for six months. Momma's doing more school; I'll go to school too. In Dhaka, the electricity goes off more days than it stays on. Momma shows us how to make birds with our hands held in front of a candle. Her bird is biggest, mine, medium, my brother's, the littlest.

I AM 6. We live in Bangkok now, with Papa. It's hot like Oahu and Dhaka, but each place is hot in a different way. Oahu has a breeze and smells like the sea. Dhaka is so hot and humid it's like sitting inside a giant mouth. Bangkok is humid, too, but less so. There's always sunshine, except during the rains. The trees are a mix of Oahu and Dhaka. Palm, coconut, mango.

I miss our family in Dhaka. If you weren't here, it'd be lonely.

Our apartment is huge now. In Oahu, our car would cough every mile, and everything we owned used to belong to someone else. Now, we have new clothes, and school uniforms too: white shirts and blue shorts or a pleated skirt. We have a car called a Mercedes-Benz. It is whiter than a smile. We have to be very careful with the way we sit inside it.

6 is much bigger than 5, so I know more things. Making faces makes wrinkles. Good girls don't do that. We also don't complain. It's much better to listen, and watch. Then you can learn people.

It's also good to be ladylike. We have a secret phrase Papa learned at boarding school called stiff upper lip. Our code we use in public is "sulip sulip," rhyming with tulip. I behave, he smiles. I dance ballet only I know, tiptoe, change, slide, dip, bow, smile, hush, that's not nice, hush, that's not pretty, hush, that's not good.

Every Saturday I have a special class at home. I wake up at 6 a.m., brush my teeth, and put on a salwar kameez. I cover my hair with my orna, a veil. My teacher arrives at 7 a.m. I'm learning to read Arabic. A good Muslim has to read the Quran thirty times in a lifetime to make it to heaven. My teacher is an old lady with a voice like smoke. We give her tea and a plate of fruit, nuts, and biscuits. I learn all the letters and sounds and read aloud for an hour. I recite the passages she assigns me to memorize. I don't know what the words and sentences I'm saying mean. I know a few of them, like Allah and insha Allah. But that's about it.

"What do the words mean?"

"It doesn't matter," says my teacher. "Just make sure to read them at least thirty times. God doesn't care as long as you follow the rules."

"But God *is* care and cares about everything. What does the book say about that?"

For an answer, she grunts. I tuck my questions into the ballerina box in my mind. My teacher spits an orange seed onto her plate, sucks her teeth, coughs. She has two fake teeth, way in the back of her mouth. They look like real molars but with sharp, silver feet. Every Saturday, she eats, then takes out one of her teeth to floss the others. She sucks on the silver feet. *Sss sss sss.* I read. *Sss sss sss.* I recite.

It's Ramadan. We go to the mosque. Papa and my brother are going to sit in the front of the room, where only men and boys are allowed. Momma and I will sit in the back with the other women and girls, behind a curtain that comes down from the ceiling, reaching all the way to the floor. Like a wall.

I won't like being away from my brother. He won't like being away from Momma and me. He starts crying.

"No," I say to Momma and Papa. "It's not okay. I don't want to."

Momma's quiet. Papa says, "Eeesh," which in Bengali means *ugh*. He sounds like a balloon losing air.

"No!" I try to make my body heavy but it doesn't work. They pull me into the mosque. Momma carries my brother, hands him to Papa when it's time to separate. I'm so angry.

The building has a ceiling curved like an egg. There are lovely patterns everywhere, of diamond shapes and a new shape that looks like a fingernail clipping. Momma says it's a crescent. The tiny shapes are in different colors, put side by side to make a bigger picture. Momma says this is a mosaic, a painting without paint, with small pieces of glass or stone. There are no faces or bodies in this mosaic.

"Why not, Momma?"

"Because it's not allowed. Only God can create human faces. Humans cannot."

We draw faces all the time. I don't like the giant room without faces but filled with hidden faces, with the big feet of men peeking through the space beneath the curtain. I miss my brother so much. I know he's scared without Momma and me.

At home, I tell Momma, "It doesn't make sense. He's my best friend. If he cries, he'll need Johnson & Johnson."

"I know, jaan. Play with your brother."

She leaves the room. He and I play one of our favorite games. We sit in our chair and hold our encyclopedia of animals, half on his lap, half on mine. We're trying to learn all the birds, lizards, fish, and animals in the world. Momma comes back to our room. We get up off our chair. She sits in the warm spot we made for her. We climb on her like pink-bottomed baboons, bush-tailed possums, and spider monkeys, because we know their names now. We tickle her. She laughs. It sounds like she has caught a cold since she left the room. She puts kisses all over us. We nuzzle into her like koalas, chinchillas, and gibbons. Her cheeks and chin taste like salt. But she still smells like honey and flowers.

We don't ever go to the mosque again.

I AM 7. Papa's reading the newspaper on the family room couch. It's one big room. I'm at the dining table doing math homework. I love math. I love formulas and patterns.

"Papa, why do we have war?"

He looks up from the paper, turns my way.

"Is it because of pride?" I ask. "Maybe we think our differences are so different and that makes people uncomfortable and scared of one another."

If it were Monday, he would've smiled and said, "Oh jaan, that may be true. What a mind you have. One day, you will be a world-renowned voice. You are my treasure."

I'd reply, "Thank you, Papa. It's because I am your daughter."

But I've spoken on the wrong day. It's Tuesday, so I'm not his treasure.

He sighs. "Stop asking questions. Just do your homework."

I read a story by Edgar Allan Poe called "The Pit and the Pendulum." I borrowed it from Nana Bhai. A pendulum goes back and forth. Although I know the pattern, I hold my breath, waiting for what will happen.

I hate when I forget the safe day from the bad. Stupid Reema. I know better.

Maybe war does come from pride. That and other invisible things that make the pendulum go back and forth while you hold your breath. Maybe that's why grown-ups keep saying, "History repeats itself." We go back and forth, believing our differences are so different, that the space between us is too big to walk nicely. So instead, we war.

I cannot shush my mind, especially my questions. Why is there a curtain? Why are some people starving and others not? Why does pigment matter when all flesh is the same color? Why do women speak less than men? Why does love make some people hard while others soft? A question I've stopped asking is: "Momma, why are you crying?" It's the only time she lies to me. It seems that whatever the questions are, they make people angry or sad. So, I swallow them for safekeeping, like a locket I need to hide. I try the questions only on you. You help unlock. We find words.

"Papa?" I try once more.

"Do your work."

I AM 8. Like you and I, my brother and I are best friends but different. He's small and thin, thinner than I was at his age. His face is so beautiful. His eyes are shaped like teardrops lying on their side. My hair is rough while his is so shiny, like the sun has kissed his head. He likes to chew on his lip or bite his fingernails down to the skin. Sometimes his fingertips bleed. He can draw dinosaurs now and loves LEGOs. We build spaceships and intergalactic kingdoms. They float in space where it's quiet.

Every day, Momma drops me off at my school, then him at his. She walks around nearby, a few hours, before returning to sit with him during lunchtime. It's the only way he'll eat.

Momma's always been love. Every piece of her and what she does for us, she learned on her own. Naan is nice to us kids but hard on everyone else. Especially Momma and Nana Bhai. Momma has a younger brother, my uncle, and a sister, my aunt. My uncle is four years younger than Momma, my aunt, fourteen years younger.

Momma raised them. She packed their lunches, gave them baths, cleaned their cuts, read them stories. My uncle says the worst day of his life was when Momma was married off.

Naan used to hide a safety pin in her sari for when my uncle was naughty. She would poke him with it until he bled. For Momma, there was slapping, and of course, yelling. That isn't anything big in Bangladesh, especially if you're the oldest daughter. Insults and being scolded are part of what we know is ours, like our name, the thickness of our waist, the length of our shadow, the color of our skin.

Naan would say Momma was too dark-skinned to be beautiful. In Bangladesh, it goes skin, hair, body, in deciding whether a girl is pretty. In Bengali, there are different ways to say dark-skinned. There's kalo, which means *black*, or moilah, which means *soiled* or *muddy*.

I'm lucky because Papa is fair-skinned. This is one of many reasons Momma was lucky to be chosen by his family, despite her dark skin. I'm light-skinned because of him. When they arrange my marriage, I have a good chance of being liked. I must make sure I don't get ugly or fat as I grow up.

I am careful about that. I don't eat much and never take seconds. I make mistakes though. I hate myself when I do. I love sweet things, and Momma's a wonderful baker. She makes cookies, cakes, pie. My favorite is apple. I imagine it tastes like America. Sometimes, when everyone is sleeping except for you and me, I tiptoe into the kitchen to sneak a tiny sliver. I like it warmed up, but I make sure to stop the microwave before the timer beeps so no one will hear. Only the purr beforehand and the scent of cinnamon confess I was there.

I watch Momma give, give, give. Why is this her story? Through it all, she is kind, sweet, patient. How can she not run out of love?

I know it's us kids who must fill her. We curl around her like wings, hints of open skies. We are small, but maybe we can be the stories Momma wanted to write. I hope we are enough.

I AM 9. I have glasses now, like Papa. I love them. They make me look smart.

Momma and Papa make their rounds in the diplomat's social calendar. There are so many parties, all the time. We kids are invited as well. I'm happy you're always nearby because these parties are important and make me nervous. During the day, Papa wears a suit, Momma wears casual Western clothes, and we have our school uniforms. For the parties, Papa wears a kurta, Momma a sari, I a salwar kameez, and my brother trousers and a button-down shirt. Everyone marvels at how mature and well-behaved I appear.

I smile, say thank you, and talk about human rights, culture, and religion. I ask questions. People love it when you ask them for their opinion—on anything. Makes them feel special.

It's Friday night. Momma and Papa have a party to go to, and this time we're going to stay home with the maid.

I hear them. Their door is closed. My brother and I are in my room, next to theirs. I hear Papa yelling, Momma crying.

I cannot sit. Anger makes me hot. I leap off the bed, run to meet Papa as he exits their room. As usual, the house is dark. I root my feet into the polished floor and stretch my spine as tall as it'll go. He looks down at me.

"Kee?" In Bengali, *What*?

"Why do you do that?"

"You don't know anything," he replies, moving to walk away.

"I'm asking to know."

"Chup!" he yells. *Silence*. He walks away.

"I will never have an arranged marriage."

He stops. Turns.

I stare.

He frowns. I keep staring until he looks away. He turns the corner into the living room.

I stomp back to my room, furious with myself. Stupid girl. I've made more trouble for Momma.

Stupid, stupid, stupid.

I turn around and there's my brother. He's crying. I half carry, half herd him into my room, shut the door. He uses his sturdy little arms to scoot himself up onto the edge of my bed. He sits, his legs dangling against the side. He cries, wiping his nose with the back of his hand. I kneel in front of him and wipe his face with my palms. I fan my hands the way I do to wash my face, except now, they smooth his face dry. His cheeks are so soft, like the skin on a peach. He looks at me, doesn't say anything. He starts to chew on his lip. He does that when he's sad, scared, or nervous. It makes his dimples pop.

"Everything's gonna be fine."

He nods. His tears gather his eyelashes into little spikes, like rays of a cartoon sun.

I gently tug at his lip with my thumb. The small tug makes his lip slip out from under his teeth. He smiles, I smile. The little tug is something we do.

"It'll be okay."

He nods. He breathes the kind of breath that is three short breaths stuffed into one.

I get our animal encyclopedia from the shelf and sit next to him. We open it up on our laps, play his favorite game, choosing which animal and which country we like best and want to travel to one day when we are big and we can go anywhere we want.

Momma comes in, glowing in her sari, gold jewelry, and makeup, and I understand now that the word "breathtaking" was invented to describe women like her.

"Momma, you're so beautiful."

"Thank you, jaan. We're leaving now. We'll be gone just a little bit."

She bends so her face is our height. She sprinkles kisses all over, light ones so her lipstick doesn't smudge. We giggle. She smells like a wish come true.

She sets up *The Sound of Music* for us to watch. You and I have learned every song. Our favorite line is "Let's start at the very beginning, a very good place to start." I love the von Trapp kids. They want their home to feel like a home. I love Maria's story. She puts her hope in a trunk and travels, searching for a place to anchor her heart. And Captain von Trapp looks like he could save the world; he is what handsome looks like. When he kisses Maria, I blush. I've never seen Momma and Papa kiss.

My brother and I fall asleep on the couch. I wrap around him like a shell holding the ocean's song. He smells exactly as when he was a baby. Sweat, sunshine, salt, and No-More-Tears Shampoo.

Momma and Papa come home. He carries my brother to bed. She carries me. It's Saturday already.

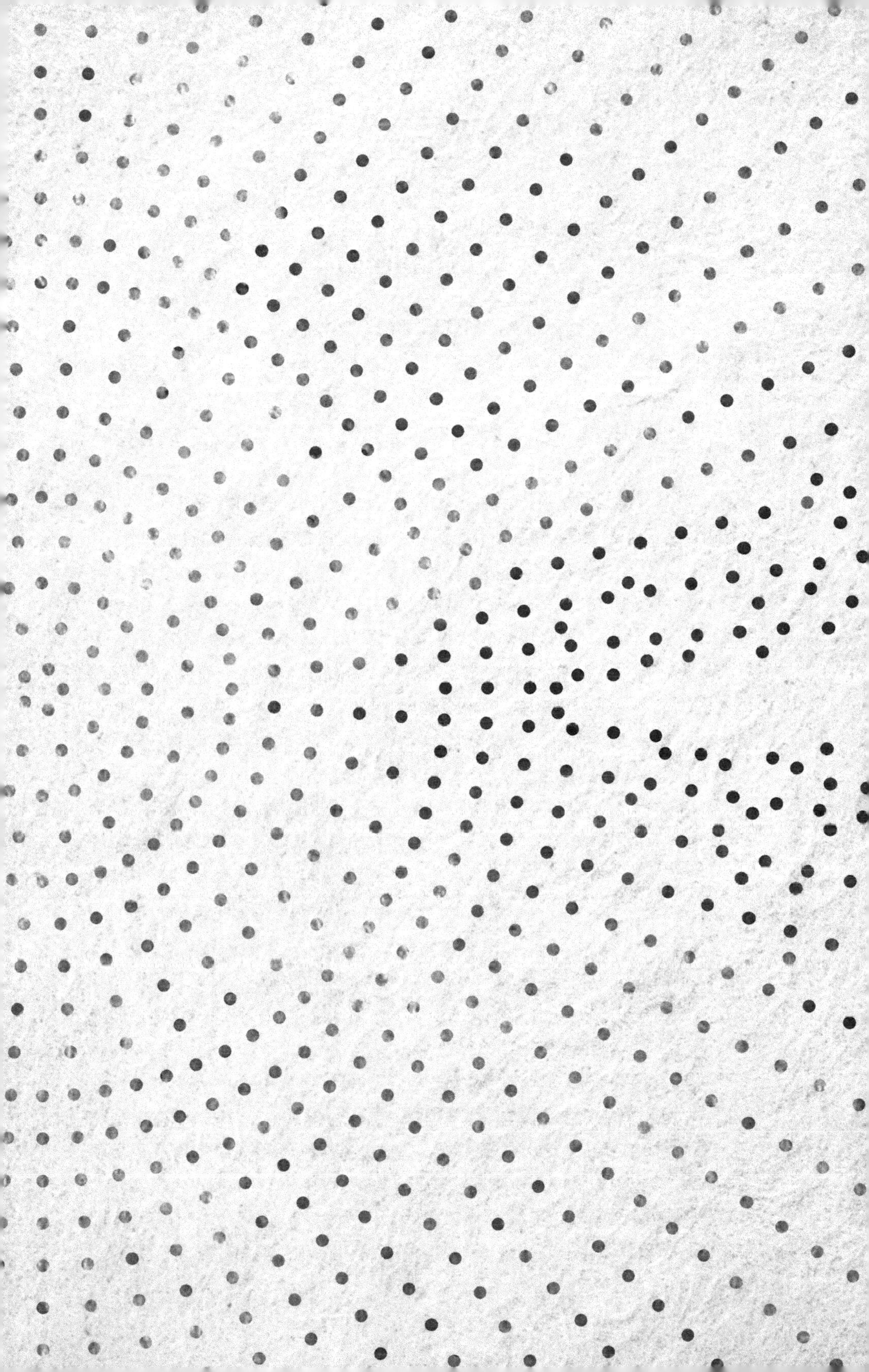

SEE

SEE

✦

I AM 10. After my family, I love books the most. I can read anywhere, anytime, ignoring noise and people. I dive, swim, almost drown in words.

My favorite books are the *Anne of Green Gables* set, the *Sweet Valley Twins*, and *The Baby-Sitters Club*. Their world is so sweet. I also love dystopian stories, like *This Perfect Day*, *The Giver*, *1984*, and anything by Ursula Le Guin. I've read "The Ones Who Walk Away from Omelas" so many times, I've memorized it. The story of an idyllic town where the people hide a specific child. Keeping him hidden allows them their beauty and peace. The ones who dare to light the secret are banished.

The magic of books is they awaken empathy. They teach you how to feel for strangers, imaginary and real. I forget myself and live for this not-so-other person, care when they care, hurt when they hurt, love when they love.

One book I really want to read is one that feels like my life. I haven't found it yet, a book that fits me perfectly. There are so many out there. There must be a book made for me.

Papa works very hard. He has to travel often and is always tired and anxious. He reads a lot for work. I wish he had the time to read about people as humans, though, and not as numbers. It would help him feel better and become better at feeling.

I have a journal now. I write in it almost every day. I love that this is but one day, one page, and there is always another to come. I write the way I talk to you. I write about us, Momma, Papa, my brother, about things I see. It helps me settle the hummingbirds in my mind. The more I write, the clearer I speak. I'm not pretty, so I can at least be smart. Sometimes I write fiction. Not all my stories are good; some feel like music while others like static. I carefully tear out the ones that sing to turn into books, stapled and hole-punched. Momma shows me how to braid yarn through the holes and tie bows to hold my words together. They have to be perfect.

"They don't, Reemani."

"Yes they do, Momma."

She smiles, disagreeing, and you do, too, but we all know it's futile. I'll always want to be better. If I stay up late to write or do homework, Momma sits on our chair with a book and a cup of tea until she falls asleep. The Darjeeling turns bitter and cold. Sometimes I stay up through the night to make sure every sentence and margin is just right. In the morning, sometimes Momma is back in their room. Sometimes she's still in our chair. Her tea will have a thin layer of dust on the surface.

Sometimes, grown-ups ask me what I write about.

"Life."

They laugh. "What do you know about living? You're a kid."

I AM 11. I have four best friends now. I have a sister! Born ten years, eleven months, and two days after me, and like both her siblings, nine days before her due date. While mine is a face of frank plainness, one that will never warrant a second glance, she is born perfect, with cheeks full and pink and eyes to incite riots. I hold her, overwhelmed with love and love's partner: the fierce resolve to keep her safe and pure for as long as possible.

On her we lavish every toy and luxury imaginable. Our lives are very different now from when I was born. Dhaka, Oahu, Bangkok, third-, first-, second-world. When my parents take her for doctor's appointments, it's in the glistening white Mercedes, not in a rickshaw painted with Bollywood scenes. We give her only the good emotions, like saving the last, most delicious bite for a favored friend.

My brother and I attend the same school now. It's extremely expensive, half the tuition paid for by the UN. A few months in, right after my sister is born, I have my first period. Momma gives me a card. Written inside is "Congratulations! I love you so much and am so proud of everything you are. You're a young lady now!"

According to the school nurse, I'm the first girl in my grade to get her period. Yay for me. I haven't a clue what the fanfare is about. It's absolutely awful, and it doesn't help my already abysmal social standing. Aside from you, I have very few friends. You're the only one I can talk to. The other kids think I'm weird. They don't speak or think like me.

All the other girls are grouped in cliques, tightly contained and guarded. And the boys are so mean. There is nothing a boy hates as much as an ugly smart girl. The other day, one of the popular boys snatched my glasses and threw them to a waiting friend. He and his friends quickly formed a circle around me, lobbing my glasses back and forth. I spun in the middle, the world a blur.

When things like that happen—and they happen often—I don't tell Momma or Papa. They're too busy in each other.

It's fine. You're here.

Momma is sweet. She asks me often if I have made friends. I smile and reply, "I have the voice in my head." She smiles, too, whenever I say this. She marvels every day how mature and lovely I am, even though my body and face are exploding. In Bangkok, all the women are tiny. I'm grosser and bigger by the second. I can *see* myself grow. It's disgusting. I'm not chubby. I'm fatfatfat.

Regardless, I love Bangkok. The sun is always bright, except during the monsoon season. Even then, the rain is fun. Songkran is the festival of water, to wash away the past and welcome a clean future. Everyone streams into the streets like confetti to dance for days. Thai culture weaves gratitude into every festival, ritual, and holiday. It's the beautiful, calm lightness of Buddhism mixed with a mentality of abundance. There's a saying: "Mai pen rai." It means *Never mind, just go with the flow.*

The one thing I don't enjoy is the nightlife. It doesn't stay confined to a time or place. Prostitutes and call girls are everywhere. Papa says, "Where there is a demand, human beings will supply." Being an economist, it's one of his favorite lines.

This summer, like every summer, we visit our family in Dhaka. While I love seeing our family, I hate hearing them say, "That's not allowed." That's not allowed because I am a girl. In the public parks, boys and men jog, run, ride bikes, and play soccer, while girls and women attract stares and catcalls if we try. I can't wear the same clothes I can in Bangkok, although my brother can. I have to cover my chest with a veil, although I don't have anything that can qualify as breasts. At the market, Momma and I meet a woman whose face was melted from acid thrown by her fiancé because she wanted to continue going to college after they got engaged.

I can still talk as much as I want when around Momma's family. But I can tell, by the way my older female relatives behave, that soon I'll have to quiet down. In a mixed group, out of respect, decorum, and habit, men talk more, while women stay quiet, smile, nod, serve tea, and corral children. I love Bangladesh. But I hate being a girl in Bangladesh.

The second we land at Dhaka airport, I start to feel different, though it's not the kind of foreignness I feel in Bangkok, or felt in Oahu. While I don't look Hawaiian, Caucasian, or Thai, I don't look

Bangladeshi either. Papa's family has Mongolian and Persian blood, while Momma's side has Indian and Afghan. In every country, we're ambiguous and foreign. Simply being a girl guarantees I'll be stared at. Add in my appearance, and the staring rises in pitch.

As the car pulls away from the airport, it's sucked into the traffic that traps the entire city in smog. Then, we meet the beggars.

Amputees. Polio survivors. Children.

Children. Children. Children. Babies on their mothers' hips, sucking deflated breasts, clutching at their sari and hair with hands so thin and dry they look like claws. Their skeletal heads, swollen bellies, shrunken limbs, sapped of life, sear into my heart.

"Why is it like this, Papa?"

He and Momma explain it's a cycle. Our lack of resources and education gives way to unemployment and poor family planning. Poor family planning leads to overpopulation. Overpopulation makes for poverty. Poverty births beggar children. Beggar children grow to be uneducated teenagers. Uneducated teenagers succumb to unemployment and poor family planning. It's a relentless nightmare that feeds and breeds itself.

"That's why education is freedom, amanjee," says Papa.

I nod. "Thank you, Papa."

The beggar children call us Ama, Aba, Apa, Bhaya. *Mother, Father, Sister, Brother*. "Eektu poisha thaan?" *Spare a few coins?*

The car moves in miniscule spits because of the crowds. A ten-mile drive takes four hours. During that time, choking on the stench of overrun sewers, we hear everyone's story. They come to the window, pressing their hands, faces, bodies, hearts, hope, hunger, thirst against the pane. We hear how he was orphaned by his parents because he was the youngest of too many children. We hear how she was sold to a brothel and ran away to live in the streets. She sells jasmine garlands now, will you please buy one for two cents? We hear how her husband died in a garment factory fire; now she and her children are homeless. The baby on her hip is the youngest of seven. His belly is taut with parasites, and his head looks enormous on his withered, sunburnt, naked body. His head bobs on his neck as he nods off from the fatigue of trying to stay alive. Each one of these stories lands like a gash. But what is just as painful is that each one is unsurprising.

"Momma, what can we do? Can we give them money? Food? Who do we call to—"

"I'm sorry, jaan. It's just how it is." Her face is etched with sorrow.

It's just how it is. The sentiment I hate most after that's not allowed.

I love Bangladesh more with each year. We simply refuse to die. We survive despite an exhaustion that never ebbs, heat that never lifts, poverty as stubborn as tar, and floods more faithful than our leaders. When I ask Momma, "Why are some people poor while others aren't?", although she tries, she can't give me an answer that makes sense enough to silence my mind. So I lay every bit of information, memory, feeling, and thought on paper, like clues to an end, trying to connect them into a constellation leading home.

Every year, we visit for at least a month, which sometimes stretches to two. Both Momma and Papa's families live in Dhaka. We stay with Papa's older brother and sister-in-law for a few days, but the rest is spent with Momma's family. Naan, Nana Bhai, and my uncle and aunt. I rush to Nana Bhai like a baby turtle to the sea. Sometimes, he reads me his short stories. He has written one with me in mind, called "Shadhina." Shadhina is my name in the story, meaning *she who leads*, taken from shadhinota, Bengali for *independence*. The tale takes place on a train. An older man tries to charm Shadhina but she holds her ground by debating every point he throws. When Nana Bhai reads, his voice curls around me like a blanket.

I love Momma's family. Everyone is vibrant, kind, and so caring. We live the way that's traditional in Bangladesh. All in the same apartment building. Each floor houses a different grandparent, aunt, uncle, and many cousins. It is happy, organized disorder. We snack, nap, and play on every floor, and eat guavas and mangos from our trees in the courtyard.

Traditionally, men and women live separate lives in Bangladeshi culture. At gatherings, except for the very young children, we sit split by gender. Like in the mosque. We're separated so we don't think about sex or get tempted to do something. It's nonsensical; being divided by gender emphasizes the exact things that are forbidden. And it makes you think sex, flirting, and marriage are the only ways girls and boys can interact. Thankfully, Momma's family is progressive, so we don't sit by gender in Nana Bhai's home.

Nana Bhai and Momma's uncle are the two patriarchs. They have little money but are wealthy with love. Nana Bhai is so effusive with hugs and affection, for all of us. Momma's brother, my uncle, is the same. Being near this love is the best part of our summers. Like holding my cheek to a lamp when I'm cold, to remind my skin what warmth feels like.

I love, too, that during these visits with her family, Momma gets a break. In Bangkok, Momma receives the full brunt of Papa's moods. I hear the thunder behind doors. I see the glares searing the air. She's always scared, always quiet. She looks tightly pinched, like an eyelash caught between forefinger and thumb before it's allowed to become a wish.

No one knows how things are back in Bangkok. Momma doesn't want her parents to feel afraid, sad, or like they have to do something. Divorce is utterly shameful in our culture. Besides, if she left Papa, where would we go? She's on a spousal visa in Bangkok, doesn't have an income, and my grandparents wouldn't be able to take us in.

Hopefully, my sister will soften things. Papa loves her so much. We all do. Babies are easy to love. They aren't complicated or willful.

I know Papa loves me. But he rarely hugs me anymore, and never in public. He pats, on the shoulder or head. It's his conditioning. Still, I feel dirty, in a way that can't be cleaned, for my mud comes from being a girl.

I have started to look more like Momma. I'm fat, she's thin, but if I turn my head the right way in the mirror, I can see her sometimes. And my voice sounds like hers, we walk the same, we like the same things. Lately, on the days he's happy with Momma, Papa's happy with me. On the days he doesn't like Momma, he doesn't like me.

I wish there was a book that could explain Papa to me. I read authors from every country, every age, dead and alive. I'm reading *A Wrinkle in Time* right now, by Madeleine L'Engle. I love it madly. But I still want that one book that could hold, hear, and answer my whole heart.

When we stay with Papa's family, I feel alien to my uncles, aunts, and cousins on this side. I can sense our mutual longing to travel the space between us and our frustration that we don't know how. While Momma's family is cheerful, Papa's is very somber.

There is one cousin who makes me wary, like an approaching group of boys. He's exactly twenty years older. A few female cousins warned me about him. "Stay away from him," they say. They tell me what he does and has done for years. He has an eerie singsong voice and always says the same thing.

"Hello Reema, how are you-oo? What a pretty girl you are."

I don't know if he's teasing, taunting, or flirting. Maybe they're one and the same. I've known to stay away from him for years, to leave any room he enters, to shift away when he sits close, to break his hold when he hugs, ever since I was little, long before my other cousins told me to. You and I, we sense this. We know from whom to hide, the way farmers know to cover their crops even before storm clouds enter their sightlines. Every year I tell Momma, "Please, I don't want to visit them. I hate it there."

"Why?" she asks.

"Because. There's loud silence and something else without a name."

I'm not afraid. I'm angry. I must tell Papa what this cousin has done to others. He has to say something. I share what I know.

"Did you know he does this? He has for years."

Papa's upper lip curls in revulsion. Good. He will do something.

"Arey, chup," he says. *Hey, be quiet.* "Boys will be boys. It happens, especially between cousins."

I swallow something that tastes like a piece of me.

We return to Bangkok.

I DON'T TELL MOMMA. She has enough sorrow. She is silent with sorrow.

When I was younger, I'd ask, "Why can't we leave?" I've stopped. My questions leach lifeblood. Each word saps energy she desperately needs.

Papa seems even angrier these days. Stressed from work, the pressure ever building as he rises higher in his field. During his moods, he leaves himself. His pupils dilate. He slips into them.

Where did you go? Where do you go? Where have you gone? Come back. I watch him, my mind howling like a trapped wind.

He moves from kindness to rage to silence with the swiftness of monsoon rains. During rare stasis, we know to remain alert. Never mistake the tiger's stillness for calm. It is steeled concentration, taut and ready.

I have learned not to cry. It makes her sad. Furthermore, crying makes me groggy, forgetful, slow. That I can't allow.

Papa won't speak. Momma can't. So I will. I must grow up to be a voice for the souls and stories silenced.

I keep reminding myself, *This is one page.*

I AM 12. Puberty has chewed me up, spit me out. Chubby, pimply, with glasses and frizzy hair. My birthday present is contacts. Still, I'm hardly tolerable. A South Asian nerd, I'm a leper in a school where white kids are the reigning monarchs.

My plainness has nosedived into ugly. I'm beyond hope, with the social skills of a piece of lint. At school, everyone else is pairing off. Everyone has a girlfriend or boyfriend, and of course, a best friend. I'm the only one without a person. I have you, and you know how much that means. But there's something about touch that we all seem to need. To lean against someone, to share secrets behind cupped hands, to giggle and swap accessories and a hug. Even with you nearby, there are days I get so lonely my skin tingles. I keep telling myself, it's okay. When I grow up, I'll find my person.

We move into our third home in Thailand, in an elite, expat community called Nichada Thani. We boast white picket fences, imported trees, McMansions, actual mansions, and pools attached to every home. Our private school sits in the middle, the sparkling nucleus in our neighborhood. Our country club flaunts tennis courts, a golf course, horse stables, a machine-forged lake, beauty salons, a massage parlor, restaurants, and of course, a Starbucks. Sleek soccer moms, blonde and thin, preening on a diet of platitudes and pills, seem to be the mascots. We baffled brown-folk stick out like Troll Dolls airdropped into Barbie and Ken's Dreamtopia.

We are a gated community, obstinately private. Armed guards at frequent check points demand neighborhood ID before entry. The manufactured, controlled, contained perfection feels less a paradise, more a human experiment. I look around, and I can *feel* the secrets. Instantly, I remember the Goldilocked Girls in kindergarten, so confident in their superiority, already expert bullies despite their age. I remember their exalted beauty, their prized music boxes bearing ballerinas, the four-note song. Spin, spin, tiny dancer.

Spin. We are dystopia breathing, trying desperately to emulate American suburbia. Most of Asia is obsessed with America because America means freedom and freedom is a universal longing. We think if we look and live like America, we draw closer to Lady Liberty.

I AM 13. BANGKOK has its own palette of color and feeling. Our sunshine is a special shade of heaven. Our people are incredibly friendly. Our beaches are glorious—if you choose the good ones. The good ones hold pristine water, clean sands, humble resorts, gracious hosts. The bad beaches are pockmarked with American, Australian, and European tourists, mostly men, parading oiled bellies, speedos, and hired girlfriends and boyfriends. Like beached whales, they loll on the sand, scratching their crotches while their Thai lovers feed them fresh cut fruit off a satay stick.

The phrase coined by the ever-skilled tourism ministry is "Amazing Thailand." She most certainly is.

My family and I walk through a sprawling mall. As always, I feel you nearby. It's December so the music over the speakers are American Christmas songs. Twinkly lights and gorgeous decorations cloak the halls. The world's been kissed with glitter.

We live inside an unwavering summer. The temperature will dip slightly in the "winter" months, turning the air simply perfect. Now is the peak season for tourists to taste our splendors. Peppered through the mall, the streets, the beaches, and, I imagine, all the clubs and hotels are couples following an unabating cliché. An older white man with a young Thai woman or a very pretty Thai man.

A huge, rotund white man in a soccer jersey leers my way. His nose is red from beer and a vicious sunburn. His clammy paw holds his temporary Thai girlfriend's hand.

Instinctively, I move closer to Papa. I try to loop my arm through his. He recoils as if stung and puts his hand in his pocket. Frowning, he says, "Don't do that. People will think you're my girlfriend."

I blink back hot, furious tears, feeling scolded but clueless to what I did to deserve rebuke. My mouth floods with something bitter. The taste lingers like a bloodstain I can't scrub invisible.

SPEAK

SPEAK

✦

I AM 14. The light in Momma is fading. A giant heel presses against her, threatening to scuff her flame.

I've learned we aren't as alike as we appear. While she is quiet, I'm outspoken. While she is afraid, fear is the emotion I most seldom feel. While she trembles at Papa's voice, I roar back. My skin warms. My pupils dilate. Loud noises still bring on migraines, but I mute the pain. Although I aspire to be like Momma, the one trait I refuse to mirror is docility. Only I will author my life.

Papa was the captain of the debate team in school and college. At work, he's an economist and lecturer. He travels the world on the wings of his words. Entire countries listen to his ideas on how to empower a nation by raising female and child literacy and quality of life. He champions women's rights to education, respect, work, and the dignity and freedom that come from working. He writes volumes on these matters. Yet Momma is not allowed to work. This dichotomy infuriates me.

The logic defended by Papa and accepted by Momma for her not working is that she is on a spousal visa in Thailand, and it doesn't include working rights. However, such logic proves very thin when held up to the light: could they not apply for a different visa that would grant her the right to work?

Thus, Papa and I don't engage in screaming matches; we debate. A debate done well is the dismantling of a topic as well as your opponent. It's an art. Each point and counterpoint is lain with the deft precision with which a surgeon stitches flesh.

We debate human rights, culture, religion. We spend long hours enjoying the athleticism of each other's words. Conceptually, we agree on every point. Then I, ever the impertinent itch, turn the conversation personal.

"How do you explain the hypocrisy, the dissonance between your professional beliefs and private manner?"

He explodes.

"You're not my daughter. You're your mother's."

I retaliate. He grimaces. I am that grotesque. I'm humankind's fiercest force. An angry girl.

"You think you are so . . . *smart*," he says, his eyes pinched into slits, spitting the final word like a bitter seed. "It's going to be difficult for a man to love you."

He stops speaking to me. A few months at a time, I'm dust best ignored. I wonder if I'd be more palatable were I a boy.

"Momma, it's been three months this time. He hasn't spoken one word to me."

"I'm sorry." Pain chokes her voice to a quiet scribble. I hate myself for telling her.

"You have nothing to be sorry for."

"I'm just . . . sorry."

The few times Momma becomes fearless are when she speaks up for us. She says, "No, my children won't have arranged marriages. They'll live however they like, and be whomever they want."

These moments are spectacular and swift like solar eclipses, when the Moon positions herself between the almighty Sun and the Earth, protecting the latter from the former's glare. I wish she could do the same for herself, to grow beyond these gates. To break the orbit that places him in the center, and begin her own.

"Momma, think of all else you could do. The woman you could be."

She looks away. I persist, unshakable as a shadow.

"Momma, what do you want to do?"

"Reemani, I can't. I can't *want*. It would be selfish."

"That's like saying an inhale is indulgent."

She smiles, strokes my hair. "You are my jaan."

"Yes, Momma. I am yours and you are mine."

As is normal in Asian families, my parents tell me everything. Therapy is prohibited in our culture. It casts shame on a family. Caught in the crossfire, it's my role to mediate and play messenger. I've long wished to know what they say to each other. Now I wish I could forget. I try to guard my siblings from the malice. I harbor secrets, soothe sorrow, mollify anger. I cup suspicions of infidelities and threats of suicide in my hands, braiding my fingers tightly lest we slip through the cracks. I revolve around moods, stoic in their stalemate, stoic in their chaos. I trytrytry to help, fix, make them feel better. At night I fall upon my pillow, drained of feeling.

Papa was called the Golden Boy in his family. He attended a chilly, grim British boarding school from age 6, to be groomed for success. His father passed away when he was 11. Papa wasn't allowed to come home to grieve. That wound has never healed or been allowed to close. Introverted, bespectacled, bookish, he spent his entire childhood, teenage years, and his 20s away at schools and rarely with family. He was starved of tenderness. Comfort. Innocence. He won prestigious scholarships to study in England and the United States. He is shaped from numbers, achievement, tenacity, and pride.

Pride is his bedrock. The structure, belonging, and protection one finds in a father figure, Papa finds in pride. As I watch my parents, their constellation begins to connect. Pride often manifests as control, because pride is another face of fear. Perhaps, without even realizing,

Papa fears that were Momma allowed certain freedoms, she would leave. Thus, the fiercely guarded walls of her life. And I think, human beings, we each tend to wound others the way we ourselves would feel, or have felt, most wounded. Papa never had a home. So on days that he is particularly angry, he commands, "Leave!" With pendulum-like habit, Momma says, "He doesn't mean it. He's trying his best."

Apathy is the opposite of love. Insofar, anger and control, so removed from apathy, are sometimes, not the absence of love but rather love that lost its way. If you grew up without being given or taught softness, the love you express will be stonelike.

Momma says what has struck her most about Papa's family, from the first day of their marriage, is how silent and unsmiling everyone is. Laughter is foreign to them, and affection is rationed. In Momma and us, Papa discovered abundant love. When he is loving, the love is enormous. His spontaneous gifts of affection are feverishly treasured, Halloween candy that I hoard, hide, count, recount. When finally indulged, my throat stings from sweetness so deep it feels sharp.

Although my mind begs them to divorce, my heart knows why she stays. We stay because we can see into him, and we love him for what we see. We stay because every now and then, we manage to draw sweetness from stone.

Momma endures and folds continually like an origami bird. She's growing thinner every day. Strange, her sorrow seems to deepen her beauty. This is her. She is poetry, growing richer with each reading.

Here we live. He, brilliant and wounded. She, tender and afraid. My brother, thankfully, gentle and kind. My sister, hopefully, too young to understand. And I, adamantly myself.

But then.

Momma begins to change.

She finds her voice. Bit by bit, she speaks. We start sharing books. Maya Angelou. Toni Morrison. Margaret Atwood. We fall asleep nightly with their lullaby on our tongue, replacing *I can't* with *Still I rise.*

Momma starts creating art. Watercolors and masks made from gypsum, the material used to cast and heal broken bones. She isn't permitted to showcase them in our home, but she shrugs it off. Creation itself strengthens her spirit.

Momma makes friends. Then, crime of all crimes, she talks to her friends.

She ignites. We have one computer, in my bedroom. In secret, Momma begins a master's degree online.

She begins to teach, first as a substitute and then full time in a school across town.

"It's volunteer work," she says. Quietly, she opens her own bank account.

I AM 15. I stare alternately at my reflection and the stylist's hands, searching myself for regret. I have none.

I didn't have an appointment for this haircut. The salon is in the mall. I ran in after an argument with Papa. The five of us were eating lunch at a restaurant, when he and I began arguing about women and "whom they belong to."

I bolted from the table, stormed into the salon, and asked a stylist to "Please cut off my hair, down to an inch and a half." She looked at my hair, trailing down my back, ending at my bra strap.

"You want me cut inch and half?"

"No. I'd like the length to be an inch and a half, please."

I watch her hands at work. The locks fall. Hair, skin tone, the body. All paramount in measuring a woman's alleged value. Hair is the ultimate temptation, and is therefore covered in conservative Muslim culture. The lusher and longer the hair, the more worthwhile the girl.

My reflection smiles. Who and what decide my value now?

Momma walks into the salon, worried, breathless. Her eyes search the room for a familiar form before making contact with mine in the mirror. I grin, and her anxious face blooms into a smile. Her hand on her chest, she mouths, "Oh, wow."

She walks over.

"Look at you." Her fingers run lightly through my tightly cropped hair. "You're a pixie."

"Thank you, Momma." I swing my head, side to side, around in circles. I reckon I've shed about two pounds in hair. My newfound lightness is blissful. Hair, aside from the root, is dead. Strange that something lifeless and listless can hold such gravity. I look at the locks on the floor.

"You used to be mine," I tell them.

Momma laughs. Extraordinary, the changes one can incite in mere minutes.

Everyone loves my haircut. I look like a mix between Audrey Hepburn and Halle Berry. Feminine, strong, decisive. Even Papa can respect it.

I AM STILL 15. The 4- and 5-year-olds stare at me with big eyes, round from bemused curiosity. Most of them grin, matching me. A few, though, are wary of this foreign visitor. They're sizing me up, their little brows knit with suspicion. These young kids have finely honed street smarts. They live down the road in a slum called Klong Toey. For most of them, this school is the only concrete building they've ever been inside. Their homes are made of corrugated tin and wooden planks.

I'm here with a group of students. We're the visiting teachers for the week. Every February, our high school has Week Without Walls. For a week, we travel or work in groups of ten to twenty. There are extravagant trips to Italy, Africa, Switzerland, costing a lot of money. Or, we can choose one of the community service programs. We do good work, and all we pay for are our lunches. My family cannot afford pricey trips for all four years. Neither can my integrity.

The school has concrete floors, polished over the years by little feet running this way and that, so smooth they faintly reflect light and images. The concrete stays cool, lovely in the sweltering heat. Air conditioning is high luxury. Most of the children don't know what it is. Like many niceties, it's folklore.

The school teachers ask us student-teachers to lead the children in a few activities. My Thai is embarrassingly disheveled. The only lessons I can walk the children through are art and music, since those don't need much explaining. I know enough Thai to ask the question, "What does your heart look like?" So, we do portraits of our hearts. Who lives there? What does your heart feel? What does it think about, wish, dream? With older kids, these questions would provoke snickers and eyerolls. With adults, I'd encounter reticence, shyness, embarrassment, sarcasm. But not with kindergarteners. They draw their hearts with brazen enthusiasm and confidence.

For music, I teach the children a few songs and ask them to teach me some. One of the songs I teach is "Four Hugs a Day."

Four hugs a day, that's the minimum. Four hugs a day, not the maximum.

After the first day, I come home feeling hollowed out, brusquely scraped with a rusty, unforgiving trowel. It's February 15th, 1999, 6:15 p.m. I'm hungry but, standing in front of the open refrigerator, looking into its cold mouth, I can't bring myself to eat anything. The harsh reality of the slum kindergarten makes yesterday's meals feel ostentatious. Last week's snacks feel downright shameful—the self-indulgent frivolities of the upper-middle class.

I slam the door, march up the stairs, return to my room. I strip and stand naked before my mirror, staring. Most of the time, my reflection holds both me and your invisible form, and that makes it easier to look at. But sometimes, it is solely, unfairly me. I take inventory of my ample imperfections. There is so much I want to change.

The average adult Thai woman is 5'2" and 90 pounds. I have fair skin for my ethnicity, but here, I'm too dark and too heavy to be thought beautiful. I cock my head, birdlike, squint, access. I have Momma's bone structure, so I'm pretty enough. But unlike her, I'm fleshy. I pull at the meat on my face, stomach, arms, legs, tummy. Disgusting. How have I lived this long without doing something about this? It's inexcusable.

The very next day, I start working out for two and a half hours daily. I attack the task of becoming beautiful like a shark to flesh. I spend every day with the kids, learning from them, cleaning myself of selfish traits. The school bus picks us up from the slum and delivers us to our campus. I walk straight to the gym. I reject all fat and refined sugar. I allow myself only brown rice, lentils, tofu, vegetables, fruit, skim milk, and the occasional helping of whole grain bread, lean meat, and egg whites. I chew each bite thirty times. This is imperative. Otherwise it won't digest properly. By the end of the week, I can numb all insipid, fleeting pangs of hunger, fatigue, and selfishness.

I start running. Miles and miles and miles. There are glorious, empowering metaphors that come with running. Soaring, flying, running the race, in your zone, on your path, running the marathon. There are metaphors of another sort. Escaping, hiding, fleeing, being hunted, being haunted, running for cover, running for safety, running for one's life. Soon enough, I am in love. After my family and you, running will be my longest relationship.

In a month and a half, I bid adieu to twenty-two pounds, a fifth of my body weight. Good. I look faintly attractive. Not yet perfect but an adequate foundation.

I feel utterly calm. Anorexia feels heavenly. I have unlocked a mythical gold mine holding every coveted treasure: inner peace, beauty, and the power to shape actual matter. All around me is chaos, but all within is still. No inkling of pain, sadness, exhaustion, or hunger can touch me; I'm becoming as invulnerable and unmortal as a mortal can be. I've started taking laxatives as well, in the form of a special tea popular in Bangkok, made from senna leaves. It's called Slimming Tea.

My face takes on a ghostly, vacant look. My eyes become caves rimmed with lavender. I wake each morning with abrasions and bruises. Cotton sheets are sandpaper against my skin, asphalt on my ribcage, elbows, shoulder blades, pelvic bones, hipbones. The place it hurts most is my spine. The polo shirt collar of my school uniform hurts, bra straps hurt, sitting down hurts, lying down hurts. I like this hurt. I control it. It is orderly. It rewards me. Makeup covers the purple. Clothes look stunning.

"How do you do it?" the other girls ask.

"You just do," I reply. "Discipline."

It's like speaking Latin to infants. They're unused to pain. Discomfort of any kind makes them squeamish.

"It's all in your mind," says Momma, her forehead stitched with worry.

"It is," I reply with pride.

Papa isn't pleased either. "What is this? A hunger strike?" he shouts. "You're your mother's daughter. You're doing this just to have something else to blame on me."

There is a plethora of ways a girl can shape herself. Cute. Sexy. Pretty. Preppy. Trashy. Punk. Exotic. Street. Urban. Sporty. Hippie. Hipster. Diva. Tarty. Racy. Retro.

I choose Beautiful. She is the most powerful of the lot, her allure spanning every demographic. Beauty is exhilarating. It is pure currency. I've morphed from chubby outsider to adored outlier. My hair is pixie short, I'm fabulously thin, and radically singular. Crowds flock, girls marvel, boys who used to bully me in elementary and middle school now fawn on my every word.

I am their queen.

I AM 16. I sing the last note of "Somewhere" before directing myself to cry a few, controlled tears. They are the quiet kind that stream down a face in delicate rivulets. The note lingers in the air, carried by the microphones, mine and his. His character has already died. His eyes are shut, but his lashes are wet too. His character doesn't usually cry in this scene, but it's not him crying. The actor is. It is our final performance.

There is a sublime pocket of silence when time has been suspended. Then, the audience erupts, leaping to their feet, sounding like a rainstorm. On other nights, the lights dim while he and I rush backstage before coming out to bow. But tonight, we simply stand up and bow. I've stopped crying, but he's openly sobbing now, grieving the end of something magical.

It is my first play, *West Side Story*. A few months ago, right before my birthday, I decided to audition and enroll in every genre of art available. Theater, art, singing, my gift to myself. Here, I'm encouraged to be as I am.

How deliciously insane.

Art gives voice to what would otherwise remain silent. We turn pain into poetry. You are the one friend I truly need, and art is the one food. I eat every moment with the ravenous pull of a black hole fighting death. I journal for long hours, take every class, am the lead in every show. I learn and create all I can, devouring light to fend off demise. The high from connecting with an invisible or actual audience is unlike anything else. But rehearsal, training, practice, and improvement are life-renewing as well. How I love that the creation of art is like the sculpting of a person. Both are the reshaping of matter, transforming the wretched into beauty, common into magic, chaos into order. On the page, body, and stage, I hound the ideal line, free of ugliness.

Nowadays, when scorned or admonished, I can look at the person and recite in my mind, *I am intelligent, kind, hardworking, beautiful, thin, and talented. What would you like to fault me for?*

I have finally found friends beyond you. There are eight of us girls. We tell one another everything but also very little.

We are a spectrum of nations and religions. Bangladesh, America, Australia, Canada, Hong Kong, Fiji, the Netherlands. Buddhist,

Catholic, Mormon, Jewish, Agnostic, Atheist. Difference is our nonchalant norm.

One of our favorite pastimes is swimming at night. Tonight, some skinny-dip, some wear bathing suits. The water is perfect, the air clear. We are the only ripple. Our hushed voices and squeals, our limbs gliding through the water, winking with moonlight, are the only movement in the inky stillness of evening. We smell of chlorine and the body sprays teenage girls buy, with names like Paradise Mist and Sunset Dream. We giggle at one another's nakedness with delight. We're the first bare bodies we've ever seen. Nearly every color of humankind, we are caramel, honey, cinnamon, amber, ivory, vanilla, alabaster, cream.

In a few years, we'll all have had sex. In a few years, we'll all break, somehow. In a few years, we'll be in college, scattered around the globe. In a few years, some of our parents will be divorced. A few years after that, some of our parents will have cancer. Two of us will contend with our own divorces, one will lose her firstborn, and one will lose her mother. The currents of grief will course through us and we will curl tightly around each woman, one after the next, like petals to a bulb.

But tonight, we don't know this. Tonight, we are only safe. Tonight, afloat in the cradle of water and one another, we are happy.

The next day, like most days, Momma and Papa continue their one battle: *You don't make me feel happy or loved.*

Devastating, for that is all they wish to feel and make each other feel. They're trying to find a way to love each other that doesn't hurt.

In an attempt to spark our family back to health like a defibrillator shooting electric life into a dying body, we move yet again. We leave our pristine, sterile neighborhood to land in the hot pulse of Bangkok. Our fifth home in Thailand, the ninth in my life. As with every move, you come with me, not my shadow but my light. There is always a window for you to sit by.

We move but carry the loud silence with us. It spreads like a pool without a floor or end. I lead and charm at school, friends with everyone, familiar with no one. I journal poems and ramblings. I read voraciously, still seeking a book that feels like my world and its cast of characters. I speak to you for longer hours and late nights, praying you send me sleep. I run longer and harder.

I run and run until my skin pulls pale and tightly over my skull like canvas stretched over a frame. Giddy with adrenaline, I fly.

STAND

STAND

✦

The night I turn 17, I decide it's time I have a boyfriend. Thus far, dating has been prohibited by Papa. My friends and I are at a club to celebrate my birthday. I'm wearing a black tank top and jeans that feel like skin, with gold glitter down the legs. On the stairs up to the club, I turn to my closest guy friend, walking behind me. I kiss him. He is a cosmos away from Captain von Trapp, but he'll do for now. The kiss isn't as thrilling as the fact that I initiated it.

Four months later, I decide it's time we have sex. I go to his house wearing a light blue, flowing sundress. With honey, I've traced a map on my body that I'd like him to follow. It all goes very well. We date for nine months. After him, I date a few other boys in rapid succession. I move through them, they through me. The same boys who grabbed my glasses, held me in a circle, taunting and laughing as my world blurred—one by one, I date them. One by one, they love me.

I AM 17. THE women hang on their poles as if held by fishing line. Men border the raised stage, their heads coming up to the women's calves, reaching to tuck fistfuls of twenty-baht bills into spandex thongs. The audience's eyes fall below the eyeline of the strippers, but the balance of power is solidly opposite. There is no question who works for whom, who exists according to the other's presence, who eats according to the other's appetite.

You and I are inside a strip club in Silom, the tangle of streets adjacent to Patpong, Bangkok's famous red-light district, where tourists, expats, and teenage clubbers rub elbows. I'm in a black tube top and jeans, with my hair now lavender and spiked. My hair has gone through black, bleached, gold, cherry, violet, and now, violet's sweeter sibling. The bright lights glint off my ears; I have four piercings in each. Much to Papa's consternation, in addition to my piercings, I now have a tattoo.

The streets are littered with Thai men and women holding crude handmade signs advertising the clubs they represent, the laminate peeling at the edges of each worn poster. There are three kinds of clubs: strip clubs, brothels, and nightclubs. In this claustrophobic net of streets, all pastimes are sated. My parents know I go out with my friends, but they don't know I slip into the darker clubs.

The strip clubs boast a variety of shows. The reps sing their glories: "Pussy show, pussy show! Come see ping-pong come out of girl vagina!"

Sometimes, while my friends are at a nightclub down the alley, I'll duck into a show. The club next door to the one I'm in now has a circus theme. In the cast of performers, there is a little person who dresses like a monkey and has sex onstage with a woman of full height, dressed like Jane from Tarzan. After the duo is Pandora, a girl famous for exhuming all sorts of things from her vagina. The classic ping-pong ball, a plastic egg that hatches a live chick, a spinning top, a wind-up car, and finally, a balloon she blows up using her anatomy. The audience howls with laughter as she stretches her face in campy shock.

Tonight I sit inside a regular strip club, "normal" compared to its neighbors. I come to watch the audience. I stay to talk to the dancers. I ask where they're from, why they do this, what it's like, if they have kids, and what that is like. I ask, *How long have you been in the industry? Did you ever try another vocation? Were you forced into this by a lack of opportunity and resources, or a relative who sold you?*

Did you grow up thinking this was your inevitable fate, the one choice in an otherwise choiceless world?

Can a choice be considered a "choice" if it is the sole option?

This project, of asking the strippers and prostitutes for their stories, began casually, a chance conversation sparked by curiosity. Who are these men and women I have grown up around, both sensitive and desensitized to their presence? But, as the stories stack, my curiosity rises in temperature. My heart now throbs with high fever.

Some of the women and men I approach meet my questions with cold or outright anger, honed from a lifetime of being attacked by others. But most of them speak with hunger, ready and desperate to give their stories to someone they sense will receive them without judgment, and only love.

Some of the men and women were lured in by dazzling promises, lines and hooks conjured by smooth-talking fleshmongers. But the majority found this path through despair; the total absence of hope. One woman began stripping and hooking to pay a gambling debt her ex-husband accrued. He left her after she paid off his debt. Another man started prostituting at 14 because his parents evicted him for being gay. Another woman echoes fears most of them harbor: *What will my children do? They were born into this life. Does that mean this, too, is their destiny?*

"What would you do if you could break out of this cycle?" I ask each of them.

"I'd own a small café."

"I'd go to college."

"I'd run a noodle cart. I'd make pad Thai and chicken satay using my mother's recipes."

They detail their dreams, their faces glowing with imagined happiness. Some poeticize the gory ways they'd seek revenge on those who have subjugated them for decades. The scars they'd cut unto those who scarred them. The burns they'd brand unto those who seared them.

Dear one, there must be a reason I'm living around all this. I brim not only with enraged questions but with the urgent need to do something. Thus, I collect stories. I'll learn my way out of these feelings, using information as my ladder to climb out of fury and helplessness. I don't know yet how to help, but I know I'm being built by these moments.

It takes everything inside me to not condemn the jeering men who jam money into the girls' and boys' G-strings, studded with rhinestones and plastic pearls. Aside from myself, there are a few women in the audience, tourists who came to marvel and laugh at the display, hoarding this experience for show-and-tell back home. I despise these women with a different texture of hatred than I feel for the men.

While the audience laughs and hoots, the women and men onstage are voiceless. The stage lights paint their skin in a kaleidoscope of eerie hues. The artificial colors are the ones you find when the sun hits gasoline spilled on a street. A manmade rainbow, its gold venomous; you know not to touch it.

MOMMA AND MY BROTHER come to all my shows. After *West Side Story* is *Into the Woods*, then *Hamlet*, then *Medea*.

We perform *Medea* outside of school as well, all through Thailand, then in Taipei for an arts conference. I win awards. Medea is the story of a woman wooed by a foreign, visiting warrior, Jason. He terrorizes her country. He takes her, leaving destruction in his wake. Her home country disowns her. She marries Jason and births two sons.

Years later, Jason betrays her by marrying the princess of his own land. Medea is robbed of her home, identity, and dignity, and is banished from her adoptive country. Effectively orphaned, she incites her revenge: She murders the land's king, the princess, and finally, her own two sons. She wounds and betrays Jason in the ultimate ways, although she does the same to herself simultaneously.

Medea will stop at nothing to direct and determine her fate, even if the resolution she forges is psychological suicide. While her decisions are horrifying, I marvel at her deathly conviction.

I play her for months, thrilled by the challenges of the harrowing script. Two days after my final performance I collapse during Calculus. An ambulance rushes me to the hospital. They needle and poke my arms, searching for a pulse they say is too weak to find. My mind screams, *My heart is a winged thing that beats furiously. What do you mean you cannot find it?*

The doctor says I'm showing signs of physical and psychological duress. I'm hospitalized for a week. It is pure sunshine. Papa didn't watch Medea, but he does make sure I'm given the largest suite in the VIP wing.

Terrified that I might gain weight from the hospital fare, I sneak my senna tea nightly, to flush every meal. I always carry a stash in my backpack.

For this week, what I do gorge on are books. In my enormous hospital bed, I get to read books solely for myself, not as assigned for school. Nowadays, I find myself choosing books more for their authors than their characters. Each author becomes a surrogate parent. I love magical realism written by Isabel Allende and Gabriel García Márquez. This week, I read *Of Love and Shadows*, *One Hundred Years of Solitude*, and *Love in the Time of Cholera*. They are all gorgeous.

Both voices are full of wisdom and compassion. But ultimately, they aren't what I'm looking for.

I am so tired. Sometimes, I feel insane; my best friend is a voice in my head. My best friend is an invisible form by the window. I nestle in the cloudlike bed, encased in wires. I raise my arm, taking in its sallow yellow. My skin is unusually thin compared to others' and always has been. Now, brighter than ever, turquoise veins web my entire body.

Where has my heart gone? They say they cannot hear it. So I search still for that one thing, one book, one guardian that can. Like you but different, to hear and answer this and other questions. A voice that mirrors my mangled world of needles, wires, love, and loud silence, and paints it poetic. It will pull my heart from hiding. I will beat steady.

I turn my palm under the fluorescent glare. This is one page, I tell myself. The next one arrives only when this one finishes. It'll all make sense.

I sleep, sleep, sleep.

I HAVE EMERGED from my hospital room and into one far worse.

The room is an open sore. A wet, hot, bubbling crater, with a sourness instinct screams is of illness and rot.

This room holds cancer, and cancer holds my Nana Bhai in its unforgiving jaws, refusing to loosen, let alone unclench.

He and Naan moved here for his chemotherapy for bone and lung cancer. It has been four months now. Bangkok's hospitals are a world beyond Bangladesh's.

This room used to be my brother's. He moved into the fourth bedroom, previously my sister's. She sleeps with me or my parents, depending on the evening's mood. The room holds a queen-sized bed, a vanity, a few closets lining a wall. Adjacent to them are French windows that open onto a slim balcony, the curtains billowing meekly, humidity tiring the wind.

Nana Bhai lies on his left, facing the windows, inhaling whatever light comes in. His six-foot frame has grown cancer-thin. The late afternoon silhouettes his body, the line of his right thigh interrupted by a sharp plunge, where cancer has eaten him. A sudden valley where there shouldn't be one, as though colossal talons have dug out a piece of him, scavenging bone and flesh.

Braided through the scent of slow decay is sweat and Prickly Heat powder, popular in hot Asian countries. It soothes the skin during extreme heat. It comes in a white tin jar with a red and green trim and silver text. You turn the top, the little holes align, the jar coughs, and wherever the powder settles, your skin tingles, instantly cooled. The powder smells of eucalyptus and mint but not the harsh medicinal mint of Tiger Balm or Vicks. The aroma is gentle. Nana Bhai has always been fond of Prickly Heat powder because of his eczema. Now, it brings small comfort for the pain, a fury-march of fire ants ripping their way through him.

Nana Bhai, my beloved wordsmith. He is too tired to write these days. He continues to hum, though, all day, a habit I've known as long and find as comforting as Momma's voice. He sings "Three Coins in a Fountain," "Raindrops Keep Falling on My Head," and "The Sound of Silence." Like his daughter, he is an unwavering romantic and optimist. The house pulses with solemnity and the nearness of death, but Nana Bhai continues to hum, smile, and speak kindly with everyone. He continues to make jokes between spasms that leave him heaving for breath, eyes rolling backward from pain. To pass the hours and distract his mind, Nana Bhai tells stories of his childhood and his time as a freedom fighter in the war. These memories are my inheritance.

Sometimes, cancer leaves Nana Bhai the Wordsmith speechless. He emits moans and whimpers when he thinks we're out of range.

Naan alternates between caring for him and resenting him, projecting onto him her rage toward the unseen forces responsible for his pain. An unfortunate but reasonable anger, her logic being love.

He is our most magnificent and gentle of giants. Some days, I can give Nana Bhai hours, reading to him, swapping tales, making him laugh. Then there are days I avoid him, in my pathetic attempt to evade the omnipresence of death and the sorrow he embodies. I hatehatehate myself on these days.

A friend asked me the other day whether or not I believe in God. Time in this family moves so painfully, I don't have the space to consider faith. Perhaps I will once I've left these rooms. I trust and believe in art, myself, and you, my invisible friend, a presence sturdier than any other guardian.

I hoped the gravity of illness would soften Papa. It hasn't. Relentless fingers pick old scabs, declaring them forever fresh with infection. Their arguments crescendo, while Nana Bhai lies dying and humming the days.

Finally, Momma confesses the truth to Nana Bhai. He looks at her, his eyes ringed with incurable grief.

"Why didn't you tell me all these years? I'm dying now. There isn't anything I can do."

"I didn't tell you, for it would hurt you to know."

"Please take care of your behavior," he pleads to Papa. Papa promises he will.

To Naan, Papa says, "You've come here to break my marriage, haven't you?"

Through tears she replies, "I'm here because your father-in-law is dying. You are breaking this on your own."

I AM 18. The letters are handwritten in red ink, on lined paper. Every letter of every word is capitalized, the handwriting slanting to a hard right, so uniformly erect it resembles font. I turn the pages over. The writing is double-sided, each letter three to five pages long. Precariously, they balance in my hands. The paper is thin, light peers through, but the pages sit heavy, sticky, warm like blood. A cool bitterness floods my mouth and spreads through my torso.

The letters are from my IB Psychology teacher. He writes that I'm a manipulative little girl too smart for her own good. Somehow, he's gained access to my schedule and calls me on classroom phones while I'm in English, Calculus, Biology. He times it so that the phone rings just as I enter the room.

"I'm recording these calls," he says.

During class he cracks lewd sexual jokes, regaling us with stories about himself gallivanting around town, with his numerous female partners, some hired, some "kept." An avid patron of Patpong and its red-lit buffet, he has long salt-and-pepper hair down to his shoulders and a handlebar mustache he strokes often, lovingly, like a soft, furry pet. He tells us "(he) enjoys (his) women young."

He flirts with female students. Some flirt back, feeling chosen and special, perhaps too, fearing if they didn't respond to his flirtation, he'd penalize them with poor grades. Most of the male students idolize him, as the epitome of "cool." They frequently request his advice on women.

I'm the only student who doesn't laugh along, who never responds to flirtation, who refuses to pander to his ego. Occasionally, I raise my voice above the chatter to say, "That was inappropriate. You're an authority figure. You're abusing your power."

In his letters and calls he doesn't commit an overt sexual advance. He is shrewd. He repeats, "You have misbehaved. You're an insolent girl. How dare you disrespect me. It pains me that we don't connect. You deserve to be punished."

The innuendo is identical to the language he quotes using with his many girlfriends.

In one letter he writes, "You think you are so perfect. That face. That body. Perfect grades, too. Well, then, you need to make me happy."

I read the words and fill with chills. He's alluding to an annual contest held by the school newspaper. At the end of every school year, students vote to elect one another for different "awards." Since freshman year, I've won "Best Body," "Best Smile," "Most Likely to be Famous," and "Most Artistic."

He has been tracking me. For years.

Therefore, although nothing explicit, this is *entirely* sexual. Control. Hunting. Intimidation. Power.

I report the letters and calls to the high school principal. My legs swing on the office chair, unable to touch the floor. The plastic back of the chair is cold and hard against my jutting shoulder blades, backbone, tailbone. I fiddle with an earring, pat my hair in place. It's dark brown now, no longer spiked, but still cropped short. The principal listens intently. A large man with thinning auburn hair who also coaches our rugby team, he seems kind. I do know, though, that he is chummy with the predator. Part of a "boys club" of male colleagues, my friends and I see them sometimes in Silom, laughing over Singha beers.

I finish listing and explaining the best I can, making sure to keep my voice clinical, flat, emotionless, lest emotion be held against the veracity of my words.

"Thank you. Would you like to involve your parents?"

I reply with the plainest truth: "No. They are unavailable."

"I'll take care of it," he says. We schedule another meeting for the following day. He requests I bring all the letters. I've stored them at home.

That evening, I approach Papa.

"The principal may call. A teacher is stalking me. He calls and sends letters."

Papa looks at me, frowning. "Kano? Thumi kee korso?" *Why? What did you do?*

"I didn't do anything, Papa. I swear."

I hold out the letters. He looks. His upper lip curls in disdain. He shakes his head and returns to his newspaper.

I feel tiny, devastated. Stupid girl. Seek not a father you won't find. When Momma asks for details, I give her everything. She replies with silence. I respond, "I'm handling it."

The next day, the principal asks, "Can you think of anything that may have provoked this behavior?"

I blink, surprised. Why do any of us do anything? Because we want to.

"Maybe this makes him feel important."

The principal nods slowly. He scribbles on his notepad. He skims the letters. He places them in a locked drawer.

Then I remember: The predator gained access to my schedule, meant to remain confidential.

"We'll take care of this discreetly," says the principal, leaning back in his chair, braiding his fingers over his gut. "Thank you for being quiet. You may return to class."

I flush with horror and outrage. The architecture of this dungeon is elaborate. Systemic. The principal hasn't taken the letters for safekeeping; he has confiscated evidence. Now, I'm to return to the monster. I leave the office. I feel like a stain. Not an ink stain from a split pen. Not a grease mark from food or the indigo left by blueberries. I'm the brown, scourged but still-visible stain of blood on a panty when you have your period and it leaks through a tampon. I feel like a stain only girls know.

I return to class, repulsed, furious. He smirks, stands a bit taller. He shakes his gray mane and touches his mustache adoringly like a penis.

When I arrive home, I go to Nana Bhai and lie down carefully on his bed. He is sleeping, his breathing a wheeze, sour, stale, like bread slowly hardening, the yeast growing wild. I watch the sun set behind the crater in his thigh, created by cancer's wrath.

How I wish I could decide who to live, who to die.

Power only responds to power. I have none. The predator is protected. I am a stain, initially irksome, ultimately forgotten. He will spend the rest of the school year mocking me to the other students, saying I fabricated the whole story due to a girlish crush. At the end of the year, he announces he'll take a leave of absence. He's honored with a glowing article in the school paper celebrating his years of gracious service.

Although enraged, I'm not surprised.

Last year, I visited Egypt on a school trip, during Week Without Walls. Every minute, I could feel something perched on the periphery of my senses. I sought words, like trying to recall evasive lyrics.

The thing was absence. The ominous absence of women. Their presence, their voices, their imprint. Droves of men unspooled through the city. Rolling coils of heat. My vision was thick with men. But try as I did, I failed to see a woman. When I finally caught sight of a few, like rare, endangered birds, they were frantic, hurrying, dodging groping hands and wolfish voices. It was a population forcibly halved, one half free to walk, the other living their days behind firmly closed doors.

It is similar in Bangladesh. In both places, I felt—I feel—powerless. Were I to act or speak back to any catcaller or grabber, I'd incur harm. The only choice is to layer clothing, keep quiet, tuck down my head, and walk as quickly as possible.

In Thailand, the air throbs with the promise and easy procurement of sex. I walk holding my limbs close to myself. Here, there is a coming-of-age ritual performed by fathers and sons. When it is time, the father buys his son his first prostitute. A passage into manhood, this tradition is upheld by select men in every social class and has continued for generations.

Shock. Horror. Gasp.

But.

It is not far from home. Anyone's home. From the red-light district to the red carpet, from pageantry to pimpdom, we have a tried-and-true pattern. A young girl, garishly visible yet rendered invisible, speaking, dancing, waving to the orders of male authority.

Her voice usurped, her body itemized, her skin tattooed by the male gaze, her story written by the hands of others.

Everywhere I look, everywhere I go, being female means varying degrees of powerlessness.

It won't be until I am half a planet and a dozen years forward that I'll feel the full bloom of dissonant chords. For now, the days race and my riotous outcry burns my tongue. I can't find anyone on whom to confer my unrest. So, hour after hour, I talk to you. Journal after journal, I transcribe my howl. I read, nourishing myself with the comfort of others. I scour every shelf I come across, in every home, bookstore, library, searching still for that singular book I've longed for since I was a child.

MOMMA GATHERS MOMENTUM. She lays out steps, preparing to leave. But then.

"I can't be pregnant. I'm taking my 18-year-old to college soon."

She's alone with the doctor. He lets her two sentiments hang in the air like sibling feathers deciding where to land. Momma repeats the truer of the two reasons.

"I *can't* be pregnant."

The doctor speaks slowly. "We don't do that here. But I have a colleague I can refer you to. Let's run a few more tests. You have a history of ectopic pregnancies and miscarriages. One step at a time."

Momma had two miscarriages between myself and my brother, then another between him and my sister. The doctor runs another test. The results will take a few days. She leaves reciting her gruesome prayer a third time. "I can't be pregnant."

The results arrive. The doctor fans them out on the desk between them, looks thoughtfully at Momma, and chooses his words carefully, letters in a game of hangman. How many have beseeched him for help, confessing their story through a handful of words?

"You aren't pregnant," he decides. "It's an ectopic pregnancy. Unfortunately, we must do a laparoscopy. Would you like to tie your tubes while we're at it?"

"Yes. Please."

The procedures are long and excruciating. Papa drops her off in the morning, goes to work. Momma plans to take a taxi home. The ordeal proves too brutal. The doctors call the school office, the office calls my Physics class, I hail down a cab and berate the poor driver as though traffic is his fault.

I walk up and wait for the sliding doors to recognize my weight on the sensory pad. At hospitals, supermarkets, drugstores, these pads always take a few seconds to realize I'm here. I hope heaven doesn't have one of these pads. A surprising scent of vanilla arrives just then, softening the sharp, medicinal air.

The sweet culprit is the coffee shop and bakery 20 feet away. Over the years, after every doctor's appointment, Momma, my brother, and I would visit the café. It's attached to the lobby and isn't your average hospital culinary affair. Our ritual was dear. Momma would have a coffee, my brother would have a chocolate éclair, and I'd have a vanilla éclair. The chocolate éclairs were traditionally shaped. The vanilla ones, though, were the shape of a swan. The pastry for the body and wings were baked in special molds, as were the necks and heads. Tiny dips carved a delicate pattern of feathers, eyes, beak, tuft of tail. The sections were artfully pieced together, held by a cloud of vanilla custard, luscious yet light as a dream. I contemplate getting a swan for Momma, but she never ate one and I no longer do.

The doors finally open. I walk briskly to the elevator, reciting her room number like a feverish jingle.

The numbers climb in the elevator, beep, beep, beep, toward the ding. My entire life, my alarm clock has been Momma. I've never had or needed an actual clock. Her heartbeat is the tick-tock I knew before any other sound. Since birth, I've slept and woken to the sound of her voice. As a baby I'd wake from deep slumber the moment she left the room. Papa says it's because I couldn't hear or smell her anymore. When he tells these stories, he turns pink with joy, and I love him so much I feel dizzy. Most moms would roll their eyes, grumbling at the task of waking up teenage children. Most moms wouldn't even bother. Not Momma though. Every morning, she says, "Reemani, Reemani, wake up." Pulling me back from wherever I've been.

At night, if I fall asleep doing homework without taking out my contacts, she brings over their case and solution, lifts my head, jostles me lightly, and holds me up while I pry off my contacts.

Without her, how would I wake up every morning? How would I see? For whom would I speak?

The elevator opens to the Women's Wing. I sprint to her room. Her door opens with a soft click and there she is, my Momma, caught for a moment without her queenly composure, looking childlike and colorless without makeup, miniscule and deflated from trauma.

"Hi, Mommani!" I feign cheer and strength.

"Hi, jaan."

She smiles thinly, pale-lipped. The times I've seen her without lipstick can't fill a hand. The sound of her voice and the Bengali word for "soul" tears me at the seams. I start crying. Our roles swiftly switch, balance returning to its known place. She retrieves her regal bearing like an ermine cape, opens her arms, and I pour into them. I gather her few things, we distribute her weight onto her legs and mine, and bid farewell the hospital. From her room to the elevator to the lobby to the taxi, her legs buckle with every step. She folds in half from the pain coursing through her, keeping determined pace with her pulse.

She grits her teeth, I grit mine. She from pain, I from fury at how little we control in life. My anger lives in an open casket tucked behind my lungs. From there it growls. When I breathe, we battle for space.

When Papa arrives home from work, she is in bed, exhausted. He says not a word. The maid makes him tea, delivered on a tray painted with roses. Biscuits, jam, the paper. He sips, eats, reads.

Aside from my Parents' Daughter, my other job is My Siblings' Older Sister. This responsibility feels heavy and sweet. It curdles and clears me like lemon and its effects. Naked on the tongue, lemon awakens, the zing pleasing. Applied to milk, it sours without forgiveness.

I take my sister on girl-dates, usually to the movies and ice cream afterwards (chocolate for her, none for me). She is 7 now and so lovely. She takes ballet. Like all little girls with the chance to dance, after her lesson, she stays in her pink tutu and leotard, her hair in a pert, darling bun, spinning pirouettes and pretending to fly. And while I would invent tales and perform plays as a child, and my brother would build LEGO space stations and play with dinosaurs, she plays "Office."

"What are you doing?" I'll ask, seeing she has cleared her pink play-table of any teacup or crayon.

"Office," she replies, like it's the most obvious answer in the world. She tosses aside her dolls with open-faced scorn, and organizes and reorganizes her office supplies for hours, until they are "just right." Pencils, erasers, notebooks, binders, and a stapler. I smile. She, our brother, and I, we all adore order.

My brother is turning 15 this year. I throw him a surprise birthday party. The cake I make is heart-shaped, double-layered, with brownie batter on the bottom, red velvet on the top. Chocolate frosting covered entirely with Twix bars and Maltesers. I don't have a proper heart-shaped pan, but it's easy to makeshift a heart. Bake two cakes, one in a square pan, the other in a round one. Place the square like a diamond. Cut the round one in half and place the halves like ears on the diamond. One day I'll track down actual heart-shaped pans, but this works well for now. There is something nice about puzzling together a heart.

I love being their sister. I clutch these smuggled moments like glittery jewels, family treasures by far the most precious.

At school, I am Little Miss Perfect. Our school is one of the most prestigious in Asia. Our grounds are an architectural masterpiece.

Our facilities are state of the art, each sponsored by a Fortune 500. Unocal. Nike. Coca-Cola. Our tuition is as high as some colleges'. The UN subsidizes half my brother's and my tuition. But most of the students are the sons and daughters of tycoons, sheiks, royalty, and the nouveau riche. Cream skimmed off every nation. Dressed immaculately, many come to school in chauffeur-driven Mercedes and BMWs, or drive the cars themselves.

We are told daily that we are the promise of the future. We walk pristine hallways, clean of any errant leaf or smudge. Sparkling fountains dot the curated gardens. Each student is shinier, splashier, prettier, smarter, richer than the previous. Each is being groomed to inherit his father's company, become a world-renowned mind, or follow in her mother's footsteps, continuing the assembly line of flawless socialites and politicians' wives.

More is our school's religion. *More, more, more* chants this generation's mascot, believing "More is Powerful." We are encouraged to dream "big" and aspire toward a "rich life."

More is the religion, and speed is the drug of choice. There are thousands of motorcycle-taxis in Bangkok and most of the drivers deal—usually pot and speed. Getting high in our town is as easy as getting a ride.

We are a city of wanton procurement, whatever one fancies. I've never tried speed, having seen the damage wreaked on close friends. And I haven't tried it because I know my personality is ideal for addiction. Speed is a perfectionist's dream drug. It enhances confidence and focus, and a person can stay awake for days. Of course it is loved. Our prestigious school breeds perfectionism.

Prestige is an illusion. Prestige comes from the Latin *praestigum*, meaning delusion or trick.

Parents pay a king's ransom, and we children, the promised prestige, perform dutifully, aided by various shadowy elixirs. All part of the magician's sleight of hand, our American-founded school hires Thai female secretaries and teaching assistants to meet Thai business and tax regulations, paying them a pittance compared to the teachers, most of whom are American and white. Very rarely, a Black teacher is hired. They stay a year, perhaps two. To maintain our impeccable reputation, through the sexism, racism, predators, and toxins, parents, teachers, and kids tend to hush things we've been taught are best kept silent. The quieter we become, the tighter we clutch our illusion of choice.

Mine is beauty. In a world devoted to denying me all other strongholds, beauty is the one privilege I'm permitted, thus the prestige I chase, wield, and grip for dear life. Beauty feels like lightning in my body. I surge with power. As Momma and I hobbled out of the hospital after her surgeries, she felt my ribcage knock against her torso, my collarbone hard under her hand.

"You really need to eat more. You're killing yourself."

She says this and I think, *In this vile planet of abuse, cancer, predators, and accomplices, why would anyone willingly surrender anything that makes them protected, special, safe, and most daring of all, happy?* When Momma says, "You need to treat yourself better," I think, *Like you?*

In a few months, I'll fly to America for college. In the land of the alleged free, I wonder what it is like for women.

MOVE

MOVE

✦

I AM 19. I'm attending Skidmore College in Saratoga Springs, New York. The grounds are classically New England: red brick buildings, rolling green fields, more trees than I've seen in all my years combined. The foliage is completely new, leaves and shades I've only drawn and painted before. Maple, birch, pine, acorn. Crimson, amber, lemon, mouse-brown, ashen gray. Seasons are new, therefore so is snow. It's as spectacular as I've imagined, but the cold makes me literally nauseous. My body feels tipped, hung upside down. I layer sweaters to no avail.

I miss my family desperately. Momma and I spend long hours writing each other and speaking on the phone. I share everything I'm learning. She shares how things are back there. We say goodbye the same way, every time.

"Thank you for being mine and letting me be yours. I love you."

I'm majoring in Women's Studies and Theater. I'm going to be a voice for those who have been silenced. I've known three things since I was 15. I'll adopt kids. I'll be a professional artist of some kind. And I'll leverage my work toward positive change. Aside from Momma,

Gloria Steinem, and Oprah, my role models are Angelina Jolie, Jane Fonda, and Audrey Hepburn. I revere them not only for their beauty and talent, but because they channeled their careers toward serving others. Actresses who became activists and UN Ambassadors, they used their fame for something good. Such is the mission I feel like a fever.

I love academia as much as I love art. I find words, and learn to transform my fury into fortitude. I learn how to mine light from life's shadows, to synthesize personal experience with studied research, to foster clarity, awareness, and a roadmap. Praxis. In addition to women's studies and theater, I take numerous religion classes. I've harbored such anger against Islam my entire life. Education lets me clarify my thoughts the way butter purifies into ghee. I separate the false, prejudiced claims from the truly sexist and justifiably infuriating.

My professors feed me assignments beyond the curriculum, tinder for a voracious flame. I'm cast in two or three plays every semester versus the standard of one. The directors negotiate a special schedule. I rehearse two hours with *Macbeth*, run through the snow-kissed campus to rehearse three hours with *Chicago*, then run a final leg for two hours with *Antigone*.

I don't have many friends. I have you, but it seems I still fail to fit with anyone else. I don't fit with the international students, or the theater or women's studies majors. Our international student population is 2 percent of the school. I'm the only international student in the women's studies and theater departments. My work ethic, ambition, and earnest friendliness are apparently off-putting. And in the women's studies department, my femininity and staunch stand against misandry, or "man-hating," are perceived as weaknesses.

I keep to myself and focus on what I'm here for. I keep at a distance from the party scene. Having grown up in Bangkok, I'm disenchanted.

Both majors claim me completely: mind, heart, body. Women's studies requires a massive amount of study, digestion of material, discussion, and writing. Theater demands rehearsal, memorization, reflection, adjustment, improvement, and execution, performance after performance. We are trained to always hit our mark, regardless of sickness, fatigue, or doubt. I am continuously on.

I wake up at 6 a.m., work out, study, write, attend classes from 9 to 6, rehearse from 7 to 11. I study and write some more, journal, sleep at 1 a.m., repeat. I Tupperware identical, diminutive, spiceless meals. Their polite, plastic containment supports the mechanics of my goals.

The people I do resonate with are my professors. I will always seek and find parents. My theater professors are kind, beyond-the-norm mentors. My women's studies advisor is a trusted kindred spirit. She is brilliant, stands at 5'2" but fills an entire hall with effervescent magnificence. Her hair is cut in a chic silver bob that volleys light with every animated, impassioned word. I'm intimidated and besotted.

On our first day, we do an exercise our professor will later explain is standard for Women's Studies programs. We're asked to describe ourselves using three sentences. There are twelve girls and four boys in the class. Once we've all written our three sentences, we read them aloud.

Eight of us twelve girls wrote as our first sentence "I am a girl," "I am female," or "I am a woman." Two wrote "I am a Black woman." Of the remaining two, one wrote "I am gay" and another, "I am Latina." As our second and third sentences, all eight wrote something to do with character or appearance: "I am kind," "I am caring," "I am beautiful." Of the four boys, two are white, one Black, and one Latino. For their first sentence, they wrote "I am an athlete," "I am 18," "I am Black," and "I am gay," respectively. For their second and third sentences, they wrote of their ambitions and vocations: "I will be a senator," "I am a scientist," "I am an entrepreneur." Our professor shares the kinds of answers collected over years, across campuses. Most white men wear their whiteness, maleness, and scope of ambition nonchalantly. Being the "dominant" race, they are the assumed lead character in the social lens, standing center amidst all orbiting matter, mostly aloof, absorbing the benefits, one of which is innocence, another, faith in their success. We girls are more conscious of our femaleness, appearance, and behavior with others, as anyone cast in a supporting "minority" role is conscious of the characteristics society uses to denote our peripheral "minority" standing. The further we are from the center, the more we're made aware of it. The world takes great pains—and inflicts great pain—to remind us of our otherness, lack of privilege, limited bandwidth, and supportive duties.

If we weren't reminded, we wouldn't know how to behave.

In women's studies, I quickly carve my niche. I'm drawn to the history of dominance and voicelessness pulsing through centuries and cultures. The psychology of misogyny, power, and abuse fascinates me. These days, I don't have the time to read books for pleasure. Everything I read is academic nonfiction, volumes by Simone de Beauvoir, Adrienne Rich, Gloria Steinem, and their protégés. I memorize countless persuasive essays and case studies on rape, domestic violence, war crimes, sexism in the workplace, and religious doctrine. I fill every nook of my mind with fodder. Stories, statistics, talking points, even self-defense classes, for lessons to use myself and pass onto others. They say information is empowering. Sometimes though, information is so painful, it impales. My heart begs my body to break for a run and while I run, I weep. But I continue learning, resolved to do what I can.

I AM 20. Momma tries to leave Papa and returns, thrice. She leaves, he promises he will change, she returns. Every time, she sobs. I hate being half a planet away.

Along with *I love you*, the sentence women repeat with equal, rabid frequency is, *He is going to change.*

"I believe he can change. People can change, Reemani."

"People can. But it's a matter of choice. And ability."

Then, Nana Bhai passes away, on December 24th, 2002. Winter break. I fly to Bangkok and we all return to Bangladesh for the funeral.

Waves of people pay their respects to our benevolent giant. Naan is inconsolable. I stay by Momma's side, so close you'd have to peel me off like skin from fruit. The tough protecting the sweet. She cries for both of us. I prohibit my tears until I'm by myself with Nana Bhai.

Strangely, there's a sliver of twenty minutes when his coffin is left alone on the ground floor of our family compound. On this small patch of cold cement, he lies in his coffin and I sit on my haunches, my back against the wall of the building, my knees tucked into my torso. He's wrapped in white linen, from toe to neck. His eyes are rimmed in violet, as though he fought sleep for days. He looks peaceful though. I talk to him. He speaks too.

We wait while the funeral procession gathers in the family courtyard. It is finally quiet. Time graces us our own nook, though it has shown very little mercy otherwise.

I weep, curling like the leaves of mimosa touch-me-nots, that fold inward from the slightest contact of rain, animals, and insects. I wonder if they, too, curl from sorrow. Momma, my uncle, and my aunt move as a flock of birds. Grief and love have stitched them seamless, and they walk, cry, speak as one undulating movement of feeling. The first and only time Momma and my aunt are ripped from my uncle is when Nana Bhai's body is taken to be buried. Women aren't permitted in the funeral procession and during the burial. Gentle Momma curses and roars. The closest we are allowed is the cemetery gate. While the rest remain in the courtyard, she and I drive over to the cemetery, and whisper our love through the iron bars.

My parents and siblings return to Bangkok. I fly back to college. My parents inhabit a stalemate but only for a few months. Momma hoped tragedy would soften Papa. It is futile. She delivers him a pithy sentence like a single rose.

"If I wish to honor my father, I must leave."

Her choice has taken time to coagulate like blood on a gash kept fresh by years of determined picking. Sometimes death is the force that stuns us alive. She travels again to Dhaka and files for divorce. Once back in Bangkok, she moves in with a girlfriend, the mom of one of my high school friends.

Papa is shocked and devastated. He never thought she'd actually leave, despite the times he told her to or she sobbed she would. Now, he calls me often, weeping uncontrollably.

"It's a mystery," he repeats. "How could this have happened?"

"Papa, you're an intelligent man. It happened because you gave her incentive."

He doesn't like that. "No," he shouts, growing bitter, crying harder. The heat he would throw on both her and me now falls solely on me.

"I have to go to class, Papa. I love you." I hang up, bracing myself for the next phone-call.

They spin, and their natures switch. She expresses anger built from decades, and he sobs. We kids dance on a tightrope, juggling fire and water, trying to keep the elements from falling.

Finally, Momma is free to be. She moves into her own apartment in Bangkok, the very first home where her name is on the lease. My brother is 17 and continues to live with Papa. My sister is 10 and lives with Momma. Visits with the opposite parent happen casually—custody is the one battle our family will not wage. The school my siblings and I have attended poaches Momma from her smaller one and hires her to found a new department. Her career grows in seismic leaps.

Then, a month after the divorce is finalized, she finds love. He is kind, a teacher who has taught on three continents, humbled and wizened by years spent alone. An introvert like myself, he is thoughtful and hilarious, used to be an actor, and is a runner as well. Born in Nebraska, raised in Oregon, he lives now in Seoul. Momma meets him at a teachers conference in Dubai.

She calls me four days after meeting him and says, "I found my person."

I promptly lose my mind.

"Momma, you've never dated before! It's a desolate wilderness out there and you're a darling, little, impressionable cub surrounded by carnivorous beasts. You spent two days together! This is insane!"

"Reema, we're in love."

"Aaaaargh, Momma!" As usual, Papa's calling on the other line, with nothing particular to say but urgent in his need to say it and feel heard. (Perhaps the multiplicity of lines was invented so one can manage the needs of all parents, all the time.) "You guys drive me crazy! I have to go to class." A beep lets me know Papa has gone to voice mail. I'll have to call him between class and rehearsal.

Lo and behold, Momma's new love holds strong. Weeks turn into months and the months move toward a year. They make their long-distance relationship work through long weekend visits and Skype. We see a shift in Momma. My siblings see it happen in person; I hear it on the phone, then experience it when I visit briefly, between summer internships. For the first time in our lives, we witness Momma relax. Have fun. *Laugh.* Her laughter is glorious, the sound bubbling and curling like sugar deepening into caramel when held over low heat. We learn an incredible thing: Momma is funny as well. She's a firecracker. She just needed to find her match.

She sings and dances. She plays jokes on us. She laughs until she hiccups and hyperventilates, until her face crumples and her makeup runs. Our poised, elegant, immaculately made Momma never looks more beautiful than when she is shaken, stirred, and unmade by joy. Love unknots her tightly stitched perfection. It releases her into something so lovely it must have a name.

Happiness.

Early on they know they'll marry, by the end of this year. I'm thrilled beyond measure for Momma, and for us as a family. Heartbreaking though, is that Papa spirals downward in his grief. Desperate to return him to standing, we kids braid a rope, throw him this line. He tries but mostly, can't grab it.

It is October of my sophomore year. I'll be 21 next month. In two months, Momma and her love will be married. An email from Papa arrives.

He writes I have betrayed him. I advocated for their divorce. I failed to save their marriage. I am failing to halt this future one. I am unfit as a daughter and therefore, disowned.

I read the letter twice. I wait for tears that don't arrive.

His love has always been a time of day I'm trying to catch and can't. As though locked in a house without windows, set free only after the sun has risen high, I now run after the light, grasping at the sun as it moves from morning to noon to afternoon to dusk, too late, too lacking to ever feel warm.

Where did you go? Where do you go? Where have you gone? Come back.

Breathe. Assess the situation for potential danger, risks, and solutions.

Tuition. I need to guarantee tuition. The UN subsidizes part of it. If he legally disowns me, they'll revoke their aid.

I'll be fine. I have been working on-campus jobs since my freshman year. I have wonderful professors. They'll help me find additional financial aid.

Wait. When Momma sent him divorce papers, he called her and his first sentences were, "Do you know what this will do to my career? And my family? My reputation? The shame."

He won't legally disown me. It would call ugly attention to his priorities. I quietly recite, *One page.* I put his words in my little pink box, home to an obedient ballerina spinning to a song sewn from a handful of notes, lingering in the air long after she slows still. I snap shut my laptop and go to rehearsal. I am the lead.

Soon it is the wedding. Given that she is in Bangkok, he in Seoul, and my siblings and I are in school, it makes sense for the families to gather for Christmas in America and have the wedding then too. We'll share a few sacred weeks before everyone scatters, including the newlyweds. It's the first time the families will meet. My brother and sister have met our soon-to-be stepdad, but I haven't.

We meet in snowy Oregon. Momma, my siblings, my soon-to-be-stepdad and I all stay in a cabin in the woods, exotic and bizarre to the four of us born and raised along the equator. We have our first Christmas, ever. I'm stunned by the audacious bounty of the holiday, the continual eating of chocolate and cookies, the music and merriment, the brightly wrapped presents. Gold for the girls, silver for the boys, with handwritten cards so lovingly penned I'm stuffed on them alone. What more could there possibly be?

There are stockings with our names in glitter. They hold additional presents: ridiculous, unnecessary, delightful things like chocolates fashioned to look like Mt. Hood, so delicately crafted that I don't want to destroy them through something as unrefined as eating. But I do, and it feels divine. There's also lip gloss, bath bubbles, fuzzy socks, running socks, miniature lotions and shampoos with scents like Cherry Blossom and Island Vanilla, and countless candles. We light a few. I'm careful to ration the light for later.

We sit inside the glow. My brother is beaming, my sister is giggling, and Momma is radiant, laughing as her fiancé attempts to stuff all the wrapping paper into shopping bags. It's like trying to pack a cloud into a bottle. His brow is furrowed with effort. We each still have our main presents to unwrap. They have gotten me one, but I want something specific. I muscle my courage and tug on his sleeve.

"For my present, may I call you 'Dad'?"

He stares. A few seconds pass. Oh God, I've asked for too much.

"Of course." His voice is hoarse with emotion. His eyes brim then spill. Momma's and mine follow. Nearby, by the window, looking out at the pillowy snow, I feel you smiling. My smile quickens to catch up with yours.

Then it is December 27th, 2004, the day of the wedding. I'm Momma's maid of honor. Everyone wears saris and kurtas. We are burnt sienna, vermilion, daffodil, peacock, rose, scarlet, sunset-pink, mango, buttercup, royal blue, and every gold imaginable. If I still had my box of 100 Crayolas, they would nod their approval. When Momma walks toward us, I feel old yet renewed, and inundated with relief. We made it. The tight fist that is my heart unclenches slightly.

Dad was raised Catholic and Momma, Muslim. They are spiritual but not religious. They found a minister who wrote them a perfect sermon on love.

"Incredible that a boy, born in America, and a girl, born in Bangladesh, can travel through continents, time, and relationships, to meet in Dubai. Incredible that their love can bring together two families, now deepened and strengthened through their unity."

I finally understand what it means to cry tears of joy. Yesteryear, the phrase was romantic affectation. Today, I live the words, the moment forever anchored in my cells by the scent of jasmine and the song of glass bangles dancing on our wrists.

Momma kisses Dad, laughs, turns toward me, and wipes away a tear.

PAPA RETURNS. He reowns me through an email, six months after the previous. He writes he'd like to see me. He is traveling to New York for a conference at the UN Headquarters. He takes the Amtrak north to visit briefly. We meet for brunch.

It's a Saturday in late January, the air freezing but bright with sunlight. We'll have only a few hours before he has to return to Manhattan. Papa meets me at school and we take a short walk through campus. The years have bent him; he is smaller than before. I will never, ever fail to be shocked by his diminutive physicality. In me, he lives so large. He wears a brown tweed jacket with elbow patches, looking like a befuddled professor, slightly lost in the walking world.

We taxi to the restaurant. It's designed to appear French, with cheerful red leather booths, small round checkered tables, and cross-hatched chairs. Big windows allow in abundant light. We sit, order, and while we wait for our food, he gives me $500 in cash and a bottle of duty-free perfume bought on his flight. Calvin Klein Eternity.

"What's happening?" I ask.

He looks at me, turns his gaze out the window. I asked for a table by the window lest we want to face something other than ourselves.

"Can we talk about the disownment, please?"

His eyes return. "You're young," he says. "I forgive you."

Astonishment mutes me. I spear my salad; he picks at his. Long minutes pass. In the loud silence, we finish our meal.

We taxi to the train station. The cold makes us shiver, highlighting Papa's frailty, the toll of divorce and distance from his loved ones, and the fact he won't be around forever. The ghastly wind catches hold of Papa's comb-over, sets it flapping like a bereft wing. With his right hand, he brushes the dozen strands to the left, a gesture as dear, loved, and familiar as Momma's scent, my brother's laugh, my sister's curls. Something in my chest twinges. After long months, my tears release. He is doing what any of us can—our best. The train careens in. We're forced a quick, sudden goodbye. We hug, both crying.

The tragic truth is that only through grief comes his softening. For my siblings, he becomes the father I prayed for. Over the coming years, I'll watch them from afar. My siblings will spend most of their summer and winter breaks with Papa. For a long while, I will decline invitations due to work and plain trepidation. It's as though I, the oldest, were practice. He parents the younger kids kindly. Loving, attentive, sweet, gentle, reliable. I fill with relief, happiness, and envy.

SERVE

SERVE

✦

I AM 21. The trees flit by, sun-bleached and wonderfully familiar, so different from pine, maple, oak. A Thai singer croons "chan rak ter" on the radio, which means *I love you*. The cab is sweltering, the leather seats sticky against my legs and shoulders. It is the summer between junior and senior year. I'm visiting my family, splitting time between Momma and Papa, and working at an orphanage three miles from our old gated community. I blink my newly LASIK-ed eyes. The surgery was an early graduation present from Papa. Blink, blink. Things seem clear.

Three miles, and reality shifts seismically. The orphanage, Baan Fuen Faa, is for children with physical and cognitive disabilities. Baan means *home*. Most children arrive as infants, orphaned by their families because of their disabilities. Some students aren't orphans but come purely for the uniquely welcoming environment. The Baan was founded by Her Majesty the Queen. The Royal Family is exceptionally generous, compassionate, and connected to the citizens and their needs, one of the few monarchies truly respected and loved by their people.

Every day, these three miles peel away the world. Every day, I arrive at 7 a.m., leave around 5 p.m. I speak little Thai, and the other caregivers speak little English. The children, from infancy to age 18, speak solely Thai. But in the infant and toddler ward, where I've been assigned, we communicate fluently. Our language is made of intuition, touch, smiles, meals, diaper-changes, and baths in an assembly line. The day begins with hugs and nuzzles and ends with lullabies.

In our ward, most of the kids have cerebral palsy. There are forty kids and four adults, but we aren't strictly assigned to ten children each. We move as a four-person unit, adapting to the children's needs.

I received this job by showing up. I completed the school year, drove to JFK Airport with a professor, wrote my final paper on the plane, arrived in Bangkok twenty-seven hours later, slept the day, and taxied here the next morning. I followed the signs to the director's office and asked her how I could help.

Due to my rudimentary Thai and my eagerness to serve, brimming deep and alive as an ocean, I've been entrusted with the lives of small children despite my staggering lack of experience and accreditation. The days have confirmed, though, that care is a thing one learns by doing. There is but one way to learn how to curve and distribute my weight when holding a child: I hold her.

We're underfunded and understaffed. The floors are cement like those in the slum school I worked in during high school. The surrounding grounds are gravel and clay, caked by the 100-degree weather. The diapers are rough linen. We wash them by hand and secure them in place with safety pins, like Momma used to with mine. Momma swears that I, like most third-world babies, was potty trained by eight months. Washing endless nappies by hand is perfect incentive to potty train a child as swiftly as possible.

Most of the cots resemble the one I used as a newborn. Government sanctioned, metal painted white, chipped and rusted by time's touch. Speckled among them are other cribs, wooden, brightly painted with teddy bear or rainbow decals and carvings, like the ones my siblings had. These cribs are secondhand, donated by our gated neighborhood or purchased by church groups.

We maintain a calm, strict schedule for meals, baths, and naps. Above all else, kids need love and stability. Consistency and routine are calming and comforting. The nurses move among the children with steady, confident cheerfulness. They teach me rudimentary physical and occupational therapy to do with the kids. It's marvelous and humbling to witness their development.

I've met an angel. Little Star is a boy unlike any other at the orphanage. He is 4 but the size of a 1-year-old. His head is shaved, like most of the kids', to lessen the likelihood of lice and for relief from the heat. But other than his shorn scalp, he bears no resemblance to the others.

He was born with all four limbs fused in place. His joints don't exist. He doesn't have rotator cuffs, elbows, hip joints or knees. His arms and legs are permanent right angles, turned downward. He's unable to move them. His spine is fused as well. He cannot sit on his own, and lies flat on his back or on his tummy. He shimmies his body, flopping like a fish, to propel himself along the floor. He has a tiny, well-defined six-pack because of this motion. The rest of his muscles have atrophied.

We're unclear whether he can grow beyond his present size. Nor is there a way to measure life expectancy—he is an absolutely singular child. Every child is unique; he is vividly so. He knows only a few words. He knows "sawasdee krap," which means *hello*. "Ahaan." *Food.* "Naam." *Water.* And "khop khun krap." *Thank you.* He forms the words the gummy, gooey way most toddlers do, dropping the consonants. He hasn't many friends. He uses the four phrases to spice his own language of sounds, gentle gurgles, squawks, and squeals that croon from his mouth in an ongoing soft patter, keeping himself company. He babbles and bubbles, a cheerful brook beginning and ending by the same rock.

He nearly always grins. If he grows hungry or tired, he'll be a little quiet. Sometimes, he whimpers. But unlike most 4-year-olds, he won't sob or throw a tantrum.

I love him madly. I nickname him Little Star for his limbs, his starfish shimmy, and the smile that rarely leaves him. Despite his lonesomeness, he smiles. He is a star, faraway light.

Solitude. A lack of frequent, consistent connection. A lack of deep love. These are the reasons Little Star hasn't learned any phrases other than those four. Attributing his voicelessness to a learning disorder would feel kinder on the heart. No. He rarely speaks because a lack of intimacy has atrophied not only the muscles in his arms and legs but also his voice. The voice, too, is a muscle.

Every week, women's groups from various embassies, NGOs, and churches visit. Aside from donations, they gift companionship. Every week, the women gravitate toward their favorites, kids particularly cute, charismatic, and lively. Little Star is rarely visited. Finding him discomfiting, most people avert their attention.

All the caregivers are devoted, loving, and well-trained. They're weighed down with countless responsibilities and dozens of children. Little Star's basic needs are met, all except for the one needed most: authentic closeness. Embraces, eye-contact, and most of all, language. Language fosters personality. Humor. Curiosity. Interests. The light in us is lit, and we begin to discover our voice. He needs stories and lullabies, jokes followed by laughter, someone to point outside to the birds and repeat the syllables back for each word, not just once but as many times he needs.

Little Star is cheerful. But is he happy? He chirps. But is he communicative or inquisitive? Does he feel wonder, and when he was 3 years old, did he ask "Why?" all day long? We ask questions when we trust Momma is there to answer them. We stop asking if ignored repeatedly. We cry first from impulse and reason, but if our cries are not met, we stop. All the orphans are exceptionally even-keeled. They've learned to mute hunger, loneliness, and their need for others. Perhaps Little Star did ask *why* until he learned his call for love and acknowledgment was rarely answered. Like his limbs and voice, his faith in others has been sapped of life, by life.

I see him trying to connect, communicate, be heard and understood, and I'm hit with memories of my own attempts. There are so many ways we humans can atrophy.

Today was like most of our days. Quiet, peaceful. It is 3 p.m. and the children are napping in rows of cots neatly organized, mosquito nets swaddling each bed like dainty cocoons. The kids are dressed in tunics or tank tops and shorts made from strong, durable cotton. Some are faintly pink or blue, assigned by gender. But time and wear are fading them into one shade of beige.

Now, watching the children sleep, I need a sudden break. I need these sometimes. I walk outside, duck behind the building, and breathe to keep from crying. I feel your presence nearby. I blink a few hard times and return to the kids.

The air is languid and thick. The ceiling fans try their best to cut through the humidity that hangs like breath, moist and close. The faint scent of antiseptic and baby powder lives forever in the air. We lather the children in both, creating a paste that cools, soothes, and protects their skin from heat and mosquitos. The song of the orphanage is gentle. Quiet humming, trills of laughter, children running and playing, giggling and cooing. The usual heartwarming sounds of childhood. Only softer.

The kids have so little and they feel deep gratitude for it all. When receiving a hug, a box of hand-me-down toys, or a new set of crayons, they smile and thank effusively. Every Friday they receive a special meal—rice porridge with steamed ground pork. The gift thrills them. They giggle, smile, and, those who can, leap to their feet to dance and applaud the meal's arrival.

There is another child I've grown very close to. Her name is Apeechaya. She calls me Ma. The women of the orphanage call me her Ma as well. She is 2 and has cerebral palsy. Her left leg is slightly bent and thinner than her right. She crawls using the other three limbs, pulling the left leg along tenderly, like a wing at rest. The staff have trained me in her physical therapy. We also do speech therapy, exercises to facilitate language, and I'm teaching her to use a baby walker so she can gain mobility and confidence. I dream of adopting her one day. If I can't grow up quickly enough to give her a home, I'll make sure she finds one all the same.

It will take a few years, but we do manage to find her a home.

Here at the orphanage, my vast desire to give love and feel love is welcome. I feel peaceful. The summer months move altogether too swiftly. I leave, promising to return.

I AM 22. IN the fall semester of my senior year, I write, direct, produce, and star in my first play, *Spinach and Babies*. My professors give me full creative freedom and theater space. The play is magical realism with archetypes for characters, a tale about a mother in search of her child, aided by a nurse, impeded by a politician. For every performance, the audience fills the space to bursting, breaking every fire safety code. At the end of one performance, a girl in the audience is sobbing so vehemently, she vomits.

Having played every role, I don't have any need to stay. I have enough credits to graduate early, it'll save money, and I'm ravenous to work. I graduate summa cum laude, with two degrees and a minor. I forgo the ceremony and move to New York City on January 15th, 2006, in a blizzard, with two suitcases, a laptop, $1,000, and the ferocious zeal to make the city mine. I have a five-week sublet my playwriting professor helped me find and a job as a hostess at a five-star restaurant, starting the 16th. My first sensation in the City is kinship; her appetite, pace, and hardened grit fit like a mother tongue. My immediate goals are simple: take film classes, get headshots, find an agent. April seems like a nice deadline.

I am the only person I know in New York City. Our family is scattered across different time zones. Momma, Dad, and my sister in Seoul, my brother and Papa in Bangkok. Phone calls are luxuries. Emails are gifts. I'll visit Thailand and Bangladesh briefly, this coming summer, to work at the orphanage and visit family. Aside for those few weeks, New York has me in totality.

The City teems with men. I've dated since I was 17 and have been dating through college, but the energy here is entirely different. Most of us who move to New York City have "I Want" at our core. We arrive with dilated pupils, hungry to make our dreams come true. Ambition, desire, and seduction take on a feral pitch. We don't simply court one another; we hound, frothing at the mouth. One man, then another, and another and another, will tell me I am his, and I will love this like water. I drink each syllable of every promise, letting their honey drip down my chin. Their words tease aside the fibers to soothe the parched place I imagine is my heart. I'm a dehydrated peach, a jolt of energy, perfect for easy consumption. Shrunken and pinched by my desire to love and be loved, to belong and hold close, so pleasing and sweet that I'm nearly cloying.

All I want is to make you happy.

Most of the time, "you" means purely you, my lifelong friend. But sometimes, my vision blurs and "you" means you, and includes him, him, her, and her, anyone, everyone, and most importantly, the man I'm with at that present time. He stands stark center.

I learn swiftly this mentality can drown a girl.

The faster a man declares love, the more likely and quickly he'll rescind. Within months, I learn not to confuse passion for proof that a man, any man, is my beloved. I learn, too, that I tend to move toward unkind and often dangerous men, and they rush toward me.

The first of my suddenly born, suddenly dead affairs is with a man who works at the same restaurant as me.

"You unhinge me," he says, and I think this means he loves me. Silly Reema.

A few weeks later, during my shift, I feel a searing pain in my abdomen. I retreat to the ladies' room. As a hostess, I don't have a uniform, but it's required I dress elegantly and entirely in black. I wear a tight pencil skirt, a long-sleeved V-neck, and four-inch stilettos. The pain keeps rhythm with my heartbeat, each throb threatening to tip me off my heels and onto the marble floor. With one hand on the wall to prop myself, I shimmy up my pencil skirt, hovering over the toilet. Something blue, pink, and veined with purple slides out of me and into the toilet bowl, landing with a sickening plop.

My body hadn't realized anything was different. Like the rest of the City, I run so hard, with jaw-clenched single-mindedness, it's difficult to separate any fatigue or twinge from the daily usual. I clean up, ball my thong in a paper towel, and stuff it deep into the trashcan with the heel of my stiletto. I flush the toilet, bid the memory of my lover and I goodbye, and return to work. He's working the same shift. I don't tell him. He's rather angst-ridden and dramatic and is likely to spin this into a sign that he must save me with his love.

As I, clearly, need saving.

A miscarriage isn't a cosmic message that we're destined loves. This miscarriage was a blessing and evidence that my body knows how to take of herself.

I brush the event aside. I send out headshots, resumes, and cover letters to a list of agents culled from *Backstage*, an industry resource. A few call me to audition. Every agency asks me to prepare one 90-second contemporary monologue. I haven't a clue what that means. My training has been Shakespeare, the Greeks, the French, and Chekhov.

For my first audition, I walk in beaming and perform three minutes of Chekhov. Nina from *The Seagull*. It isn't light, lovely fare. By the end of the meandering monologue, Nina and I are crying. When I return to my body, I scold myself for my stubbornness. I should've adapted. I have completely botched this opportunity. I look up to find all three agents have tears in their eyes. Sitting center, a beautiful man with the slightest Southern swing in his voice asks, "What are you doing tomorrow?"

"Hostessing."

"Thursday?"

"All yours," I grin.

During our meeting, he shares the agency's philosophy. The company was founded by two powerhouse women, pioneers in the industry. They're a boutique with a roster of carefully selected clients. Thus, they are able to closely understand and guide each individual on their unique path.

"I always ask actors two questions," he says. "What made you choose acting, and when did you know?"

I smile. "I've known since I was 15. That I'd adopt kids, and be a voice for those without one. For me, that's the best way I can serve the planet."

He looks thoughtful, a slow smile stretching like light breaking through morning clouds.

"I grew up in a Southern Baptist community," he says, "in a very small, insular town. My dad was our minister. When I realized I was gay, a thought that helped me align my homosexual self with my spiritual self was that maybe one reason God makes gays is so we can give homes to the orphans of the world. We are all one big Self, one big love."

"Where can I sign?"

He laughs and we share our first hug. It is the first of April. On this same day, across town, I sign with a different agency for modeling, commercial, and voice-over representation. I begin auditioning for theater, television, film, commercials, and print.

My body is now a fine science. I am now a 00. "Doublezero-doublezerodoublezero" is the mantra I chant while running on the treadmill. My anorexia feels like an omnipresence residing inside me, more a siren than a disease. It bewitches my arms, legs, mind, actions, trying to lure me toward hostile waves. It nestles within me just like you do, but it is shadowy while you are lit and pure. You are my better self, while Anorexia is the name of my punishing voice.

As with any behavior that is self-admonishing, when things feel calm, I eat, rest well, and speak to myself kindly. When around chaos,

I revert to punishment, tucking tightly into my harmful habits, like a centipede recoiling from the world's graze. This, now, the life I've chosen of an aspiring actress in New York, dating the kind of men I date, swarms with chaos.

I let six of my eight piercings close and decide to grow my hair. I've kept it pixie short for seven years. My hair is *mine.* The look at any given time is less about appearance and more about my controlling it. I decide its importance, its length, its style, when it grows, and when it's cut. In three months, my hair grows from two inches to my chin. By the end of the year, it touches the middle of my back. I guess it yearned to grow.

Quickly I realize the length of my hair parallels the amount of power it commands over others. Unsurprising yet stunning. I now viscerally understand why hair is revered in Bangladesh and tied tightly to a woman's worth. Why it's lusted after and feared to the point where women are ordered to hide it in certain religions. Hair tempts, distracts, seduces, impresses, and is therefore very threatening to mindsets that preach women matter very little. How offensive. How volatile. Of course it must be hidden.

A year is all it needed to grow. Now, when I turn my back to the mirror and peer around, I see locks down the length of my back, covering sharp shoulder blades. Lightly, I toss my head. My hair sways languidly, moving like a sheet of lava.

FIGHT

FIGHT

✦

I AM 23. My hand pulls at the plastic ring attaching me to the subway rail. My wrist grows sore with each tug as the train lurches, burping noisily without rhythm or apology. It couldn't be more disinterested in us, this mass of bodies, compacted and caught, willingly. My palm and fingers slide along the grimy ring, the plastic soiled by countless hands, each leaving their oily imprint. I curse myself for forgetting my gloves, necessary not only for warmth but for cleanliness and peace of mind. As much as I loathe the cold, the layered protection of winter attire is much welcomed.

The man standing behind me pushes his crotch against my lower back. I'm grateful for my thick coat. Among all the clubs, predators have the most inclusive membership. They come in all forms: politicians, businessmen, lawyers, teachers, students, electricians, construction workers, old, young, white, black, brown, and everything in between. This one burrows his hard nub into me. The pressure makes me recede as far as possible, which is scant given our cramped quarters. He knows this. He revels in this, sucking it like juice spilt from a ripe bite. I turn to glare at him. He feigns nonchalance.

The doors open. A mouthful of us spit onto the platform. We scurry, spread, each person in a different stage of gritty swift. It's rare to find a born-and-raised New Yorker. Most of us have come here with a fervent purpose, arriving on the wings of a wish. We plunge into the flow, weaving our narratives with one another's, moving as one pulsing organism.

I emerge from underground. The crisp evening envelops me in a gulp. I don't need to check my bearings. My pace matches the quickest foot. A few loiter, drag their feet, second-guess their direction. Not us, the urgent ones.

I make it home, now in my fifth sublet, and on the good nights (like tonight, as the man on the subway decided not to follow me home and has slipped into the past), I exhale with relief. Another day closed, and thankfully, safely. I hang my coat.

The months rifle through me like mismatched fruit in a slot machine, failing to land in line. Then, one mundane Monday, I stumble into an old colleague. An actor like myself. A friend.

"What a great surprise!" he says. "We have so much to catch up on. Dinner? Friday?"

"Sure," I reply.

We met a few years ago in the summer between my sophomore and junior year, while working at Williamstown, the most renowned theater festival in the nation. He was a bit older than me, in graduate school at Brown. We became quick, close friends the way everyone does in a community of artists.

In the performance arts, we cultivate closeness through specific practices. For weeks or months, we do exercises crafted to foster trust and loyalty. We divulge achingly personal stories. We spend long hours rehearsing, suspended from reality, in the studio, onstage, and on the road. Therefore, by the time we perform, the audience believes we are family, siblings, lovers, or best friends. It's our job to communicate intimacy. Thus, once two artists have worked together, we are allied for life. We are part of a larger, loving tribe, generations deep. It is understood that we don't dishonor this.

Now, years later, he and I have run into each other in the City, the way most of us do and will. We catch sight of each other in the waiting room of a studio, the way most of us do and will. We hug with the easy affection all actors who have worked together do and will.

Dinner is wonderful. He's wearing a button-down shirt and jeans. I'm wearing a short sundress and ballet flats. We share stories and laugh. My apartment is around the corner. I invite him up for tea. We talk and feel the attraction. He kisses me. I kiss him back. It's all delightfully harmless.

It's getting late. I walk him to the front door, adjacent to my bedroom.

"Good night. Thanks for a great time."

He wants more.

He kisses me again, harder. He pushes me against the wall, my 5'4", 105-pound frame feeling pitiful to his 5'11", 180 pounds.

"You have to leave now." I keep my voice light but persuasive. He tries to push me onto the bed, forcefully, not remotely playfully. I hold my ground.

"No. You have to go."

"No," he says, grinning, his teeth glowing in the darkness. "I'm not going anywhere."

The air has thickened like blood clotting. Dread curls around the edges of the room, like the scent of rain before the sky slits open. He comes toward me. I back away. I breathe slowly through my nose to calm my lungs and pace my heart. My mind sifts through every case study and self-defense lesson I've memorized over the years. I bolster myself with tactics, ready to use them: Place one hand on each side of his head, poke hard into his eyes with my thumbs. Knee him in the groin. Bite, kick, scream. Urinate. The shock and disgust might unsettle him, letting me run.

He grabs me. I steel my body against his. I try to take his hands off me, twisting my arms and torso the way I was taught to do with assaulters. My teeth and hands tingle, eager to bite, to claw, to obey my orders.

But.

The vile truth, as bitter as bile: He is much too strong.

Somewhere nearby, I feel your heart clench, mimicking mine.

I fight with all my might, flaying like a fish caught on a hook. He keeps his hold on me, and the tussle flings us onto the bed. My left cheek is pressed against his shoulder and turned toward the wall.

My room is pink. I painted it this way, pink with a daisy-yellow trim. Growing up, I always wanted a pink room. There's a Benjamin Moore a block down from my agent's office. The day I signed with him, I gave myself a pink room. I've been trying to create something soft for myself, within the black and gray bruise that is New York.

Life is surprising. Just as crayons fail to taste like their names, paint on a wall will be much brighter than paint in a can. I envisioned a light, blush pink but ended up with pink as vivid as flesh sliced open.

Now, I'm inside a mouth.

Lining the flesh-pink walls are stacks of books, arranged in a way I think is pretty. My bedframe is lovely too, black wrought-iron in a delicate pattern of leaves and flowers, much like my tattoo on my ribcage, tucked into the small spot between my breasts. I chose that area for its sweet privacy, believing no one would see it unless invited. I found the bedframe on Craigslist. It didn't come with a bedspring so I balance it on plywood boards.

I haven't stopped fighting. I am still trying to wiggle out from beneath him. He's pinned my wrists above my head, first with both his hands and then with only one hand to hold my wrists down. With the other hand he's undone his jeans and hiked up my dress. Now, he knees apart my legs, and enters. As he jams in, I order myself to imagine that what I'm feeling is an inanimate instrument, like those found in a gynecologist's office, which given my age, I've been to only thrice. Now, he grunts and grunts, his upper lip, forehead, palms, and torso growing clammy with sweat, saturating the room with his scent, musky, male, yet acutely his own. Cracking like lightning, the wooden boards break from our combined weight and exertion. The mattress tilts down like a split bone. It juts into the air at an awkward angle, shaking with each thrust. The broken boards scratch my flesh-pink walls.

"You're just too beautiful," he hisses between groans. Astonishing, the power of the human word. Through a meager handful of sound and suggestion, I feel guilt for being myself and fury for having it used against me. I wish to be anyone but myself, to be anything but attractive, to disappear and remain hidden, indefinitely. I wish these things and I hate him for it.

I've looked left, right, down, so now, I look into him. His sounds, scent, and desire have filled the room full of him, yet he has completely left. His pupils have dilated so deeply his entire eyes look black, dulled of light, dead of any humanity. I'm still repeating, "You have to go, you have to go, you have to go," although I don't know whom I'm referring to anymore, him or myself. I'd be grateful for either one of us to vanish. I switch to saying loudly, "No, no, no!" spitting the words like seeds that won't take.

Here we are. This. Is. Happening.

The horrifying certainty hits me like raw steak slamming a chopping board. Perhaps because he, too, believes this is an assured acquisition, suddenly, his hold on my wrists slackens. His moment of sloth is all I need. I slip my wrists out from his hand, press the heels of my palms on his shoulders and push with all my might.

"NO," I yell. The sudden volume and physical force are enough to shock him backward. He comes at the same time he falls. If this weren't rape, if I weren't terrified, if my voice weren't hoarse from being ignored, I'd be embarrassed for him.

I scoot back until I'm against the headboard, hugging my legs to my chest. My throat is chapped. I taste blood. I must've bitten my tongue. It'll hurt tomorrow. He puts on his clothes, swiftly, silently. I say it once more:

"LEAVE."

He does. After his sentence, "You're just too beautiful," he hasn't said a word.

I don't call anyone for help. I sit in the dark for fifteen minutes, listing my options and weighing the costs of each. Speaking of this to my family would hurt me further and dishonor them. To negotiate any legal retribution for rape is a brutal ordeal. I'm here on my OPT visa, my agents will sponsor my next visa, and if I accrue enough professional credits, I can obtain a green card. Every minute and penny is devoted toward the next meal, audition, job, and rent check.

I am working so hard to live here. In addition to the grueling interrogation I can expect from most medical, police, and legal staff, and loved ones, I'm wary that if I press charges against my rapist, the legal process will cause me further injury given my Bangladeshi citizenship. The fine print of my immigrant status claims I'm entitled to the same justice as an American woman, but often, the promise of justice fails to influence the reality of justice. All the more if you are brown. All the more if you were born in a Muslim country. Similarly, the minutiae behind immigration include nothing to suggest that pressing charges against a rapist would compromise my status here, or when I file for a green card. But all it would take to endanger my life is for my case to land in the hands of that one male immigration officer who believes women should be shamed and punished for the crimes inflicted upon our bodies.

Momma's face flashes in my mind, my storyline reflecting hers in a unforeseen way: why is it that more often than not, a woman wishing to live, work, speak, and succeed must first consider the imprint, response, and threat of the men around her, caught as we all are in architecture built and run by men?

A question that answers itself: it is the way it is because of the way and by whom it was created.

I fill with a soundless anger so complete and piercing it feels like a scream.

I cannot jeopardize my chances at staying in America. I love this country beyond words. Here I'm allowed to be who I am. I don't have a place in Thailand. Nor in Bangladesh. I'm profoundly American. I'm independence, grit, and freedom of speech, personified. Staying here is crucial for the life I want, to be a voice for those without one. The irony is acutely painful. I won't press charges. I have to be quiet now to be a voice for others later. The hardest fact to reconcile is that my silence allows him the liberty to do this to other women. This thought of hypothetical others brands me with guilt.

What now?

In unison, you and I answer: *Get him off you.*

I take a shower. Scrolling down and along the walls like the stock exchange are statistics and stories I've learned and lived as a girl and student. What a twisted joke. I feel the rise of tears build and with them, my heartbeat, sounding like the decisive march of soldiers, resolute and approaching. So immense grows my panic that it drowns the sound of water and sucks in my breath. I begin to choke.

Stop.

Breathe.

I breathe. This is rage and self-pity, two faces of fear. Fear, like justice, is another luxury I cannot afford.

This is *my* story. He is but one page. One character. I refuse to feel small, dirty, or somehow damaged. This wasn't sex; this was assault. He is neither a man nor all men combined; he is one predator. He is a scab, and Momma taught me not to pick scabs. Especially if they are human.

Under my makeshift waterfall, I speak these words. They bloom then distill into one sentence: *Only I author my life.*

I step out of the water. In the mirror, I find my reflection. As it tends to, your invisible form mingles with my lines.

You are always here.

"Hello, you," I say aloud. I tilt my head, birdlike. Our reflection follows.

I smile ruefully. I've been trained to smile like a movie star. Not an aspiring star but a star. A smile big, bright, and symmetrical. However, left to my own devices and late at night, my smile is wry and lopsided. You don't seem to mind.

Now the wrecked bed. I return the wooden slats to their precarious balance, angling them on the thin lip of metal, making sure they don't succumb to the Earth's pull. I lift the mattress. So recently overpowered, I now smile, not from the strength in my arms, but the lack of trembling in my hands.

I sleep.

The next day I have an audition for *Gossip Girl*. *Gossip Girl* is presently the most coveted job for girls my age. More often than not, I'm asked to read for the exotic vixen. I don the requisite tight black dress, five-inch heels, and maneuver my mouth around the vapid script. No one in their right mind will believe me in these roles.

"Try a giggle," says the casting director. "Tone down the intelligence."

The producers nod in unison.

"We need you to be a little *less*." The casting director's hands gesture as though tamping down gravity.

I'm certain there are brilliant actresses who can achieve such feats. But I'm a mediocre pretender. Some things I cannot act.

I subway to my hostessing job and clock in a few hours. I mute my brain, play pretty, let everyone believe what they need to believe. Afterwards, I babysit for a family I met a few weeks ago. The mama is a Broadway star and daddy a tennis icon. He is as steadfast in person as he is on court. She sears through life, blazing with the audacious confidence of an enduring flame. Their firstborn is nearly 1 and will be joined soon by two other daughters, all three golden-haired, blue-eyed beauties. The family resembles characters I've read about, never believing they might actually exist. They are *that* idyllic. Their apartment is the same. The first time I enter, a wondrous warmth spreads through me like hot tea renewing a body. So this is what it feels like. Home.

I balance the baby on my hip and look into her eyes, blue as the skies in sonnets. We are safe in each other. All she wants is for me to be present. I fill with a love so authentic it arrests my breath.

Mama and Daddy return home, I to my pink room. Another day arrives, followed by another, the days form into months, months into years. I don't hear from him but I will run into him. I will run into him over the years because we are both actors, our world is tiny, and life has a harsh, wise way of doing what she does. She will give us things as provocation to die sooner, or to grow. I will read about him in the *Times*. I will see him at auditions. One time, I will sit across from him on the subway.

"How are you?" I will ask, looking him in the eye. In response, he will move through every shade of pale and burn. He will sputter and shake. I will refuse to break eye contact. I will smile. I will think, *Have you become more than your past self?*

Over time, I will meet an uncanny number of men like him. With each person, I grow better at sensing the volatility beneath the sheen. I feel it like incoming rain: he holds the dormant capability to inflict pain. Tally the encounters, and I run out of fingers and toes.

The idiom *everything happens for a reason* has never sat well with me. One cannot blurt "everything happens for a reason" to a person who has just lost a loved one, been raped, or been diagnosed with cancer. "Everything happens for a reason" sounds passive, as though all the power in one's narrative has been surrendered into the hands of others, or, to life's harsh whims and winds, to decide one's path, destiny, identity, and sense of self.

The truth I prefer is only I assign my experiences their reasons.

I choose to believe the reason this fateful evening intercepted my path was not to destroy my faith in men, life, or my instincts. The reason this night arrived was to prove and nourish my resilience. My beauty and youth will fade. People and money will come and go. But my formidable will to live is mine evermore.

Startling. Realizing this lights something within me. For the first time in my life, I like myself.

Papa visits during a UN conference. Time and loss have softened him like butter left on a countertop. He says the City terrifies him. The pace, scale, crowds, remarks. A terrain dotted with magic unlike anywhere else, but otherwise cacophonic, putrid, and obstinately gray.

"Don't you get scared?" he asks.

"Sometimes."

Life is masterful at being fearsome. But dear one, you are my loyal witness. You have stayed although life has grown painful. You haven't put me aside. You haven't disowned me. You haven't said, "Enough."

For that and more, I love you.

I AM 24. It is a Saturday afternoon at the restaurant. I am alone in the office, printing menus. We are closed until dinner. It is quiet. The celebrity chef and sommelier come in. They lob a few sophomoric jokes. I make polite small talk. They take a joke too far and suddenly, I'm pinned against a wall by the chef, his mouth on mine. The sommelier laughs.

When I share the story with the guy I'm presently dating, he says, "Well, you're just so cute and sweet." As though that exonerates the behavior.

I report the event to the manager, who is appalled.

"What would you like to do?" he asks, fearing a lawsuit. As if I have the energy, time, and money for one.

I want the chef to publicly own his behavior and apologize. To me and the other women I know he has harassed as well. Surprisingly, he obeys. A rare win.

Sad, though, that something so little as a man apologizing is considered a win.

My love, to remain and thrive in this city, I will need to fortify my spirit.

I leave the restaurant industry to work strictly in childcare. I start practicing Buddhism. I say goodbye to any friend who leeches my lifeblood. I begin studying nutrition, and cut out gluten, dairy, and alcohol. I have never enjoyed drinking. I hate anything that compromises my mind.

I spend more hours journaling. I run longer and harder. I write "Love" on the back of my left hand, a daily reminder and medicine. I start meditating and logging gratitude lists, writing every morning the names of loved ones and the qualities I admire in myself. I write my first screenplay, about a group of wrongfully incarcerated women in a Thai prison. I use the public library to research justice systems around the world. I don't share my writing. It feels like practice toward something else.

I read as much as I can, filling myself with the lives of others, drawing solace and strength. I search still, though, for that one author, one book, that will feel like my personal lifeline of love. More than purely love, I find myself craving kinship. As the years pass, the likelihood of ever finding that in a book grows dimmer. As the events of my strange life tally, finding a voice who may closely empathize feels increasingly impossible.

I leave the pink room and move into the next sublet, the sixth in what will be fourteen. I join a nondenominational church in Chelsea where most of the congregation is gay. The minister is a vibrant, witty lesbian. Her electric intelligence sizzles the room. There is much joy, togetherness, support, and quick and easy friendship. There's holding of hands, praying, singing in unison. After years of not crying, here I do, holding the hands of strangers. I'm seized by sobs I cannot place, coming from a wash of years. The tears sat on the ocean floor, submerged with creatures in various stages of decay and birth. Now, they rise to the surface and break to breathe.

I weep and weep. The woman holding my left hand gives it a squeeze and turns to smile at me. She's in her 50s, deliciously round and soft. From her billows a delicate hippy breeze of rosewood and incense, her bangles and charms tinkling as she dances to our collective song. The tall, Black man to my right pulls me to his bosom.

"There, there, sugar bean. Cry. You are okay." His Southern drawl curls around me like caramel hugs a tart green apple.

Slowly, I feel stronger. My day is an eccentric mix of jobs. I run from auditions to babysitting to acting class to rehearsals, performing endlessly. Occasionally I'll model, but it's not something I actively pursue. By the time I return to my sublet, tiny and bare, the sun has long bidden the world adieu. Within these walls I shed the roles I'm hired to play and resume the work of understanding who I am. When a month is particularly grueling, I'll remind myself, *This is one chapter. It is vital. Hold steady your flame.*

Auditioning is a marvelous, beastly enterprise. Every audition is a mix of a first interview with a dream boss, and a first date with a dream partner. The stakes are staggering, the investment deep. Acting is an exercise in vulnerability. I'm measured not only on experience, skill, training, and talent, but personality and soul. My ability (or inability) to impress and endear in a memorable, unique, authentic way is paramount. The better I know myself, fill into myself, and express that truth, the stronger my art.

They film me. They observe the way I walk into, command, and read the room—or fail to. They study the way I perform, sound, laugh, and hold myself. They scrutinize my body, height, weight, skin color, hair, smile, and degree and type of attractiveness.

"You're beautiful but not too beautiful or intimidating, so you'll appeal to a wide range of markets."

Great. I'm easily digestible.

"But."

There is always a clause.

"How tall are you? How much do you weigh? Okay. So you're not short-short but you're not tall, and you're thin and definitely not curvy, but not skinny-thin either. You're just . . ." the casting director trails off, waves a hand. "And you don't look like anything particular. Where are you from? Asia? But you're not *Asian* Asian. Bangladesh? Is that India? No? Bangladesh is Bangladesh? I thought you guys were darker. I mean, yeah, you're exotic enough, but you don't fit with the look we need." Then, a long sigh, for the egregious faux pas I have committed by, ultimately, being too much myself to prove palatable.

They then ask, "So, who are you? Tell us something about yourself." They're still filming. I make sure to answer eloquently, and be humble yet impressive, earnest yet charming. They give direction, ask that I perform the audition sides a different way. They ask I do them once, twice, thrice, differently, to test how adaptable, egoless, and quick I am. They'll wave me away without eye contact or praise me extravagantly. I thank them, leave the room, button up my heart, run to the next appointment. Every day, I have three to six auditions. I'll open and close the valves of my heart three to six times.

Countless variables are beyond my power: the production company's agenda, market statistics, a director, casting director, writer, or producer's personal biases, prejudices, and backstage politics. In the occasion I'm rejected, I won't be given straightforward closure. We don't receive automated or personalized rejection emails or calls. It feels like a string of passionate love affairs, each followed by complete heartbreak, silence, and abandonment.

I'm perversely adept at handling this industry. And lifestyle. There's nothing romantic about being a struggling or working artist, and to think it will be is the first step toward disappointment. One evening, after a seemingly endless day of auditions and babysitting, I'm greeted home by a toilet overflowing with feces and vomit. My druggie roommates are nowhere to be found. I kick off my heels, pin up my hair, glance at the contrast between the moment and my immaculately painted face, and clean up the everyday mess of being human.

Occasionally, I'll date. Men know how to find me, I fall into them. The more pieces of myself I lose, the more men I attract. As far as I can tell, falling in love feels the same as forfeiting contact with my voice. No one lasts beyond a few months, though. Thankfully, the families I babysit for become my source of constancy. The mom I met a few months ago, the Broadway star, connects me to other families.

She and I met through acting. We kept running into each other at auditions, first at ABC then CBS. She asked me where I'm from. I told her, "I'm not entirely sure."

She immediately declared, "I'm adopting you."

She is my Warrior Mama. She is exuberance, audacity, and fire, embodied. I watch how she mothers these qualities in her three daughters.

I have always made sense with kids. My hummingbird heart matches theirs. They make me feel the way you do—safe, accepted, and known. They keep me soft. They don't care about pedigree, intelligence, attractiveness, failings, successes, or how much I weigh, earn, will produce or be recognized for. All they measure is the quality of my love. They sense when I'm distracted or halfheartedly reciting words and pantomiming motions. They'll tug at me to pull me from my ego, toward what is true.

I fall in love with each child I babysit. They squeal with delight when they greet me after an audition or a photo shoot. I'm their real-life fairy princess. My hair is braided by little hands sticky from apple juice and childhood.

Children are always watching. They'll wear their parents on their skin. If the parents are unhappy, the child wears the sorrow like a rash. She'll draw pictures of people without mouths or with huge red mouths, devouring the entire face. The face she won't draw is one that is smiling. Smiling hasn't a place in the portrait of her life.

I can sense familial tension the moment I arrive for a first interview. It's like walking into a section of a forest where there is a nest of hornets nearby. It is out of sight but the air is thick with warning.

Faintly trills the little pink music box. The ballerina spins. Although I know I have vowed to protect myself and develop boundaries, the call of a family in need is still something I cannot ignore. They find me, I find them, I stitch my heart to theirs, to help however I can.

The days fall into a pattern of acting, auditioning, and kids. I swim a fantastical ocean, the water heavy with carnivorous adults, and life-buoyed by sweet children.

ACT II

LOVE

LOVE

✦

I AM 30. My sister's desk is blessed refuge. She has left for college, and I've moved into her teenage bedroom. I sit in her place. I type. I dig. You help.

Writing one's memories is essentially the act of recovering oneself. To unearth, to retrieve, to mend. There are mornings I find by the feeling around my eyes that I cried during the night without waking myself up. The salt has dehydrated my skin, and it hugs my eye sockets tightly. I ask our reflection, "Where did we go last night?"

I'm given a thin-lipped smile, a shake of the head, and a few words: *You don't need to know. Eat something. Write. This is all you need.*

And then you add, *I am here. I love you. I am yours.*

I AM 25. I meet his dog before I meet him.

May 30th, 2009. I'm at a summer rooftop party in the East Village, in a stunning home owned by an elegant gay Filipino couple. I'm here with my manager of a few months. My love, I'm torn over her. I'm wary of her combination of cocaine and a frenetic work ethic.

We have grown very close, though. She leans heavily on my arm from today's cocktail of summer heat, drugs, and Chardonnay. I need to let her go but I can't. I understand her. Insight and empathy, deepened by ego; it feels good to be needed.

She's in her 50s, but her exact age is indiscernible. Life has been hard and she has tried to rally with multiple surgeries, refashioning her face as neither old nor young, neither beautiful nor unattractive.

The patio brims with sparkly people monologuing about their films at Cannes and their weekend jaunts in the Hamptons. The air is saturated with scent: perfume, sweat, alcohol. I'm in a white strapless dress made of cotton lace with a sweetheart neckline. I have my signature red lips and manicure. My hair is in ringlets. I look like the crowd's mascot. A life-sized doll in full costume, part of the team but not quite. I sit in the middle of the milling bodies, my hands clenched tightly in my lap, one ankle tucked behind the other, my torso straight, shoulders back, trying to withstand the moist breath and weight of the intoxicated woman beside me.

I attend these parties because I must. I make sure to connect and be gracious with the host and guests. I keep a gentle hold on you, and the hours pass.

A German shepherd ambles my way. He tilts his head. I mirror him. His eyes hold the filmy blue of cataracts, but I know he sees more than most attending this soirée.

I'm not much of a pet person. I know that's as terrible as saying I'm not looking for an everlasting love. I like pets just fine. But I don't go all gooey when near one. My first two pets were baby chicks in Hawaii. They didn't last long. In Bangkok we had four guinea pigs. They died after a few months. Then two rabbits that also died after three months. Next, two ducklings and a terrapin. After a few months, they were set free into the lake by our house. Then, a bichon frise. Buddy. When Buddy was 3, he was stolen. Then, two other dogs, a poodle and a mix. Coco and Peppermint. Each lasted for a few months before they were given away. Then, a kitten. She fell off the balcony from our ninth-floor apartment. We had as many addresses as we did pets.

Why grow attached, to pets or people, when so often they disappear? I've had exactly ten in-depth relationships from age 17 until now, 25. I keep being drawn to harmful choices. Every person has delivered a fervent proclamation of love, which I was foolish enough to believe. Every relationship has felt like a consumption, as in the illness and the synonym for a devouring. Every bond has begun with dilated infatuation and has ended with me dismantled limb by limb, a spider toyed with by a cruel child.

Although 25, I feel old, earmarked with all this love and letting go. I yearn to slow my racing pulse and rest my head on a pillow made by someone's nearness. But I know better than to count on it or trust myself when it comes to men. I need to somehow rewire this mind and heart of mine before I can fantasize a life with a husband and children. And pets. For now, all I want, all I should allow myself, is a quiet, sunlit room of my own.

This dog trusts me. I can tell he's too wizened for his trust to be unconditional like that of a puppy. He senses solidarity in our mirrored stillness. Surrounded by noise and ego, he and I float suspended in tranquility. I place my hand lightly on his head. It feels strange. In Thailand, it's disrespectful to touch the top of anyone's head if they are one's age or older. This dog exudes such wisdom I feel it'd be more appropriate to sit on my knees and look into his eyes. So I do.

Suddenly, a gravelly voice butchers the peace. "There you are."

I look up.

It is like staring into the almighty sun. He emits light. Gorgeous, tall and muscled, lean and full at the same time. Radiating sex like a coiled spring, taut and ready. There is something haphazard and worn in about him, like a well-used boot. Twin feelings surge my veins: I want to sleep with him and take care of him. He hunches down, his arm around the dog.

"I see you guys have met," he says, his tone stamping ownership over the dog and certainty over our meeting. The grit in his voice lodges into my chest.

He asks my name, and I hand it over like a child surrendering her milk money to the school bully. My face is warm, my fingers cold, tingly. My blood has lost its way. He wears white, matching my dress. A linen button-down shirt with the sleeves rolled up and tan cargo shorts. Later he'll say, "I knew she was my bride. She was in white, and I just knew."

"Want a glass of wine? Red or white?"

"Neither, thank you. I don't drink."

"How about some ribs?"

A slow smile that I cannot help starts tickling my mouth. "I'm vegan."

His grins, undeterred. "How 'bout some water?"

"I can have some water," I nod, blushing.

"Can you now?" His smile cuts through me like a hot knife slips through butter.

We swap stories. He wants to build sustainable communities around the world. I share where I'm from, and my dreams of building safe havens and schools in Bangladesh and elsewhere. He asks where I went to college and what I studied, and upon hearing, says he's a feminist man raised by a feminist. It has been fifteen minutes since we exchanged names and already our identities are on the brink of merging.

"My website's under construction," he says. "Like me. I'm looking for my muse."

I feel his smile, temperature, and scent move into me, coursing through my cheeks, neck, torso, down to my toes and back up again to nestle into my heart or between my legs. I can't quite tell the difference.

I look him in the eye, smile without an ounce of flirtation and say, "I am not your muse."

He is unabating, a storm that pushes on. He asks me four times for my number. I reply I'm not dating right now. He persists. I can tell he's very good at this. He has been watching me, I've been watching him. He moves with the superior aura of one who has always been the most magnetic in the room. Everyone here is smitten with him. Smitten comes from the word *smite*, which means to strike with a hard blow during battle, to defeat and conquer land, or, when used in the context of disease, to attack or affect severely. Funny and fitting that we also use smitten to describe feelings of attraction.

His manner defies "charm"—that's too small a word. "Magic" is more appropriate. He conjures something from nothing.

"Come on. Not a date. Coffee or a walk."

"I'm flattered, but no, thank you."

"If you won't give me your number, take mine. I'll wait for your call." He nudges a scrap of paper into my hand. I hold it tightly, in vain hope that doing so will still my shaking. Desire always makes me tremble.

Thankfully, my coked-up manager decides to become belligerent at this moment. Her husband has arrived and she's yelling obscenities.

"It was lovely to meet you," I say, hurrying away to neutralize the commotion.

The crowd's collectively cringing, fanning themselves to keep her words from landing on their skin. Her husband looks at me. He sighs, angry and resigned.

"I can't control her," he says. "She's yours. I'm leaving. Please get her out of here and bring her home."

"I will," I nod. We've been here before. He leaves, I take her hand, we sit on a patio bench.

"Honey, I'm going to get you some water, then we'll get a cab and go home, okay?" I stroke her hair, tuck a lock behind her ear. She nods enthusiastically, defeated and drained. For a moment, her eagerness paints her young. A kid who has thrown a tantrum from being over-tired. I bring her water. She drinks, gripping my hand like a raft. We make our way toward the door to leave the apartment. I sense him looking, the man in white. We share a smile. He waves, not with the wrist but with the top of his hand, just the fingers. Nodding up and down.

He mouths, "Bye bye."

We finally find a cab, drive a few blocks, before she realizes she's left her attaché case back at the party, with her laptop, a stack of headshots and resumes of various clients, and her wallet. We turn around. I go upstairs to retrieve her things. The elevator opens and of course, there he is.

"Missed me already?" he grins.

"Kind of," I laugh.

I walk past, find the attaché case, and she and I leave. She lives in Soho. I tuck her in and decide to walk the 67 blocks home. The air is alive with students and hipsters out to hooligan the Lower East Side. I love the electric, ravenous ownership with which they attack the night. I watch them laugh, hear their vernacular, observe them fall over or be sick or get into fights, only to laugh, get up, and keep doing what they were doing. Night after night after night. There's such cacophonic energy on the ground that we forget to look up at the skyline we're so famous for. As for those living in the skyscrapers, I wonder how often they peer down.

Walking helps me think. He has unnerved me. I feel around for you, dear one, and thank goodness, there you are. Between him, and her, and the party, I started to feel us slip. I buy three oranges from the fruit-cart on 5th Avenue and 14th Street. I eat the first, then the second, then the third orange, as though feasting on fruit will sate my curiosity and bed my wanting.

The futility is embarrassing. Of course I contact him. He is a magician. He has stolen my reason. It's in a box somewhere being sawn in half.

He texts back, "Princess, let down your hair. Where's your tower? The frog man comes." Which I take to be Rapunzel and Frog Prince references, mashed together. He sends two then four more texts to explain his mangled lines, but they all contradict one another, similes and subtexts falling in exhausted tangle.

"It's okay," I text, "I know how to translate you."

Our first date is the next morning at 10 a.m. Excitement makes me run toward the corner where he and his dog are waiting. I have to cross the street to meet him and we float for giddy seconds, waiting for the light to say Walk. Come on comeon comeoncomeon. I have to keep myself from running as we move toward each other. He waves the same as the night before, the top of his hand nodding up and down.

The three of us walk through Central Park. We come out the 72nd Street exit to lunch at a French bistro, then pile into his Westfalia van for New Jersey, where his sailboat's docked. We pick up a picnic to eat while sailing. Right before he climbs up the mast to ready the sails, he kisses me.

"Just in case I fall," he says.

I'm too seduced by the sun, the heat, the water to care about the cheesiness. For all I can tell, it's perfect. The sea air has made my hair curly, and his skin tastes like salt. He hands me a flute of champagne. I take a hesitant sip, telling myself *No* even as I do. It has been a peaceful sober year. I'm instantly queasy from bubbles, alcohol, and breaking a promise to myself. But the moment's delirium is delicious.

We sail around Manhattan, dock at 10 p.m., and eat at 1 in the morning back in his apartment in Chelsea. As a rule, I don't eat after 8 in the evening. I keep slipping today. We eat from each other's plates and spoons. We split everything down the middle and eat them our own ways. He pours balsamic vinegar and olive oil into his half of an avocado, and I eat mine naked. Before we get into bed, we take a shower. Not together. One at a time. I go first, washing away the last remnants of my makeup. The ocean's breath has smudged the lines.

We share a toothbrush and he reminds me to floss, his insistence both startling and endearing. I put on a faded yellow T-shirt that belonged to his father and we fall into bed, tired but wide awake. We feel like we've done this forever. I nuzzle into him and he unwraps me like a present he packed, sent to himself, and has been waiting to open. We stay up late in the nonsensical way one does when something extraordinary has happened. He asks to have sex and I say, "No, thank you." He asks to do other things and I repeat, "No, thank you." He says, "I'm amazing, I promise!" I stare at him, mouth agape, astonished by the scale of his confidence.

"I'm sure you are, but I'm fine, thank you."

He makes a game of it: "Can I do this? Can I touch here? How about here?"

He pesters and persists, growls and grins. I keep repeating, "No!" growing pink with both pleasure and exasperation. He finally accepts defeat and attacks a dead slumber at 4 in the morning. I'm sleepless, unused to being in another's bed, unused to a day and night like this, unused to straying from my tight routine.

At 6 a.m. I run away. The last thing I need is another man who wants, wants, wants, then spits me out. I'm foggy-brained that day from a lack of sleep, a sip of champagne, and an overdose of spontaneity and touch. I scold myself and later, drop my phone in a mug of tea. I'm relieved to be unreachable for a few days. He is not dissuaded. He finds me on Facebook, and emails a story of himself in the third person, a lost, wandering man and his dog in search of love, softness, and completion. A place to rest, a person to rest with, a person to be. I want to think the letter is a crafty ploy, but it feels beautifully earnest. The tender hope threaded through it moves me. The least I should do is call, to tell him I'm not the person he seeks.

My love, you may think I'm being coy or overly cautious. But I'm neither. Despite his openness, I'm unconvinced. One can't make a meal out of dessert. He is walking, breathing, grinning decadence.

"Thank you, but I'm not your girl. You're an incredible man, and I'm positive you'll find the woman you need. But I'm not her."

Somehow this conversation doesn't proceed as intended.

He asks, "Why not? What would keep you from being her, and keep me from being the man for you? What are you doing right now?"

"I'm on my way to the gym. But, in general, I don't have time for a relationship."

"Right now, what're you doing?

"I'm walking. To the gym."

"Okay. Where?"

Every detail he needs trips out of my mouth. I hang up and gape goldfish-like at my phone, furious with myself.

I turn the corner, and he's waiting by the gym. "Don't you ever take time to relax?" he asks.

"I *am* relaxed."

He smiles. "Just give me half an hour. Just a tiny, thirty-minute interlude in your schedule."

"Fine."

We walk to the Natural History Museum. In the Late Jurassic hall, he sits me on a bench in front of a stegosaurus. Staring longingly like an orphaned puppy seeking a teat, he announces, "You are my perfection. I refuse to take 'No' for an answer."

His pitch is impressive and I've received the best. Every proposal in this city is masterful, and every man, given the personality of this town, proclaims he is not one to take "No" for an answer. He's here to conquer and succeed and the woman he presently desires is the prize to win.

Past the museum wall is Central Park. In there, around the west 70s, is a bench that heard a similar speech a year ago, and another, further north in the Conservatory Gardens, that witnessed an impassioned soliloquy two years ago. A grassy knoll near John Lennon's memorial garden staged a similar scene two and half years ago. Professing love or receiving a profession on a bench or patch of grass in Central Park is almost a rite of passage to being a New Yorker.

This, though, is the first I've been pitched in front of a stegosaurus.

His argument is particularly emphatic. His concluding sentence:

"You are mine."

I smile. "But I haven't said that I am yours. And I'm far from perfect. Besides, declaring me your perfection doesn't automatically make you mine."

He grins, tipsy with excitement and challenge. "You're gonna love me."

Stunning, his engorged entitlement. The beauty of his features is remarkable; his is a face to drown in. No one has ever denied him. Least of all a woman. I wonder what his mother is like.

I remind him we want different things and are incompatible. He is wanderlust. I am discipline. I am an LED lightbulb while he's an outlaw firecracker singeing any hand foolish enough to touch it. He wants to live in Connecticut and rebuild a half-burnt, dilapidated barn he just bought. Acting is my calling—I cannot leave New York City.

He says, "We'll make it work. All I'll do is support your dreams, like you'll support mine."

I agree to date him. Still, I'm hesitant. It's unsettling how panicky and frustrated he becomes on days I have to be away from him for work. Every emotion, he seems to feel aggressively, from joy to anger, lust to fear. After two weeks, I end it.

Momma doesn't like that.

"He's so good for you. He's so much fun and makes you happy. You need to be happy!"

"Momma, I *am* happy! He takes too much. We're too different."

"That's a good thing. You'll balance each other. He can bring lightness into your life, and you can infuse order into his."

He calls three weeks later. "Come over for dinner," he says. "A dinner as friends."

He makes sushi and surprises me with an easel he's built, refurbished from an antique wrought-iron chair. The back of the chair is shaped like a heart. He built a t-platform that hooks into the chair.

He bought me two canvases to go with the easel, one three by four feet, another four by six.

I trail my fingers along the white expanse, hungrily, dazzled. Could this really be mine?

I turn to him. His eyes are pools of want and tenderness and hard as I search, I cannot find danger. I realize in a sudden rush that my trepidation has come from being wary of my *own* dangerous tendencies regarding men. My heart and mind are sinister and untrustworthy but his are pure and open. I have been punishing him for my past. Shame on you, Reema.

He hands me keys to his apartment. I've been given emptied shelves by men before, but never keys.

"Stay," he says. "Stay or come and go, but stay longer than you stay away. I'll always be safe for you. You can trust me."

After two months of exceptional romance, I leap. I don't move in, but I do stay.

Dear one, have you ever been in love? I'm unclear on how your reality works. As for me, I've lived my entire life with you, and shared every detail of remote importance. So you know I've never felt true love before.

But now, I feel love happening.

And, dear one, have you ever, by chance, fallen in love in New York City? If you haven't, please consider putting it on your list of things to do before you die. Falling in love in New York is sublime. Do what you need to do: reorganize your schedule, pay sacrificial alms to the planets, surrender the limb the Devil asks for to make this happen at least once. The entire City will conspire to make this wonderfully easy for you. All our lives, like kittens to milk, we obediently lap up movies, songs, novels, and short stories depicting glorious scenes set in Manhattan that we now perform. Here we are, he and I, finally floating in a serenaded montage of our own. Here we are on the cobblestone streets of the West Village, people-watching and playing hopscotch with witty innuendos. Here we are looking out the window at the Empire State Building flanked by adoring skyscrapers. The view is made all the more marvelous by our horizontal vantage point as we lie on his bed, our skin warm, blushed, dewy, recently enjoyed and quenched.

A few weeks are all it takes for the inevitable. I'm a little shy to say it so I write a note and tape it to a pineapple I buy for the purpose of being my messenger.

"I bought you a pineapple," says the note. "Because I love you."

He understands. He laughs. Feeling exposed, I hide behind a basket of laced fingers. He peels them back one by one to kiss my face.

I cut the pineapple the way we do in Thailand. We cut it whole, nicking out the eyes in dainty, delicate slivers in a spiral, surgeoned on an angle. This way you retain more of the fruit than if you were to hack at the hard skin, chucking chunks of fruit with the shell. This amazes him and I love him all the more, for how easily the little things delight him and his consequent unabashed joy. We eat the entire fruit in one go. Our mouths itch the way anyone's will when hell-bent on eating a whole pineapple, pausing only to lick the juice off your lover's fingers, lips, chin, neck, chest, wrists. Love is the sweetest itch.

I HAVE NEVER BEEN loved this way. This love feels like coming home to children and puppies, tumbling, spilling, pouring in feverish haste to welcome and adore me. He likes all of me. My mind, personality, goals, my many flaws and idiosyncrasies, the motorcycle muffler burn on my right ankle, the little red mole on my nose that I hope isn't cancerous, the spot on my lower back that's extremely sensitive when blown on or licked. He assigns every forgettable detail a nickname, claiming them as his evermore. Under the hot glare of his love, I feel special.

I have been dying to love and be loved. Whenever I think of my initial wariness toward him, I scold myself for being so cruel and unfair.

I have now surrendered all trepidation, to love him with full intensity and abandon. After a lifetime of finely honed alertness, I soften. The long hours I used to spend writing in my journal or talking to you, I devote now to him. I would never let you slip from me. It's simply that he occupies so much space. There's barely any left for you.

We are that couple. Into a room we walk wearing smiles wider than the parting crowd, delivering laughter, presents, and music. He brings his guitar and sings one of the songs he has written for me. He writes a song a day, a practice he adopted long before meeting me, although he slips in and out of the vow, so that a song-a-day becomes a song-when-I-feel-like-it. Many of the songs have lyrics that sound Spanish but are actually nonsensical. He invents the words, and his carnal charisma and confidence pass them off as real. The audacity horrifies my work ethic and thrills my spirit. In the middle of a moment, he'll start singing invented words, will pull me into a playful samba, and paint me in kisses. All other tasks are forgotten. My favorite song he writes for me is "Sunshine."

"You will always be my sunshine, and I will always your man."

My love isn't an accomplished man. Neither is he exceptionally intelligent, talented, or cultured. But he has the invaluable ability to make others feel good. The moment you're around him, you feel unique, adored, and needed. You feel meaningful. You vow your life to his and believe him when he says he has done the same.

On our first date I told him, "I'm a touch person."

He replied, "I'm the same. That's mainly why my last relationship fell apart. My ex-wife was different. Cold."

I hear him in me and me in him. We fuse need to need.

"You are mine and I am yours," I decide, murmuring into his chest, nuzzling at night like a small, sleepy pet into that warm nook where his heart beats loudest.

After three months, we know. We're going to be married.

I cannot wait for him to meet my family. In the meantime, he needs to meet my New York brood. He comes to a christening, for the twin daughters of my closest friends. The Broadway star and the tennis icon, my surrogate older sister and brother. My Warrior family. They adore him instantly.

We stay at the christening reception for a few hours and leave to walk while the light is still young.

Somewhere along Jane Street we come across two women he knows. They're coming this way, we're walking that way, straight toward them, the only people on the block. One has auburn hair, the other blonde. The blonde has a lovely smattering of freckles across her nose, a trail that begs tracing. She smiles a small smile, raises her hand in a little wave.

"Hey there," he says in his molasses drawl. "How are ya?"

Both women seem a little shy. He pulls them into hugs. He introduces me. I smile big, trying to warm the space between us, sensing their reticence and something else. A cloudy sadness fills the air, making it feel like bathwater once you've soaped the day away, the milky gray of long, tired hours spent working, toiling, trying.

We exchange small talk. He does most of the talking. He asks what they're up to, explains we just came from a christening, hence our dressy attire. We didn't mean to, but his button-down shirt is the identical blue as my chiffon dress. I chose the dress for its color, the same shade as his eyes when they decide to be more blue than green. He chose his shirt because I sewed back one of its buttons a few days ago. He declared it thus his favorite. My hair is pinned with silk roses, and we are glowing from the summer and the nearness of each other. We are embarrassingly picturesque and something about the women makes me feel guilty.

He says, "I'm so happy we ran into you guys. I'm glad you're doin' good."

He takes my hand, we walk a block in silence. He exhales deeply.

"That was my ex-wife. The blonde. Our divorce finalized last December."

It is September. He looks sad and worn.

"I didn't know what to do," he says, the sentence unzipping everything. Years I cannot see, memories fading to sepia, matters never reconciled, questions still unanswered.

I nod slowly. "She seemed nice," I say, squeezing his hand. "She was reserved but friendly. And you were so kind and warm. That's a testament to you and her. There was a lot of love there once." I kiss the back of his hand.

He looks miserable, still.

"You are so dear," I say. "You feel your feelings in such a big way, don't you?"

He nods. "I can't help it."

I smile. "It's a rare and beautiful thing." I take his hand. "Let's sit down somewhere."

He nods okay. We tuck into a little Italian café. He shares what happened, the explainable parts and the pieces that remain elusive.

"It's okay," I say. "It'll be okay."

He nods. I place my hands on either side of his face, propping my elbows on the little mosaic-topped table. He closes his eyes and rests the weight of his head in my palms. We sit like this for a while. The balmy summer days are so long. They begin cool but warm as the hours pass. The sun keeps us dutiful company. I watch the light move from lemon to gold to amber. He opens his eyes and suddenly I'm looking into an ocean, a blue so vivid I can smell the salt. He keeps his head where it is, his jaw nestled in my palms as snuggly and decidedly as a body fills a hammock, and the hammock bends and gives to hold the body seeking rest. This is why we are here. To share the weight.

MERGE

MERGE

✦

My love is a stunning adventure. A temperamental sparkler to my steady flame. He has started working in Connecticut, at the Barn, where he intends for us to live. Every day, he drives a Suburban recently inherited from his deceased father, and the Bus from our first date, too old for long drives, sits parked in front of the Barn. Thanks to a bank loan and a hefty gift from his mother, he puts aside all other work and focuses solely on rebuilding the Barn. With the help of hired labor, he takes down walls, puts up new ones, digs ditches, wires electricity, and starts mapping out a vegtable garden. With him away, I'm able to maintain the kind of day I like. And, although I don't tell him, I do prefer to live in my own apartment, with roommates, and devote only the weekend nights to him.

Every minute of my day is scheduled. Every bite of food is accounted for. Every ringlet is hairsprayed into obedient position. I wake up at 4:30 a.m., drink my green juice, and am on the treadmill by 5. I babysit from 8 a.m. to 1 p.m. After the 2 year-old goes down for his nap at 1 p.m., I make dinner, dessert, and snacks for the family. I eat a carrot, a cucumber, a grapefruit and set off for auditions at

2 p.m. I'm home by 6 or 7 to eat a bag of spinach, half an avocado, and a pear. I eat birdlike portions, run like the Devil's chasing me, but at least I'm eating regularly. I've started writing essays on topics I find interesting, like Buddhism, feminism, anorexia. Nightly, I write for a few hours and sleep by 11 p.m.

I am in awe of his unrestraint. In his hands, life becomes so fun. He hasn't the slightest routine aside from being routinely spontaneous. He doesn't eat. He grazes and wolfs, continuously. He has tried all sorts of professions. A self-professed "idea man" who finds follow-through difficult, he says it's another reason we are ideal for each other. He'll spring spontaneity in me, I'll help him structure and achieve his goals. I love that he is deeply focused on the Barn. He says he'll complete construction by next summer, in perfect time for a wedding.

He's eleven years older but has a gorgeous, carefree youthfulness. I often feel like I'm the older one, withered and uglied by my past. He imbues me with lightness. I keep from him most of the things that have happened in my life, like the assaults in New York, the predator in Bangkok. He doesn't have to know. They'd only make him spin into frenzied emotion.

For some people, the idea of being with one person for the rest of your life is what makes them hesitant about marriage. One person forevermore is my favorite part of the concept. The forever part of forever is what makes forever sublime. All I've ever wanted was to belong to someone indefinitely, and for them to belong to me. To know each other through the aging of life. To know I'll be known only by him. Sometimes, when we're lying in bed or making dinner or curled on the couch watching a movie, I'm hit with a sudden wave of relief and gratitude so giant it holds my breath captive. I'll never have to navigate the world by myself again. He is, we are, home.

It is a Saturday morning. Usually he's up and singing, climbing on top of me with growly kisses. Today, though, he lies still, pensive.

"Honey, you okay?"

He turns. "Can it really be this easy to love you?"

I have had many opinions thrown at me. This by far is the most shocking.

"I hope you keep thinking that. You're so effortless to love too."

"I feel like I'm gonna get a call from your mom and she's gonna say, 'Oh yeah, thanks for finding Reema. She escaped from the asylum again.'"

I laugh. "It feels insane and unreal, doesn't it? But I'm not crazy, or a runaway, and I'm not going anywhere."

A few weeks later, I have a cancer scare. Ovarian cysts. It isn't the first time. They flared up in college, turned out fine. For the first time in a long while, I feel something close to fear. He and I grow scared for different reasons. He's wracked with the terror of losing me. I'm devastated by the thought of him feeling pain. When the results are benign, we cry for the profound gift of being alive.

OUR PLAN WAS to wait until the Barn was finished to be married, sometime in the summer. But six months into our relationship, he suggests something new. My yearly visa renewal is coming up in February. He proposes, suddenly and over the phone, that rather than my applying for another artist visa through my agents, how about he and I apply for a green card instead, through marriage? We'd be doing that anyway once we were married, so why not move up the entire process? And, being married alleviates taxes, which are coming up in April. With all the recent expenditure tied to the Barn, we need all the help we can muster.

"What do you think, baby?" he asks. "Let's do it."

Briefly, I question whether I want to become a woman whose ability to work and reside in a country hinges on her husband.

He loves me; everything will be fine.

"I am yours," I reply, synonymous with "Yes." Three words that are both assent and reason why I would do anything to make him happy.

So, we'll have a large ceremony with all our family in the summer, but City Hall it shall be, in January.

A few years ago his life took a quick and devastating turn. He lost his father, a calm, gentle, man. A personality opposite to his mother's fiery temperament. The family shakes still from the reverberations of his death. I wonder if my love has fully recovered from the grief and shock, if that is at all possible, for anyone.

"You remind me of my dad," he says. "You're the missing piece."

What a wondrous thing to hear. As his father did with his mother, I find him through the smoke created by the fires he ignites. This, our compatibility and our crucifix. I wonder what he'd do if I ever upset him. Not if but when.

When I meet his sister, she says, "I get what he meant on the phone. You're the one. You understand him."

"I've never been happier," I reply. "He lights up the entire world, doesn't he?"

"He does," she laughs.

His mother is thunder and lightning manifest. The first time we meet, during a weekend visit, she grabs me in a back-cracking hug and interrogates me. She towers half a foot above me, athletic and quick still at her age, with a smile wider than a canyon. A voice so thick with gravel it reverberates in my breastbone, just like her son's. We spend the entire weekend engrossed in each other, I by her side, cooking, baking, and answering a litany of questions. She declares her evaluation with a slap on my back so enthusiastic I nearly fall into the vat of cookie dough I'm mixing.

"You're it," she decides. "You're exactly what he needs."

I'm so relieved. "Thank you so much."

"Stay on him. Make him see things through."

I nod so vehemently I fear I'll lose my head.

I turn 26. All my presents from him and my family are books I've asked for. *Eva Luna* by Isabel Allende, *Room* by Emma Donaghue, and *Me Talk Pretty One Day* by David Sedaris. I love their voices. Intelligent. Witty. Haunting. Money is so scarce, I've rarely the chance to buy a book; the birthday bounty is a blessing. I seek still that one voice, a book that will feel utterly my own. Although now my need has grown more complex. I wish the same qualities as before but also a place to confess and heal. There is so much I have to keep to myself. I hold so many pieces of my past precariously in my hands. I wish for someone to mirror how to lay them down.

My birthday tends to fall in the same week as Thanksgiving. We spend it with my family in Oregon. Momma and Dad left Seoul and moved here last year, into a house they've actually bought, and in the suburbs to boot. No more apartments, lease to lease, moving between cities, countries, time zones. Entering their new home, I feel the faint beginning of peace.

My parents adore him immediately. Dad aptly arranges the words.

"He just makes you feel good," he says.

"It's like being at a party all the time, isn't it?" I say.

"Exactly," Dad nods. "He's that guy. The life of the party and the party itself."

This Thanksgiving, we laugh more, talk more, become livelier and funnier. Dad and he do yardwork and install a new garbage disposal, while we girls cook and bake. Dad's father, Grandpa, passed earlier this spring. We've grieved deeply, a grief that won't end. Missing isn't something one can quit. Dad says grace before Thanksgiving dinner. He lifts his wine glass and toasts Grandpa and recalls beautiful memories. He speaks of the sadness swirling through the family like a loyal, resolute wind. He reflects on the passage of time and the introduction of new moments and friends among us. We cry, eat, laugh, rejoice, and have a sing-along after dinner with songs from the Beatles, Stones, and of course, Joni. I look around at my loved ones, thinking how love makes us form to one another like plaster holds and hardens around a broken bone. I feel around for you, dear friend. I find you and I well with relief. You're still here although I've been giving you less than I should.

We spend Christmas with his family, at his sister's home. She has two young daughters, whom I love instantly. The adults in his family have one mode. Full-throated intensity, moving between emotions like erratic violins. They celebrate, compliment, fight, and throw obscenities casually like ice into a tumbler, fully expecting them to melt and be swallowed.

Christmas Eve is his sister's birthday. We call Papa, for it's his birthday as well, in Thailand, twelve hours ahead. His birthday is Christmas. I shyly share the news.

"I'm getting married."

He is euphoric. "I'm so happy! You found someone!"

"Thank you so much, Papa. That means the world, to know you're happy." I tell Papa of my soon-to-be-husband's background, that his mother was an extremely successful doctor and his father a CPA. Papa is pleased.

We return to the living room. His family is a few cocktails in. His mom walks over and cups her right hand around my neck, gripping tight enough for my pulse to rise. Her palm and fingers are cold from the ice in her gin and tonic, which she balances on my shoulder with the other hand. The condensation on the glass seeps through my shirt, inciting a quick, complete fever through my body. She speaks.

"If you ever hurt my son I will kill you."

I'm pinned immovable. I look at him, believing and expecting with every cell that he'll say something. He doesn't. Instead, he laughs. She joins. Everyone else—his sister, her husband, their young daughters—is silent.

In eight days, I will be theirs, evermore.

"I love your son more than I can explain in words," I say with labored precision. "I promise I will never, ever hurt him. Let me go check on the dessert. I'll be right back."

I escape to the kitchen. His sister follows.

"I am so sorry," she says.

"It's fine. It's your birthday, sweetheart. Let's celebrate."

We sit to eat. I stare at my plate. Brussels sprouts. Wild rice. Sweet potatoes. Grace.

I AM 26. Happy New Year, my love. It is January.

Due to the Barn, he has been living in construction overalls. He buys me my own pair from Tractor Supply, from the kids' section. They're bubblegum pink. For our big day at City Hall, I planned on wearing the white dress I had on when we met, but he insists I don the overalls instead.

"Come on, baby, please!"

Has saying No to him ever been something I've done well?

He chooses the date for its alliteration: We're getting married by the Mayor of Millerton on a Monday. In matching overalls. My Warrior Mama gives me my something old, something new, something borrowed, something blue.

We're late but we make it, speeding from the train station to City Hall. I change from babysitting clothes into the overalls in the car.

"Sweetheart! We don't have rings!"

He laughs. "Oops."

He used his grandmother's ring for his previous wife. His sister has earrings belonging to their grandma. She suggested we take the stones and have a jeweler fashion a ring once we have the money. For now, we must conjure something from nothing. I think I read once that Ancient Egyptians made wedding rings from reeds that grew along the Nile. They believed there is a vein traveling directly from the heart down through a particular finger, the one we call our ring finger. Thus it was decreed this finger would be the bearer of our promises. I've cherished and told this story since I was 9, unsure whether I read it or imagined it. I haven't fact-checked its authenticity because sometimes, loveliness doesn't require the validation of logic.

During work today, the girl I babysit gave me a small ball of yarn, in a sweet lavender-pink hue. She is 4. When handing me the gift, she said, gravely, "This is the yarn of love." At City Hall, before the mayor, using the yarn, we tie rings on each other's fingers. His dog is our best man. A policeman offers to be a witness. You witness for us as well. With every encircling of the yarn, he and I share a promise. I will love you, celebrate you, respect you, and support you. I will keep you happy and strong. I am yours.

We take the mayor out to dinner to celebrate. We eat, drink, laugh, and tell story after story. We toast the entire world. We drive through the five feet of snow to a cabin we're housesitting for friends. I've left my sublet in Tribeca. He is subletting his Chelsea apartment to bring in extra money. We'll stay here for a few days before moving onto his sailboat.

It snows hard that night. We wake up enfolded in incandescent, white silence. The car battery has died. We are completely out of gas. We used the last bit of cash on last night's dinner. We rifle through our pockets to find $2.17, all in coins. I put them inside a pink silk pouch.

"Honey," I say, "Let's never use this. These coins will remind us where we began. Full of love, fearless, facing the weathers together."

We're forced to stay put and skip work. We laugh. A surprise honeymoon, a wedding gift from sly Mother Nature. We stay in the cabin for a few days before he's able to rouse some cash from generous friends, buy some gas, and drive to the Boat in New Jersey. On our way, we drop off his dear German shepherd, to live with friends. Our lifestyle is uninhabitable for any creature other than ourselves. We arrive at our new home, which is bone-chilling but toasty within minutes—he has lined the entire inside of the Boat with electric blankets. Our very own radiant heating system, aided by a few space heaters. I'm pretty sure we are a fire hazard.

It's my first time living with a man, and we make the improbable work. The boat is twenty-nine feet in length. At 6 o'clock, there's a short staircase leading into the living quarters. At 12 o'clock, tucked into the nose of the boat, we have a tiny sleeping alcove in shape of a triangle. At 9 and 3, there are two thin windows running along the torso of the boat, with padded benches beneath them, separated by a table that folds down. At 8 there's a sink and an icebox. At 7, a nook mirroring the sleeping area, where we store our clothes and books. At 5, behind its own door, there's a toilet that has to be pumped and filled every time it is used. Living on the Boat teaches me leagues about water conservation, and deepens my reverence for this resource I've often taken for granted. Any water we use, we gather from pumps on the dock. In the dead of winter, middle of the night, when I need a drink of water, its preciousness and my gratitude startles me awake.

We have very little and need nothing else. We have our laptops, hot plate, tiny icebox, electric teakettle, and rice cooker. We move around each other fluidly. We cook simple meals. For dessert, I have fruit while he inhales chocolate. I tease, "My husband loves sweet things, especially women and chocolate." He tells stories while I wash dishes with the slimmest splash possible, thinking of a method used in Bangladesh. Villagers use coal and coconut husks to scrub dishes, pots, pans. While we're continents away from where I began, I'm proud we live humbly, in our own way.

I am amazed by this love. I'm flooded with bizarre notions like, *I love this face so much I could devour it, stubble, bone, grin, and gristle.* How have I become this person? I pull at his face and body, saying *Mineminemine* like a toddler declares a toy hershershers. He laughs, pulls, decrees me his in return.

Every morning, we wake up nestled in the front of the boat, our bodies curled into a triangle, our limbs a tangled mystery. Which ones belong to whom is a puzzle I'm happy to leave unsolved. Eyes barely open we reach for each other, for warmth, conversation, closeness, touch.

We make love while it's still gray outside, under the skylight frosted with a million tendrils of ice, a delicate tapestry of unreplicable beauty.

"This design is absolutely singular," I tell him, tracing the crystals. "Never will it visit the earth again."

The biting pane freezes my fingers. He puts them in his mouth to warm. Outside the world is bitterly cold. Inside, our planet burns to the wick only to light again. Our heat kisses the windows with mist. Through the fogged glass, I can see Lady Liberty.

Every morning he drives to work on the Barn. I take the train into the City to audition and babysit. In the evening we make our way back to our floating nest. I write, he pencils construction plans, we make dinner, drink tea, he nibbles chocolate, we squirrel into each other for warmth. We make love again under our skylight, now a clear window to the moon and the North Star, our fellow travelers, our sole company on the ice. Into sleep we fall, full-bellied with the warmth of our simple life.

It looks like the Barn will take longer than he thought and won't be finished by the summer. Our plan is we'll spend these few months on the Boat, the summer and autumn in the Bus, and by winter, move into a livable section of the Barn. I'm excited. Sometimes he and I look at each other with wonderment, murmuring, "I don't know anyone else with whom I could do this."

WHEN ANGRY OR ANXIOUS, he pulls out thin locks of hair, a habit begun as a toddler. Trichotillomania. "It comforts me," he says. He roars, pacing like something caged, not an animal but an element. Were it possible to contain lightning in a jar, that'd be him.

He grew up in wealthy, sunlit California. His parents loved each other madly, fought with equal ardor. His memories are thickly threaded with daily fights, like fat marbling an expensive cut of meat.

"It was normal," he grins, rolling a little ball of hair between his forefinger and thumb, knotting it like a cherry stem, depositing it into his jeans pocket for safekeeping. He saves the knots for later, to calm and distract himself during dark moods or when he's procrastinating.

I find them like mementos left on tabletops, in bed, inside backpacks, marking his trail.

When I'm around loud noise, I'm visited still by migraines. People advise, *Love is compromise*, and I guess the pact includes pain. When I grow visibly shaken from his volume, or from hearing unkind words, between him and family, he laughs, declaring this is part of my education in adulthood. He's probably right; I could do with some wizening.

I attend a self-development conference for a few days. It's the first time my husband and I are truly apart. I start writing him a daily poem, a little email to greet his morning.

"I'll do this every day, regardless of whether we're in the same place or apart."

He is exasperated.

"You're silly to write a poem a day, or to say you're going to. It's too much pressure. You're gonna miss days. And if you say you love me every day, it dilutes the meaning."

"Honey, given who I am, you know I'll follow through. Besides, it's not a pressure. It's a privilege to love you—"

I stop, having traced his frustration. My poems will shed light on his song-a-day habit that he breaks more often than not. Underneath all his peacocking lives a tender boy.

I'm sad. Love isn't a meritocracy; we give for the sake of giving. He and I don't have much money. Words are what I can give. But I abort my idea, not wanting to shame him. I tuck my poems into my music box with the tiny ballerina, twirling dutifully to her thin song. I draw him angels instead. He smiles, puts them in a folder, to be seen only by him.

"How sweet," I think.

THE BABY DIED. My girlfriend writes, her pain reverberating like heat through her email, that she found him, five months old, caught in his blanket, her words *good morning* curdling into a scream.

In our childhood band of eight friends, she was the first to have a child. I cannot fathom her grief. I don't have the money to go to her.

Here in the Boat, my husband sits on the opposite bench, arms-length and an ocean away, watching me. Coiled by sorrow into a tight ball, sobbing, I've forgotten how to breathe. Silent, he plays with his hair. Twirl, yank, a new curl to knot and pocket.

"Where are you going?" I ask. He's putting on snow boots.

"Out for a drink."

"Please don't. Come here. I need you."

"There's nothing I can do. It's done. It happened."

"Stop, please."

"There's nothing I can do!"

"You can stay with me."

He leaves. Thus the moment arrives, the one that arrives sooner or later in any relationship, when tears cease to affect him. It smugly moves into our floating home, seeping into the hollow where my heart should be beating.

One page, whispers my mind, like it's the ghost of Christmas past.

Being left alone jostles awake my ability to breathe. I breathe, my pulse resumes its beat, and then, I hear you, truly for the first time in a long while. I hear you say, *I am here. I love you. I am yours.*

I email my girlfriend. I write all my girlfriends, wash my face, brush my teeth, and count my breath to fall asleep. One, two, three, four, forty-seven, forty-eight, sleep.

I'm pulled from slumber a few hours later by the acrid sour of tequila. He's home. He holds a cupcake his friend's girlfriend bought me when she heard I had "a bad day." I blink and will my lids to remain closed.

I HONOR MY HABIT of withholding from him the hard things about the present and the past. I shouldn't burden him, and he lacks the bandwidth to respond kindly. He says, "I'm passion, you're love." He says, "I'm fire, you're water." Bristling energy and soothing softness.

Passion incarnate, never have I felt attention like his. If each human is a landscape, then the area denoting my childhood is marred with patches of cracked earth. Landmarks where affection and attention felt sparse and difficult to obtain. His abundance is rain for my parched heart.

Keeping me warm is an obsession for him. He whips up soups and hearty pastas. He buys me thick, heavy sweaters despite our thin wallets.

"Baby, you're brown! You need to be warm! You're from the equator! When we get pregnant, we have to move somewhere tropical. That's where you and the baby will thrive."

That's him: every statement, every feeling, charged with vehemence. He attacks arguments with the single-minded zeal of a dog. A dog can bite down on a chew-toy or a hunk of meat with equal addiction, growing more obstinate and ferocious when challenged. It isn't the thing he wants that is important; what matters is he must have it.

I'll never be able to say my husband doesn't challenge me. Which is what anyone desires; a partner who stretches your heart, tutors your patience, disarms your stubbornness. I'm learning exasperation and expressions of anger won't serve my marriage or him. I'm learning to rein them in and speak only cautiously.

Loving him makes me grow. My life is bigger—farming and rebuilding a ramshackle barn aren't choices I'd naturally gravitate toward. He's expanding my mind. He's good for me, my love. This is good.

WE DRIVE HOME after dinner with another couple. It was a gorgeous evening, the conversation and laughter bountiful and easy, moving seamlessly between art, religion, politics, film, books, and sweet trivialities. Happily replaying my favorite bits, it takes me a while to notice our comfortable silence has mottled.

"Honey, everything okay?"

He waits a few seconds. "Baby, nobody needs to know you're smart, all the time."

"Okay."

"Don't talk so much. I love you, but it's arrogant to think people want to hear your opinion."

"I'm sorry." I'm mortified. "Do you think I come across as arrogant? That's awful."

Eyes on the road, he nods. "I don't think you can help it. You're really good at making people uncomfortable. To the point where some people hate being around you. Like my mom, and I feel it from your mom and sister too. You're just so sweet, calm, polite, all the time. It must be insufferable for you, and it sure is for us."

I'm stunned silent.

"I know you don't mean to, but you're condescending by being yourself. Just be less. Don't talk so much. And dress down. You attract too much attention. It's embarrassing. You're supposed to be a feminist."

"Yes, my love." Now is not the time to clarify feminism is about equality and choice. For every person to have the right to choose their choices without hurting or overpowering anyone else in the process. The irony stings.

I turn toward the window, draw a heart in the condensation, and our initials inside. I've kept my own last name. It was never a discussion.

"I'm glad you understand," he says.

"Of course, honey. Thank you for letting me know. I'll be more careful."

He sighs, content. He touches my chin affectionately before moving his hand to massage the back of my neck. "Oh, baby," he says, smiling. "You make it so hard to love you."

Dear one, I take it back—there *is* something a boy hates as much as an ugly smart girl.

A beautiful smart girl.

"But I do love you," he adds. "That's why I'm warning you."

"Thank you, my love."

He is my husband. He wants the best for me. He loves me. I repeat this to myself, to the trees sweeping past, to the night holding us in her icy embrace.

BEND

BEND

✦

SPRING ARRIVES. The ice around the Boat thaws. I book my first professional lead. The play is a world premiere. My character is 15 years old, half Pakistani, half Caucasian. It's a radical, powerful play, the story of an American woman, a former interrogator in Guantanamo Bay. The American woman is my mother, while my father is a prisoner she interrogated. Fifteen years later I discover their story and my beginnings. I learn the man who I thought was my father, isn't. The family falls apart. In trying to better understand my parents, I become obsessed with replaying torture methods. I accidentally asphyxiate myself, dying in the final scene.

The play of only four characters is performed in the round, on a stage just big enough to be grand but small enough to be intimate. It's ideal for the extreme intensity and pace of the story. I can feel the audience collectively breathe, cry, panic, gasp, drown, and die with me. The tale is a stark examination of desperation, cruelty, manipulation, prejudice, and love, and how we're all capable of these forces.

My husband and I move out of the Boat. I travel to West Virginia for the show. He moves north to the Barn. He sleeps in his Bus while he works everyday, all day, to make the Barn inhabitable. While sad to be apart, I love having my entire day to my work and myself again. Every moment is peaceful. The weather is heavenly. Having only myself to contend with, without him occupying the space he generally demands, I get to sleep, meditate, write, paint, run, read, and make contact with you more freely. And this work itself is precious. The cast is incredible. I'm honored to learn from my peers daily.

Never have I felt more alive. I start eating larger portions and more grains. I increase my daily runs to seven miles. I run and write in the morning, begin rehearsals at 10 a.m. and perform in the evenings. It's a repertory company. We perform five plays, and most of us are cast in two plays simultaneously. I play a small part in the other play. Between the two, I have sixteen performances a week. My job is to emote, fall in love, destroy, sob, fight, and die sixteen times a week. An exhilarating vacation I'm being paid for.

The season kicks off with a reception, and he drives down to be there with me. He and I are photographed for the front page of the local newspaper. We are picture-perfect, multiracial, young, an embodied promise. He surprises me by coming again on opening night. I don't know he's there until I see him in the lobby after the show. I run and jump onto him like a koala, laughing. He spins me around, proud of his girl. He comes to seven shows, driving six hours each way. My parents fly to see the show, as do his mother and stepfather. I'm so grateful and thrilled. We're growing close.

Once the shows close, I join him in the Bus. While the Boat had a pretty elegance, the Bus is pure humorous charm, tan and rust-brown. A 1981 Vanagon Westfalia, transported from a free-spirited era. The top folds up, the stickering on the windows dark and peeling. The laminate, vinyl, plastic, and rubber inside, on the trays, dashboard, chairs, and sides, smell of time and look happily aged, like a traveling musician who has seen everything and done the crazy. The back seat in the Bus opens like a trunk and out fans a bed, narrow but wider than the Boat's, in the shape of a rectangle. Gone are the months of sleeping in a triangle. When visiting friends or family, we've sometimes slept on queen- or king-sized mattresses. They feel absurd, like we've fallen into a world of different dimension and shape. When we're with a large group and the rooms are being doled out, we volunteer to take the one with the twin bed. The other couples sigh with relief, thanking us as though we've done something nice for their sake.

The months are simple and good. We grow our own vegetables on the small plot of land that came with the Barn, and supplement what we need from nearby farms. We pick apples off our trees for breakfast and friends. He fishes. We still don't have indoor plumbing, but at least now we have warmth, sunshine, and wheels upon earth. Inside the Barn we have electricity. It's the first thing he hooked up, for powertools and a landline telephone. Tucked as we are in the woods, so removed from civilization, we don't have cell reception. We cook our meals on the hot plate or on a small camping grill, compact and sturdy despite its years. We make an adventure of everything, luxury mined from imagination. The dollar store is our whimsical cave of possibilities. Anything can be found, and if not, he and I build it from scrapwood, nails, rocks, branches, paint, and gumption. I hang a heart-shaped sign inside the Bus. It says, Home Sweet Home.

"Baby," he grins, "Just imagine all the places this heart will hang."

I love being a wife. I love the feeling of cultivating something together, a team. While he works on the Barn, I write on the grass, essays purely for myself, and a book of poetry for kids and parents. I commute into the City to audition and babysit. I land a few art commissions and build my first websites. He digs ditches for a septic system and puts in the roof. Watching him, tireless under the sun, bathed in dirt, sweat, and tenacity, pulls forth the seemingly impossible; I grow to love him even more.

One side of the Barn needs complete remodeling. Sometime in the 70s, a fire devoured the entire wall. He nails new planks to resemble the other three sides. He wants to recreate the original beauty, weathered, accidental, but now deliberate, through paint. I select a few grays and browns at the hardware store. After a few tries, we learn to mimic the effect of time, rain, and wind, using different brushes for an aged texture. We walk across the field, waiting until we're two hundred feet away before turning to gaze at our work. We stand, tired, sun-kissed, proud. How sacred, these stories we are writing for our children and grandchildren.

We make love in the field with nary a covering except the sky. He feels heavier on me, nicely, his body wider, more muscled, tanned, and toughened from months of hard labor. We're now closely brown, I only slightly tanner.

I come and he says, "You're blessing our land." I blush. We lie half asleep, suspended in the fuzzy warmth found after sex. Few things are better than this nook only we know.

I trace the calluses he collects daily, feeling proud of his strength and the enormity of what he has decided to accomplish. I kiss the hard knots, one by one. He has great, strong, builder's hands. He slips into a nap.

A butterfly lands on his arm, tiptoes along its length. It treads lightly lest it wake the dozing dragon. Suddenly, I see beads of light dancing over the grass.

"Baby!" I nudge him awake. "Fairies!"

"Silly girl," he laughs, groggily. "They're fireflies."

It is my first time witnessing such magic. Fireflies are fascinating, not only for their bioluminescence but the nature and reasoning behind it. Their light is a "cold light," devoid of the more common infrared and ultraviolet wavelengths. And, the reason fireflies alight is so to attract both mates *and* prey.

I turn to tell my husband these things, but he has already fallen back asleep.

He is furious. He bought a wedding ring to replace the yarn but misplaced it. The ring was a slim gold band with a gold heart curved like a shell, nesting a tiny, perfect, white pearl. I saw it at a vintage store, touched the glass case reverently, but didn't cave. We cannot afford it right now. Unbeknownst to me, he returned and bought the ring.

Now he has lost it. He rips apart the Bus and Barn trying to find the ring, roaring, yanking chunks of hair, knotting them into tiny balls.

"Baby, it's okay. I don't need a ring to know you're mine and I'm yours. Our love is too big to live on a finger."

He hurricanes still. I pull him down to sitting and get on his lap.

"Shhh, it's okay," I murmur into his neck, hair, chest. We sit like this for long minutes, my lips pressed to his forehead. Against my mouth, I feel his frantic pulse slow down, like a hammock swaying softly to rest.

"Let's get pregnant," he says suddenly. He likes saying this often, throwing me the sentence like a dishtowel or beach ball, as if to say, *Think fast!*

I kiss the back of his hand. "Not yet, my love. Let's wait until we're on solid ground."

He nods, yawning. He has exhausted himself.

Sketches surround him like a growing lake. Different plans for the Barn, scrawled by expert hands. I adore his handwriting and the way he draws, the sophisticated penmanship characteristic of architects and engineers. Their lines have a masterly flare different from my civilian scribbles. He sits on the bed we can't use for sleeping yet, covered in plastic for safekeeping from sawdust and plaster. It's a mattress and box spring, the one piece of furniture I've ever owned, that's traveled with me sublet to sublet. The walls of this first floor are nearly finished. Stacks of plywood punctuate the space, with piles of nails and cans of paint eagerly waiting to be used.

He has sawn out most of the windows. They wait patiently for the glass panes. The paneless windows are covered with plastic construction sheets to keep out wind, leaves, and summer rains.

I tiptoe over to peer at the beautiful designs. I want to frame some of these for their artistry and also, their meaning. "Here's how Daddy built our home," I'll say to our son or daughter, balancing him or her on a hip they'll believe exists solely for their perching. They'll trace the lines with their pudgy fingers, smudging the glass with the stickiness of childhood, a sweet mix of applesauce, playground, sweat, and sand.

"They're so beautiful, my love. They're treasures."

"Thanks, babe. They're just sketches."

I play with his hair. "Which section of the house is this?"

"The second floor. I'm trying to figure out how to use the light best, so it comes through every side, with the rooms mapped out with the rise and set of the sun."

I love that. He has marked the coordinates on the plans, east, west, north, south. I can see where the windows and rooms would make most sense.

"May I make a suggestion?" I ask.

"No, I got this."

"Okay, honey. I'll leave you to it."

I'm working on a commission, a child's portrait. It needs the final shading, then I'll mail it. My art brings in some welcome cash. Recently, two large paintings of nude angels sold for a sweet $1,000 each, which helped immensely with our bills.

I work.

A few hours pass. The light shifts, nudging that it's time to decide dinner. I package the finished portrait. "Are you hungry, baby?"

Balls of banished paper pockmark his pool of designs. He angrily toys with a knot of hair, kneading it between forefinger and thumb.

I slip my hand into his, lace our fingers, tease away the knot. He retrieves it, puts it in his pocket.

"Is it the windows?"

"Yeah. Everything feels wrong."

"You'll get it done. Perhaps, if we place the master bedroom here, with two windows facing here and here, we'll capture the sun's path perfectly." I motion what I mean.

He rises. "No. It's all right. Design isn't your thing. You're not an artist. You wanna cook at home or order in?"

I blink. "Home. We can eat outside. The sun's still out."

We cook, falling into our familiar rhythm, donning the blessed wordless dance like a sweatshirt that knows your every groove. Chop vegetables, measure rice, add water. A few minutes pass.

"Did you finish your piece?" he asks.

"Yeah, I did. And actually," strangely, I become shy, "I found the folder of drawings I've given you. We can start framing a few, maybe hang them up."

"It's vain to hang your own work." He delivers the verdict with echoing finality, the gavel hitting my breastbone, declaring me guilty of petty desires.

"Oh. I was thinking about painting something for that north wall, since we have that expanse to fill. It'd be lovely, to hang a painting I've made, on a wall you've built."

"No. It's like when a person puts up photos of their kids everywhere. How many reminders of yourself do you need?"

The rice steams. From habit, I draw our initials in the condensation on the mason jar behind the cooker, the one holding oats. I eat them by the bushel like a horse. I run nearly as much as one.

"Here." He walks over to his makeshift blueprint. With his toe, he indicates a miniscule square on the paper resting on the dusty floor, for a six-by-six-foot structure. "I'm building you your own space. Out in the lawn. Like a shed."

"It's small," I carefully calibrate the inflections in my voice, lest I sound ungrateful.

"It's just right. Big enough for you. Your writing. Your drawings. You can hang whatever you want there. The Barn's for family."

"Okay. Thank you."

I check on the vegetables. We take our bowls to the lawn. We have been brave with our garden, recently planting cabbages, peppers, kale, carrots, peas, and tomatoes. Along the perimeter of the lawn are wild apple trees. The fruits are coyly dimpled from being left to their own nature, boasting a rich tartness that can't be bettered. The plastic sheets covering the window frames billow like wings, the wind having her way with them. We balance the bowls on our knees, waiting for the food to cool. I slice an avocado in half, scoop his into his bowl, mine into mine. He returns inside, brings balsamic vinegar and olive oil for himself, water for us both. We murmur, "Thank you, love," to each other. For dessert he picks an apple off a tree, cuts slices to share. I take in our empty bowls, bring out almond butter. He likes it with his apples.

We snuggle into a favorite conversation. How our kids will look and be. We volley back and forth a gentle patter of hopes and qualities we most admire in each other. Our kids will always seek and find the beauty in others. They'll give love generously and easily. They'll celebrate the little things. They'll be caramel skinned with blue eyes, huge smiles, and thick hair that grows like weeds.

"They'll be amazing athletes like their father," I say.

"They'll be sweet like their mama," he says.

"They'll build things like their dad."

He smiles. "They'll create something out of nothing like their mom."

"You'll teach them how to sing."

"You'll teach them how to be funny. You're funnier than me."

"Funny-looking," I quip.

"It's because your mind's quicker. You're smarter."

"Not true. You'll teach them how to play guitar and make people glow just by being around them."

He reaches for my hand, resting it in its rightful place; inside his. "You'll teach them how to be kind."

"We both will, my love."

We braid our fingers, breathe in the fall air that's beginning to cool like a temper deciding to settle. The sun paints us gold then tawny-brown then lusty, earthy red, before enveloping us in solemn blue. We sit quietly, lulled by food, pensive with love and other things hovering nearby, shadows we try to catch or chase away, succeeding in neither.

I DON'T KNOW HOW to drive. I dodged lessons offered by Papa during high school. The occasional nightmare visits me still, where I crash his Mercedes. I've never sat behind the wheel of that car but I know in pristine detail how it feels to destroy it. My head and neck snapping forward, the sickening crackle of knotted vertebrae coming apart. The sound of shattering glass, high-pitched like a shy request. The accordion crunch of metal, the squeal of tires on asphalt, the pebbles, rocks, branches fleeing the scene. Finally, my primal scream pulled from the little ballerina box where I hide unspeakable things.

My husband is very excited to teach me how to drive. He says the Suburban is perfect for teaching, because it's huge and heavy, with a stick shift—if I can drive this car, I can drive any. I'm told it's good for men to feel like they can teach you something. It's important to him, and me, although his enthusiasm is colored by competitiveness. I don't mind. I want nothing more than for him to feel knowledgeable and thus, hopefully, more confident and secure.

He chooses a winding road up a mountain for my first lesson. The path is choked with snow. The lesson happens spontaneously, like a forest catching fire due to extreme heat. We're on the way to visit friends when he stops the car and demands I take the wheel.

"Come on, baby. Where's that famous focus of yours? Let's see you put your discipline to good use. Go."

So I do. I wind up the mountain, a wall of rock and snow on our left, empty space on our right. A steep drop, thousands of feet high or deep, however one wishes to see it. I do rather well.

PAPA COMES to visit us. He's in New York for another conference. He takes the train to stay with us for two days and nights. Ecstatic and so anxious to see the man I revere and fear, I can barely eat or sleep for three days prior to his visit. This will be the first time the two men meet.

My husband's taken aback by how tiny Papa is, the father who resides so largely in me. They embrace each other like long-lost friends, and it's clear that Papa's enamored with my husband. My heart soars. We have a detailed schedule planned for his visit, filled with possible joyful memories yearning to be made.

Papa is astonished by the Barn, our partly constructed, partly scorched life. I show him our makeshift kitchen with our hot plate, rice cooker, vegetable steamer, and my husband's latest flash purchase, a gleaming refrigerator bought from a bankrupt restaurant. Everything is powered by electric cables, exposed in plain air.

"Ayta thomar shongshar?" *Are these the makings of your life?*

"We'll get a stove and an oven soon," I reply. "Maybe in a few months."

We show Papa the small vegetable patch with kale, carrots, green beans, peppers. My husband worked quickly to ready a space for Papa in the house, on the second floor, where we've placed the mattress and box spring. Papa will sleep here while we sleep in the Bus as usual.

"I wish you could've come to my show," I say, smiling. "I had a leading role."

"Well," he says, an answer and an end to the conversation.

"I'm here to see my son's work. His vision is enormous." He pats my husband on his back. He looks at the architectural plans, gazes around, wonderstruck, his face a canvas of pride, admiration, and delight.

"He's an artist! We have an artist in our family!"

"We do," I agree, feeling my familiar joy and rejection. Don't be selfish, I scold myself. Be grateful.

I have nearly mastered driving. My husband is determined to show Papa I can drive, believing this can be a watershed event, when we bond and I release my fear of him. But I don't feel I'm ready to drive, not with other lives on the road, nor do I think we can force an epic turning point in our relationship.

"Come on, baby," my husband urges with characteristic relentlessness, biting down on his opinion and refusing to relinquish the caught animal.

I consent, both Papa and I viscerally nervous. Nearby, my love, I feel you tense.

"You don't need to," Papa says. "It's okay."

"It's okay," I parrot. "It'll be fine."

We begin smoothly. The day is clear, the sun is shining, I've driven the Suburban and this loop a dozen times. Papa sits behind me and speaks in Bengali.

"Slow down, look at the rearview mirror, signal the turn, slow down, slow down, slow down, you don't know what you're doing, slow down."

My husband sits beside me and says in English, "Speed up, hurry up, push down on the accelerator, signal the turn, speed up, speed up, why are you doing that, don't do that, that's not the way to do it."

Both voices, one nasal, one gruff, contradicting each other, quickly escalate to yelling, devoted to the same cause; to drive me as I drive. Within minutes, we create our effortless norm: distilled cacophony and my acquiescence. Soon, neither man speaks coherently, only loudly, caught in the vortex of his need to control.

I calmly repeat, "Please stop talking. Please let me drive."

The instant I stray from this tone, all will be lost. I focus my entire concentration on the wheel, the road, imploring myself, *Don't listen, don't break, don't let go.* As I approach the turn into our driveway, their voices reverberate against the glass. I feel their tag-teamed efforts battle-ramming my chest. I'm struck by a horrifying thought: they'll stop only if I crash.

I don't mean to.

But perhaps I do.

I press down on the accelerator. We smoothly careen into an oak stump, three feet in diameter, at forty miles an hour. The tree receives us without any hesitation, the impact unlike anything I've felt before or since: a stoic, solid end. We halt so firmly, so casually, the air bag doesn't explode. My chest slams against the wheel, my hands gripping it still, like a child refusing to unclutch a security blanket.

The doors swing open, the car spits us onto the grass. We spill more than we walk. I buckle in half as if kneed in the stomach, crumpling like a soiled paper plate a person folds without thinking before throwing it away.

I burst into huge, gulping sobs. I collapse onto the asphalt, the pebbles hot and sharp, creating indentations wherever we touch. I'm so scared. How could I have failed them so terribly? They'll be livid.

Neither man comes to me. They stand a few feet away. Watching.

Suddenly, my husband starts laughing hysterically, so hard he cannot stop, holding his stomach from the effort of his mirth. His eyes tear up.

"Baby, I have never seen anyone cry like this before! I'm sorry, but I've never seen you like this at all, it's amazing!" He takes out his phone and snaps dozens of photos of me, finally unhinged, weeping.

Papa takes a few steps toward me, unsure of what to do, what to say, how to comfort.

I peer through the salt, my eyelashes caked with the dirt and dust of the ground where I burrow. Our combined personalities have orchestrated a car crash. How humiliatingly unsurprising and inevitable.

Humility is the moment you realize your universe is neither original nor special. You're scathingly human, mostly alone, and now you must stand.

I stand. I scream: "Someone please hold me."

I cry this with all my might. I'm terrified they're both furious with me, but still, I scream my plea.

My husband continues to laugh with unwavering enthusiasm. Papa tries his best to hug me, tying his arms around my face and shoulders like a loose, warm swaddle, patting my cheek with one hand.

"Shh, shh, jaan," he says. I love him so much for this I feel I'll collapse again.

"I'm so sorry," I sob. "I'm not perfect. I know that. And you can't keep yelling at me for it."

My words shock me as much as they astonish the two men in my life. I feel I have sinned. I've exposed a vicious truth known and hidden by everyone. I return to my tangle on the ground.

A few long minutes pass. Papa pulls me up.

"Shh, amanjee." *Little mother.* "It will be okay." It's the sweetest thing I've ever heard.

My husband continues to take photos, capturing every moment, of Papa trying to hold me up, of the two of us standing in front of the demolished car and the stump. He calls over a neighbor, asks him to take the photos so he can strike a pose. He joins us for another dozen, him grinning, flashing a thumbs up, me weeping, Papa looking stricken. He texts and emails the photos to our families. Momma calls, horrified.

"I'm sorry, Momma. Please don't worry. Everything is fine. No. I'm not hurt. No one's hurt. I just. Messed up. Tell me about you guys. Please."

My brother is with them in Portland. He recently graduated college. He's visiting Momma and Dad for a few months, for this period between graduation and beginning his corporate job. The wise investment he is, he was recruited straight from school by a Fortune

500. Everyone is so proud. He, too, didn't learn to drive during his teenage years. Dad has taught him over these past months. My brother wanted time with that pairing of parents for exactly this sort of reason. To feel and do things that escaped us before. I'm so happy for him.

On the phone now, Momma talks about my brother's achievements and how confident he is on the road, knowing that anything regarding either sibling always raises my spirits. She gushes, I laugh from joy, cry some more. I miss them with a hunger on a cellular level, a longing that travels my veins, replacing my blood. I feel so far away from them, not just physically. I've tried tracing when this feeling began. I think I've always felt it.

It is evening. My husband asks, "How're you feelin'?"

"I'm fine. Thank you."

"It's okay to cry."

"Thanks for your permission." I sound like water turning to ice.

"G'night. Love you."

"Love you too."

Of course I do. If I did not love him, who would? Everyone else has left. Who would love these men but me? I close my eyes.

I wake up to his usual morning kisses and playful growls that always make me feel lucky and cherished.

"Wake up, baby. I love you, I love you, I love you. You're so beautiful when you sleep. So peaceful and young. You're my little fairy queen. Today will be great, I promise."

I open my eyes and just this hurts. My whole body throbs with every heartbeat. I sneak a peek under the covers; my breastbone is vivid indigo. I breathe and stretch beneath the press of his body. I giggle despite the bitter ache, still smitten, still susceptible to him.

It's Papa's last day with us. We have a blessedly gentle day. We picnic in the field next to the Barn. For dessert we each have an apple from one of our trees, the fruit green and red, speckled with little black freckles. The car is drivable albeit dented and scratched.

We drive Papa to the train station. We thank him for making the trip to see us.

"It's been a wonderful visit," he says.

"I'm so glad, Papa. Thank you for coming to see us. I'm sorry about yesterday."

"It's all right, jaan. You'll learn to be better."

My husband slings his arm around me and echoes, "Yup, you'll get better."

I look at my men. I smile, nodding in agreement.

AN IDEAL FALL DAY, the sky arrogantly spectacular, the leaves a bonfire of color daring us not to swoon. We are driving into the City for his godson's birthday party. The little guy is turning 1 today. The Suburban has held up, although it groans and wheezes. My husband is singing. I join him for a few lines before letting him have his airtime. I love his voice. He's a much better singer than I am. He says I sing like a Disney princess. Sweet, wholesome, without much personality, and not a smidge of sensuality. His voice is pure sex, rich, thick, and coiled like syrup. He's singing "I Wan'na Be Like You" from *The Jungle Book*, jazzing it up, weaving in some reggae.

I'm wearing my favorite dress. It's silk, light pink, short, and fitted with spaghetti straps and delicate ruffles along the neckline and skirt. It's the second time I've worn it. I'm excited for the chance. I bought it a month ago as a rare treat, to wear to my agent's birthday party. A few years ago, my agent enfolded me into his tribe of close friends and family. They're a safe, loving clan. Every year now, I'm in charge of my agent's birthday cake. His favorite is strawberry shortcake, but the tribe favorite is banana chocolate chip. I layer one of each.

I have framed one of my drawings for today's birthday boy. It sits tucked beside me. On my knees I balance his cake. We offered to make it, and his mama was happy to have one less thing to do. All my baking pans are heart-shaped. I found them, finally, a few months ago. I've been baking more for the kids I babysit. All of them are toddlers and older now. With a picky eater who needs more vegetables, fruit, or a higher calorie intake, I've learned to get crafty with ways to woo their taste buds. I create recipes for each child off what they need and like, cakes sweetened only with fruit juice and purees, folding in carrots or zucchini for more veggies and nuts, seeds, dried and fresh fruit for richness, flavor, and healthy calories.

I love being a part of so many lives. It's such a joy, and I get to brainstorm recipes and lessons I can use one day when I'm a mother.

Suddenly, my stomach is clutched by a thing that hasn't a name, like the creature that lives under our bed. My skin prickles. The climate in the car has changed. The light hasn't shifted, neither has the temperature. But the air is clotted with emotion.

"Honey, is everything okay?"

He looks at me, sideways.

"I don't know why you dress like that. And all that makeup. You look like you're dumb. What's that line from *Hamlet*? A painted whore?"

I order my face to remain immovable.

"I don't know why you work so hard to make women hate you. Everyone at that party knows my ex-wife. Now they're gonna think you're my child bride, a rebound. They won't even pause to see the real you or that we love each other."

I play with the extra button sewn into my cardigan. It's cherry-red. The dress is the kind of blush-pink that allows for this. I like to think the ensemble makes me look like a valentine. *Valentine, Valentine, please be mine*, my mind sings while I look at passing trees, blinking to keep tears from falling.

"A woman can wear—"

His voice rises to drown mine. "It's like you're trying to be the most perfect thing in a room." He shakes his head. "Who do you think you are?"

I remember when we first met, observing he moved with the entitled confidence of someone accustomed to standing center and spotlit in a crowd.

He hits the glove compartment, the mouth drops open, he grabs a handful of takeout paper napkins and thrusts them toward me.

"Here. Wipe your face." He swabs my cheeks a few times, showing me how, before dropping the napkins into my lap.

I cradle the napkins like petals from an enormous rose, withered and falling apart in my hands. I blot my cheeks, lips, eyelids, dimming myself.

Fitting that the word blot means to erase or wound.

"I don't wanna go to the party," he says. "I'm too frustrated."

"But he's your godson. We have to."

"Why d'you have to be like this?"

"I'm sorry," I reply automatically.

He sighs. "I know. You can't help it."

Suddenly, he swings a sharp turn, pulling into a Toyota dealership. "We need a new car. This one's not gonna hold up."

We walk in and in a matter of minutes, he has leased a new Prius. The dealership takes the Suburban to help with the cost of the new car. It'll take about an hour for the paperwork to go through. In the dealership restroom, I slip into running leggings and one of his sweatshirts. One value to the way we live is there's always a backpack of clothes within hands' reach, and both clean and dirty Tupperware and Ziploc bags for our many on-the-road meals. I gingerly slip my pink silk dress into a fresh Ziploc, like a nefarious clue from a crime scene, a phantom detective sneering, "Why were you wearing a short dress?"

We walk to a Barnes & Noble across the highway. I'm happy. Bookshops are the cathedral for this hunchback. I hate that lately I haven't been able to read as much as I'd like. There is hardly any energy for reading by each day's end. I lovingly touch the spines of stories I wish I could buy, like an impoverished, hungry child desiring food, walking through a vast supermarket, gazing reverently at cereal cartons and boxes of cookies, the fluorescent light blanching her shrunken face even paler. Money's extremely tight right now. He has emptied the loan he took to rebuild the Barn on materials and hired labor. We are both working shifts at a neighborhood restaurant. I'm babysitting as much as possible. And now we have a new car for which we'll have to pay, somehow.

I let a few books open to the page they decide to share with me and read what the author has chosen to confess. I smile, remembering my longstanding fantasy of finding that one book that will feel like my clear thread of love. How I yearn for it. So many longings feel impossible.

He isn't a reader. I wish he was. Sometimes, before bed, I read aloud passages from books, hoping the words will spark the kind of discourse I, as a young girl, dreamt would be part of my future marriage. My attempts fall listlessly to the ground like rejected love letters.

I close the book in my hands. *Naked* by David Sedaris. My finger traces the author's name on the spine.

Maybe I'll write a book one day.

"You wanna get that?" His voice startles me from my thoughts.

"Can we afford it?"

"Absolutely."

"Wow. Thank you."

He pays with the help of his mom's account. We chitchat with the cashier. He rubs my back, humming a sweet nothing. I order my body to not tense at his touch.

"Thank you for changing, baby." He plays with the cord of my sweatshirt hood. "You look more comfortable now."

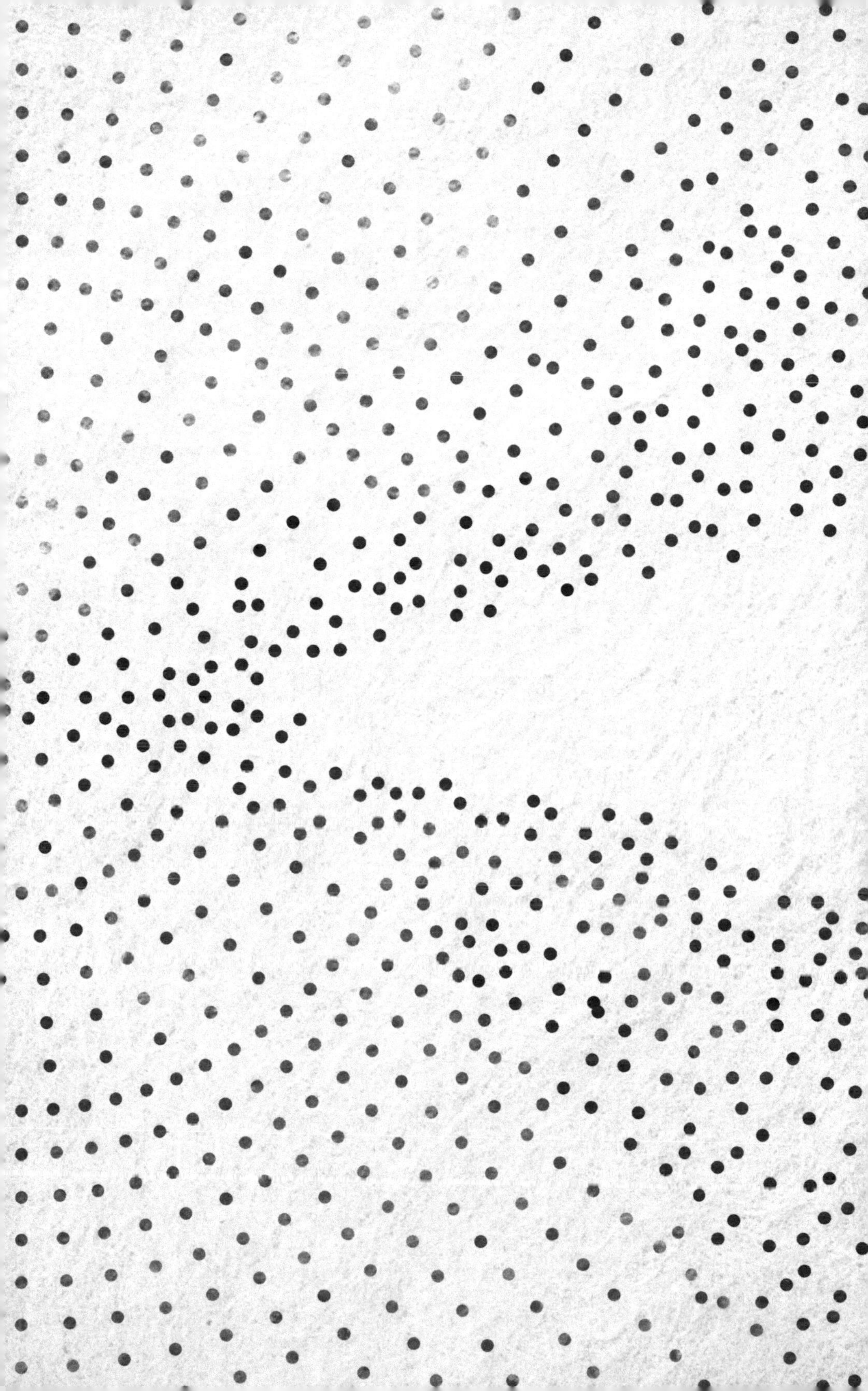

CHANGE

CHANGE

✦

SUDDENLY, HERE IS WINTER, vast, waiting, a great cat lying patiently for her kill. He quickly figures how to heat a small corner of the Barn with space heaters. We bring down the bed and finally sleep on it. We bring home as well his dear dog. Some of our walls are missing still, as are many windows upstairs, but we have a blessed roof. A blessing even greater is you, my love, loyal through the seasons, though there are hardly any windows to sit by without falling through.

Without the loan and its monthly installments, he and I barely scrape by on what we earn between the restaurant and babysitting. As there isn't anything left to pay for materials or labor for the Barn, he has halted all progress. Unable to be purposeful, he spins. He grows more and more insecure.

We have an enormous number of bills, possessions, and properties. While I've always lived an ascetic life, he enjoys collecting and buying. We have the mortgages for the Barn and his City apartment. He has the Bus and the new Prius. We have two sets of car insurance, homeowner's insurance, two storage units in Connecticut and one in the City. Two cars, two properties, and we live like church mice. Ashram mice. Ashram mice who live on steamed veggies cooked on a hot plate.

We live week to week, dollar to dollar. While I try to persuade him to relinquish some things, our frugality and uncertainty don't weigh on me or make me feel as though we haven't enough. I feel I always have enough. And I love the feeling of building something together. He and I are working toward stability, comfort, success. While I thrive on adversity, it daunts and depresses him. I sometimes succeed in pulling him from his melancholia and frustration, only to return home and find him back in bed, perusing porn, YouTube, Netflix.

I look at him. Born with every privilege under the sun, including being treated as the sun. Perhaps this is why, here he lies.

"Just get famous and rich already," he groans.

"I will, I promise. I'm a million-dollar idea that works." I keep my voice small and soft like a molten M&M, lest he declare me vain and grows angry.

Without meaning to, he teaches me: We humans become the expectations we assign ourselves. We grow to the limits or limitlessness wherein we place our identity.

His temper has grown worse. Or, I'm not as effective as I was at calming him. He has grown used to me. I watch this storm in the form of a man. I sense him on the lookout, daring life and me to prove his disdain for us correct.

"Why are you quiet?"

"Nothing, sweetheart. Just a bit cold, that's all. What would you like for dinner?"

"You're always complaining!" he yells.

"It's not an affront to you. You asked and I—I'm sorry."

I'msorryI'msorryI'msorry. Please tell me. How does it come undone so easily? Like pulling one end of a string and watching, disbelievingly, the entire spool unravel in a messy heap in my lap. A cat's cradle without an exit or solution. He manages to weaponize every event and twist every word into incentive to feel angry, hurt, disappointed, threatened, insulted.

Where did you go? Where do you go? Where have you gone? Come back.

I want to bring him back. I want to smooth away his anger like an iron soothes cloth. At night, his back to me, I want to turn and return him to face me, look at me, please, again. His trichotillomania has grown worse. Little knots of hair scatter our bedsheets like lost punctuation.

I see a moment to nudge my way in. I lull him, bring him back. I make him laugh. I remind him he is loved. He croons his favorite song. "I Won't Grow Up" from *Peter Pan*. He smiles again.

In place of work, he devotes most of his day to Netflix. He rifles through actresses, pointing out parts of their bodies more attractive than mine.

"You're too bony. *Those* are breasts."

He concocts stories of having sex with various actresses. The alleged rendezvous took place years ago in Europe when touring with his band, or out in LA, or in Manhattan. He claims if he wanted to bed them he could, again.

On his bad days, he tells me I am his wife for "greensies," not "realsies." On the rare good day, I return to being his wife for realsies. He calls me wife for greensies to remind me that my green card is dependent on him. To remind me that power only responds to power, and as a mere Bangladeshi immigrant woman to his white, male American privilege, I have no power. To remind me that his love can be withdrawn so easily, that I can be disowned and perhaps deported so casually. To remind me I am caught by a noose woven partly by my complicit hands.

I am stunned by the nonchalance with which he wounds.

America's almighty son, around him I orbit. Sometimes, he adopts a baby voice. I've known girls to do that, to be cute or coy. It's disconcerting. He pouts, dons the voice and puppy-dog eyes during apologies following his daily explosions.

"I'm sowwy, baby. I yelled at my boss. I might be fiyurd." He sticks out his bottom lip, raises his eyebrows, his enormous blue eyes beckoning like the sea. He means to endear me.

I don't feel endeared. I feel like his mother.

I voice nothing.

One followed by another, my flaws stack, a looming monolith of traits he finds insufferable.

"You're too calm," he says.

"Too ambitious," he says.

"Too intelligent."

"Too disciplined."

"Too polite."

"Too thin."

"Too measured."

"Too responsible."

"Too young."

"Too mature."

"Too optimistic."

"Too realistic."

"Too perfect," in a way he no longer finds attractive.

Imperfect, in a way he no longer finds charming.

It seems my lifelong crime is that I'm obstinately myself. He desires for me to change my molecular design.

Seemingly overnight, I can do no right. I morph from perfection incarnate to a cancerous blight.

"MAYBE I NEED a girlfriend."

I stare, stunned. I'm laying out lunch while he sorts mail. His previous sentence was, "Car payment, mortgage, homeowner's insurance—that looks great, honey, and put some hummus on mine."

"A girlfriend? Why?"

"So she could take the pressure off you."

"I don't feel . . . any pressure."

"Pressure to be more of what I want. Need."

"Okay," I nod slowly, "What more would you like me to be?" I arrange each syllable carefully. Nearby, my love, I feel you sigh.

"I wish you were more sporty. And outdoorsy."

"Okay. We've lived outdoors for our entire marriage, sweetheart."

"You're complaining again." His voice is low, toeing the line between teasing and menacing.

"I'm sorry. I didn't mean it that way. If you'd like, we can start going on runs and hikes together."

"No. I just think a girlfriend is a practical solution. Like, she and I could ski."

"I've never known you to ski."

"Exactly. I need someone to inspire me."

A pause. He is still looking for a muse. Someone he could defer responsibility to.

"Here, honey. Lunch. Extra hummus."

His idea festers into a maniacal campaign pitched daily, persistently, decisively. He argues, pleads, bargains, rants. I marvel thinking of the man he could be were a morsel of his determination redirected toward work, health, a hobby, a business. I love that imaginary man. He, as the self he chooses to be, flaunts his desire for other women the way a child threatens to run away from home. A tantrum means *Look under the bed. Find the monster. Ask its name.*

"It's not cheating," he insists. "They'd be like sister-wives. A sisterhood—it's pretty feminist."

"Feminism is equality. Would I sleep with other men, then?" Such is not a thing I desire but a point he needs to hear.

"No way. I'd kill them."

The conversation rests for an evening but, like a trick candle, lights up again.

"You want me to be happy, don't you?" He frowns. "I deserve to be happy."

"Yes, of course, love, but at the cost of my happiness?"

"When I was dating a few women at a time, I'd last longer." He paces. "Sister-wives would be a win-win, baby."

"Sweetheart, I don't want a polygamist commune. I want a marriage."

"I know." He sighs. "Me too." He starts dancing a light, sexy samba, sings a song in characteristic gibberish, draws me to him, spins me, pulls a laugh and kiss from my lips.

The next day, another bill, another setback, another fit. He throws down a stack of mail and curses.

"Honey, you're offended that life's being lifelike?"

"It's too hard," he yells. "Let's get a divorce."

"A divorce won't nullify the electricity bill. We can't get a divorce simply because we're having a hard day. You can't pop marriages and divorces like Skittles."

He explodes, this time with laughter. Just like that, my love returns.

He goes to work. I return to mine. The birds sing, the wind whistles, the light shifts and time redelivers the proposal, laced with a new chemical the way dealers enhance previous iterations of a drug to make it stronger, costlier, deadlier.

"Women love me. It's one of my gifts. I make them feel loved and appreciated. You're holding me back from sharing my talent."

I look up from my laptop. I rub my eyes. "What you propose lives contrary to our values, and our families' values. Monogamy is nonnegotiable. And this sort of talk . . . these words lack dignity."

"I'm being honest," he says, a rationale he repeats like dawn follows night. "You want me to be honest, don't you?"

"The root word of honesty is honor," I reply, "Synonymous with integrity. Authentic honesty isn't honesty unless it contains integrity."

"I don't, can't, un-der-stand you," he says, drawing his syllables like the arrogant wind pulls the clouds. I've committed my usual misdemeanor: uttering sounds that swerve him entirely.

Days turn into weeks, weeks into months. He crusades for sister-wives. My patience holds steady. But finally, one night, I feel my frustration swell and tolerance fade. I try to warn him.

"Please, baby. You're exploiting my compassion. Don't push me into a debate."

He pushes. Hard. And then, my love, I commit treason: I unleash my wrath. I descend and eviscerate like a murder of crows, an unforgiving mouth sent from the heavens. My father's daughter, I gut my husband, his innards spilling with slippery ease: "Which woman, aside from my insane self, would find you attractive? With what promises would you lure anyone into this pit of a life?" I stare at him. I smile. "You're an aging Adonis losing his light, threatened by anyone more intelligent, beautiful, or strong, in other words, nearly any woman. Do you think you're actually capable of sleeping with another woman?"

"Absolutely!" he yells. "Anyone would love—would be lucky—" His words hang flaccid in the air. He visibly shrinks, and I hate myself for it. *Stop*, I order myself. *Do not attack the weak. Do not attack, period.*

I resume my usual soft manner. There I stay. I apologize. I listen. I comfort.

The following day, another claim:

"I need more attention."

I close my laptop. I'm baffled. In the spectrum of emotional, verbal, and physical affection, I, akin to a boarder collie, will shepherd, protect, and love on anything with a pulse.

"*More* attention?"

"Let's go on a trip. Let's get in the car and just drive."

"We can't, sweetheart. We have work in the morning. We have to show up."

The next day, he adds another spin: "Leave!" he shouts, the exertion mottling his skin red and bloated, as though drunk with petulance. "I can't do this! Get out!" Again, I'm visited by Papa.

"I love you. No one is leaving. This is our home."

But tomorrow is the same as yesterday. He petitions, I try to defuse the arguments with food, sex, jokes, distractions, keeping my voice calm, wanting neither to lose his love nor to exacerbate his temper, especially without another soul for miles. I try to soothe his anxiety over work, money, identity, and feelings of purposelessness. I remind myself everything in life is about love and its absence: every gesture is an act of love or a cry for love. These words become my prayer beads, and my morphine.

"You're an amazing man. This is part of your path. It'll be okay. I believe in you."

Finally I say, "Love, a girlfriend won't address the underlying issues. A person isn't a solution."

He exhales, wilting. He walks over. We hug for what feels like an eternity.

"You are my wife," he says. "You are my life."

He says this after every outburst. He says, "Thank you for staying. For understanding. I would die if you left. You are my wife, you are my life." The couplet I adored from the moment he first tied my ring, I've now grown to loathe.

"Of course, my love," I reply. "I am yours."

In sickness and in health goes the vow. Insecurity, the most common sickness, more than the cold. Feeling small, he wishes me the same. These countless changes fall into my hands like broken-winged chicks orphaned of their nest. I, a profoundly ordinary creature, am meant to mend and save these lives. These nights, insomnia hounds me like a vicious rumor. I am his wife. This is our life. I repeat the words, hoping they'll induce me to sleep, a lullaby at once sacred and scathing.

LEARN

LEARN

✦

The biting wind makes my eyes tear. But the sun is glorious. Daily I run these woods, through elegant pillars of oak and maple. The trees wear their stillness with the same ease a matriarch purveys her brood of children and grandchildren, at complete peace with her life's solidity.

The trees watch me. I watch them. I run. I talk to you. I tell you my wishes. I harbor the same ones I know Momma and Papa always had: to love and be loved in a way that doesn't hurt.

I've been running for eleven years now, the same length of time I've acted and performed. I'm not exceptional by any means. I don't have the inherent physical strength for speed nor the sparkling talent of prodigal athletes. But, as we know, I have one thing in my favor: zealous commitment. If I tell myself, *Today you'll run fifteen miles without pause*, I will.

"Come run with me," I say to him.

"Babe, you're a distance runner; I'm a sprinter."

As a sapling, the earth around my roots were ever-shifting. The nourishment sometimes failed to reach me. As I run, I retrace my story, to see so clearly that if a person is raised and loved in a way that conflates love with pain, they will grow capable of loving beliefs and characters that hold the potential to wound. I page through the partners I've gravitated toward in the past, to arrive at my husband. Most of them were chosen for their alluring passion, charm, and shadow. Hardly solid ground.

I have always been my first response and line of defense. When drawn to a man or a friend, I have never prioritized emotional strength, self-awareness, wisdom, integrity, or accountability as traits to seek. I've learned to accept that as long as I have you and myself, I don't need anyone else to give me comfort, kindness, support, and protection, so it doesn't matter if they can't.

I'm feeling the harsh effects of my beliefs. In a relationship, all of this matters. Equal ownership, tenderness, responsibility, investment, maturity, willingness, and capability matter. Fault lines are cracking apart our love. Depleted and lonely, the distance between him and me stretches like a mouth without a hinge to snap the jaws shut.

Where did you go, where do you go, why have you gone, come back.

I have looked under every stone. I've expunged every method to improve us, scouring books and articles for answers to the riddle that is my husband. We've lost the only glue we began with: affection. Where is our common language? The further I dig, the more I feel we can't be mended by discussions about rapport, flexibility, love languages, quality time, and cultivating deeper connection.

I don't think he wants us to succeed. I don't think he wants happiness. I don't think he likes me very much, and I think he'd enjoy it if I were unhappy and unsuccessful.

More often than ever, I think of Momma and Papa, and how impossible it is to understand the narrative between two people. Love draws forth our most beautiful and jarring faces. Rarely has any tale a tidy verdict. Something about feeling my own marriage come apart so messily, so easily, helps me lay my parents' marriage to rest. It is effortless to become mean. And we are all capable of it.

Daily, I collect miles of thought. Such is the grim blessing of this love. A hill crests before me. Although the weather is still cold, the asphalt has absorbed the sun and the heat makes the road buckle like a mirage, the air shimmering as if wrinkled. I'm getting stronger. I'm running farther. My muscles are more alert and able. Should I need, should I want, I could run my way to safety and freedom.

While I run, I write in my mind. Running always helps organize my thoughts. But today, unlike other days, what I'm mulling isn't a poem, play, screenplay, or short story. Last week, while memorizing sides for an audition, reading them off my laptop, a stern order sent from that spot where my spine meets my brain told me to open a blank Word document. The white filled quickly with paragraphs on love, family, pain, trauma, healing. Paragraphs turned into pages.

I stared at the screen, stunned. What are these words? Where have they come from? Did you send them? Are they the harmony of our voices, yours and mine? I wrote for what felt like minutes but were actually hours, in a trance, until he came home. I haven't had a chance to return to the pages. But every day since, while on my run, my mind keeps writing. Writing words whose fate is as much a mystery as my marriage's.

I finish my run and return to the Barn. He is on the bed, his laptop's light illuminating his face in the dark Barn. He quickly shuts the laptop, looking suddenly like a teenage boy caught red-handed.

"Porn?" I ask, half jokingly.

"Yes," he laughs. "I needed a pick-me-up."

"Oh. Did you get one?"

"No. I was interrupted." He yawns, stretches, curls a lock of hair around a finger. "How was your run, mottu?"

Mottu means *fatso* in Bengali. On a recent call with my parents, Momma mentioned their new dog was rapidly layering on pounds, a veritable "mottu." My husband promptly anointed this my new nickname, explaining it will obliterate any relapse of anorexia.

"You'll hear just how ridiculous it is to call you that, so you won't think the same of yourself either. I'm protecting you, mottu. You gotta get the crazy out of your head."

"My run was great, thank you." I sit down on the bed, pull out my laptop. "Will you read something I wrote, please? It's not much, just some thoughts on love and family . . ." I trail off.

His eyes skim the screen. My heart begs, Please hear me. He brands a kiss on my forehead.

"Too many words, baby. Papa's gotta go."

Papa or Papa Bear are his nicknames for himself. I take off my tank top, sports bra, shorts. Naked, I perch on our bed.

"Baby," I reach for him. "We need to feel connected again."

"There you go, again," he says. "Complaining all the time."

He strolls out to the car. I collect my clothes, hastily cover myself, from whom I don't know. I hear him whistling, the engine growling, while the wind's thin cries keep me company.

THE SUBWAY LURCHES and groans. I stand, swaying with its rhythm, nursing a paper cup of coffee like a broken wing. I swallow my coffee quickly, scorching my throat. That's me: a tongue perpetually burnt.

I've been babysitting more, and the week is generally divided as three days in the City, four with him. It's Monday. He is miles away.

I love the subway. It's a chance to be alone while with others. It is soothing to feel like I'm part of something bigger. Even though the togetherness is sweaty, smelly, messy, uncomfortable, it is all the more human. We need these reminders of our oneness. Interdependency. Impact. I'm reminded I can always give someone my seat. I can share or abuse space. I can grimace, avert my eyes, or smile.

Today, as always, I have my journal. During these years with him, I've written my thoughts less than any other period of my life. And I keep breaking my habit of logging daily gratitude lists. As with nearly all my qualities, he has grown to resent this habit that he once admired. So I skip days and wait to write my thanks on the sly, as if gratitude were my clandestine lover.

I cherish this time on the subway for exactly that sort of thing: to be. I've started carrying another journal as well. A Moleskine notebook I use for love notes for other people. Friends, acquaintances at auditions, and mostly, strangers on the subway. Some notes I have prewritten, ready to tear and pass on. Others I'll write from a spontaneous feeling, off a person's expression.

The note will say something like, *It will be okay. Own your voice.* Or, *You are the spine of your life. Stand tall.* Or, *Thank you for you.*

At times all I write is, *I promise you are loved.*

I look around the subway car. There are a few here who could use a note. My pen gets busy.

I don't know anyone's details. I don't know what happened, how long ago, or if it's happening right now. But I can read emotion. Especially pain. I can tell if something hurts. Like now, standing by the far window, is a woman, looking like she's being eaten from the inside. Something or someone is atrophying her spirit. Shaken and tired, she's trying now to maintain her balance through the roar of the subway mouth.

I deliver her love note like a crumpled Valentine from a clumsy, not-so-sly admirer. I try to time it so she gets it right before her stop. Sometimes this works, and the person opens it before disembarking. Sometimes they tear up. Sometimes they mouth "Thank you. You too."

It takes her a few seconds to realize what has happened. She isn't able to open her note until she's on the other side of the doors, on the subway platform. The doors slide closed. She reads it. She looks at me through the glass as the subway jerks, readying to move. She places the opened note on her heart, like a rose pressed inside a book for safekeeping. She smiles. The subway moves on.

Sometimes, a scrap of sentences is the match that lights a flame. If I ever write a book, it will be to give all of us more than a hurried line of love.

THROUGH THE DARK OCEAN, my anchor and lighthouse are the families for whom I babysit. In particular, my Warriors and Healers. The Warriors are the actress, the athlete, and their three daughters, who charge through life with spectacular flair. The Healers are led by a wise, calm mama I met a few years ago, when my husband and I were living on the Boat. An ethereal beauty with a smoky-sweet voice like spiced apple cider, she says I'm her spiritual daughter and she my spiritual mother. She and her husband have one son, whom I've taken care of since he was four months old. I think of his mama as my Healer, for she has slowly, over the years, been monumental in my relationship with food and anorexia. She talks to me. She has taught me how to cook. She has taught me how to enjoy food.

My Warriors have two nannies now, but I still peek in from time to time. The baby I met all those years ago is now 5 and her twin sisters, 3. The memory of their christening feels like a dream, when he and I wore matching blue, glowing with love.

In each home, there is a room called Reema's Room. These are the addresses I've known the longest. One for five years, the other for three.

It's spring break and the Warriors are hosting the kindergarten classroom pet, a guinea pig. The poor thing is a little ruffled from all the travel. He squeaks and squeals something heartbreaking. The cage is on the island in their kitchen. The girls surround his cage, worry tensing their faces, dedicated as they are to making him feel better. I'm mixing the ingredients for dinner and banana chocolate chip bread. Their dad, the tennis legend, sits at the dining room table a few feet away, scrolling through emails on his iPad.

The oldest girl frowns sweetly, her forehead furrowed in concentration, her chin set, determined. It's the look she wears on the tennis court. The twins are fraternal, looking similar yet completely different. One's taller, athletically built, a cherubic cannonball of tight curls and giggles. Her eyes are now wide with despair. The smaller, lithe twin has an angelic perfection to her face, a delicacy and symmetry that feel painted. She dons glasses and a delicious lisp.

"Daddy," says the oldest, "What do we do?"

Dad comes over and hushes the girls with a few comforting words. He opens the cage, gathers the guinea pig into his hands. It's wonderful to see these great, weathered hands, famous for strategy and strength on the court, cup a tiny, terrified, trembling creature as carefully as water. It quiets down immediately. The girls look at him with awe and reverence, as if he has just willed the world to change. For them, he has. They stroke the guinea pig's head, their little hands the length of their dad's thumb.

"See," he says, "All the little guy needed was to be held close, to know he's safe. We all do."

This moment will drift into those girls' hearts quietly and unnoticed like dust in a column of sunlight floating to the ground at its calm pace.

I smile, thinking how incredibly blessed they are. And, how lucky I've been to witness and share this abundant love, for years.

One day, I will have a husband like that, who will be a remarkable father for our kids.

The thought flits through me like light playing hopscotch along the sea. I'm singed with horror and guilt.

I *have* a husband. I'm already married to the man with whom I'm supposed to bear and raise children.

A chill races along my skin. It leaves goosebumps in its tread despite the sizzling stove, the warmth of the oven, and the beauty before me.

A SATURDAY NIGHT. THE moment my husband leaves, his dog defecates, a geyser erupting with a three-foot radius. The poor beast slumps right into his mess, his eyes rolling back in his head, keening and panting. The sound, the sight, the smell: it is death, approaching. I run to the animal, pull him out of his swamp, and begin cleaning it off him and the floorboards. I call my husband's phone, leave one, two, three messages begging he come home, saying, *This may be the end.* He texts, "Take care of it. I'm out." I wash the dog, give him water, then sit with him until both he and I, exhausted, fall asleep. My last thought before sleep is, *He loves his dog so much; he must really hate me.* I awake to the pungent stench of tequila. Papa Bear is home.

"We needed you."

"Oh come on, baby, I'm sowwy. I made a boo-boo."

"Please stop talking like that."

"Aw, mottu, I hadn't seen those guys—"

"Please stop pouting."

"You're being a bitch."

"Don't call me a bitch."

"I didn't say you're a bitch. I said you're being one."

No one tells us love can curdle so quickly. Like milk, when love decides to sour, it seems to happen instantly.

He paces and yells, pulls out clumps of hair, arguing he has every reason to be furious with me. How dare I ask he come home. In the end, the only way to make him stop is by placing my hands over my ears and screaming, "Stop it, stop it! Stop!"

He leaves the Barn to prowl outside. Because of love, I yearn for his return. Happily, warily, like the earth sensing incoming rain. She wants it, needs it, while knowing the love will land hard.

He comes back. Drained, we opt to sleep. He snores. I watch him with the clenched-jaw tenderness you feel for a child who has a stomach bug, hasn't kept anything inside, and you can't remember a time when your life didn't smell like bile and feces. Due to our gutted septic tank, half-constructed toilet, and the sweet, aging dog, this isn't hyperbole.

He snores. Unconsciously, he throws an arm over me. By habit, my fingers engage in a nightly ritual: to search his skin and along his hairline for telltale hard knots where deer ticks may have bitten into him. Deer ticks can lead to Lyme disease. I've lost count how many I've found and pinched off during our years together. He turns his head and from under his pillow comes a crackle of plastic. An empty condom wrapper. Bizarre. A year and half into our relationship, I still insist on him using a condom. Even more bizarre, he amiably complies without argument.

One by one, telltale symptoms are coming into view, of a disease demanding diagnosis. "It'll be just you and me, baby!" he had said. Miles away from cell service towers and other humans, I now see our seclusion for what it is: isolation. Perfect romance has festered into perfect hell. Although all my emotions and earnings are invested in our lives, our future, the Barn, the car, he insists only his name appears on every lease. Aside from our marriage certificate, the sole contract that bears my name is blame. Everywhere else I look is evidence of my slow erasure.

How peaceful he looks when he sleeps. I imagine we all look this way, when the face finally stills, the day's worries subside, and the chaos we carry calls a truce for these stolen hours of rest. The raging mind and heart decide for these hours, we won't battle.

Sometimes, I wish he would physically hit me. Then, I could point to a bruise as a receipt, proof of grief, permission to leave. The catch with emotional warfare is it's inflicted with far more stealth and elegance than abuse delivered by touch. Making it easier to accept, rationalize, ignore, forgive, page after page.

I author my life. How have I let it come to this? I had so much promise. Talent. Intelligence. My high school friends and teachers, my college professors, my parents, would be devastated with the state of my story. I have let everyone down. I have let you and myself down.

He turns away, then I. We lie this way, as if repelled by the other's skin.

Strange, to lie next to someone you miss.

He is making it increasingly easy to fall out of love with him. From our very beginning, I have moved around him, traveling the space between us. Now, I let the distance lie. As I cry, I try to do it soundlessly. The thing is, though, constricting sobs makes the body shake. My muted tears ripple the bed, confessing my secret without meaning to.

"I hate hearing you cry," he says suddenly, his voice boomeranging off the far wall to lodge itself in my heart.

I say nothing. Faintly, I hear the ballerina's song. I feel the love leaving me as though I've been pierced.

ACCEPT

ACCEPT

✦

I AM 27. Dear love, I am a terrible wife.

I don't love my husband the way I did before.

I saturate with guilt. I feel I have committed an awful betrayal, one I'm trying desperately to undo, to return my heart to its original tick.

Only you know about us. You are my one confidante. Were I to tell Momma and Dad, they'd say, "Leave. Come here."

I wouldn't go. I have my young but promising trajectory. Dad says I have an uncanny ability to work, give, and achieve far more than a normal, healthy person could under normal, healthy conditions. Such is the blessed training from a childhood and industry like mine, and years spent anorexic. I've learned to live on very little. But what would be possible were I not living a starved life? So much of my day is spent buffering and calming his storm. What would I discover if freed of him? Who could I be?

I'm grotesque. Dreaming of a life without him feels like I'm cheating.

"Honey, I want to write a book one day. I think there's one inside me."

He laughs. "That's pretty presumptuous, baby. Stick to the comedy."

Quietly I work, his opinion exactly that: his. His oblivion is a an illness I cannot contract. You and I have inborn and life-honed immunity. Everything I earn goes toward our bills, but I've started keeping money aside. I continue acting classes. I start improv and sketch writing classes. I secure a spec-contract and music producer for my first song. I keep recording pages on my laptop, sent from the ether. I work, silently, tirelessly, trying to kill the suspicion that I will live a smaller life should I remain his wife.

I once marveled at our love. Now I loathe our ugliness. The other day, during a shrieking match, he lobbed his favored line: "I'm going to sleep with other women." For months, I have alternately cried, battled, negotiated, debated, and placated when slapped with that threat. But this time I replied, "Please do. I'm completely disinterested in arguing. Whatever the route you need to let me be, please take it."

How gruesome we are. I catch myself staring at him, willing myself to feel more love than I do, to return to the ease and bliss and certainty of our first months, when I swore he was the most incredible man I'd ever met. Momma says an excellent way of getting me to do anything is to dare me. I'll follow through and die trying.

I look at him and I dare myself, *Love him, enormously and entirely, again.*

This dare, I fail. I trytrytry to muster the conviction to no avail.

Daily, nightly, I ask you, *How can I possibly leave, where would I possibly go, how could life apart work?*

There is always a way, you reply, steely in our hard-earned confidence. *There is always a way, and you will always thrive, by the simple skin of who you are.*

Then you add, *You can trust yourself.*

Thus your words are my air as I lie on a rock hewn from my loneliness. The distance between him and me unspools like a river without an end. There is an ocean of difference between loving well and loving carelessly. Separated by this sea, he and I lie beside each other, each wishing the other was different. In my mind jeers the song "I Won't Grow Up" from *Peter Pan*. His favorite. He sings it, hums it, drums its beat, whittles its lyrics into the bones of our love. Should I remain, I would be doing the same; refusing to grow. In the dark, I raise my hands, palms facing me. They shimmer with two sentiments, separate but connected. The space between them grows slimmer by the day.

I am a terrible wife. There is always a way.

IT IS COLD in the car, parked in front of the Barn. The snow persists stubbornly, surrounding the Barn in three-foot-high banks. My fingers are numb. I blow on them. I sandwich my hands between my legs. It doesn't work. I bite the ends of my gloves and pull them off. I put my fingers in my mouth. There, warmer.

He has banished me here. I, a misbehaving pest, am not to return. Whether now or indefinitely was left unclear. Given that our cellphones don't work here in the belly of the woods, I swiped the house phone before coming outside. At long last, I call Momma and Dad, confess what happened, what has been happening. Appalled, they urge me to leave immediately and stay with them. I can't. I won't.

Momma asks her three preliminary questions, asked in any conversation, and I reply with my usual half-lies.

"Are you eating enough? Sleeping enough? Do you have enough money?"

"Yes, yes, and yes, Momma." My rationale: *Enough* is an opinion, highly subjective. Is the veracity of an answer determined by the ear of a receiver or the mouth of the giver? Anyway, what is the parent-child relationship but a braid of truths, well-meant lies, and omissions, all designed to preserve each other's happiness?

"Does he hit you?" she asks, pain ripping her voice into ribbons. The sound of her hurt makes me close my eyes, and I hate myself for arriving to a place where my mother is brought to ask this. I reply with the sincere truth.

"No, Momma. He doesn't. And if he ever tried, I promise I'd know what to do. I'd talk him down."

"You're so far away from any other person. Aren't you lonely?"

"It's all right, Momma. I've got the voice in my head." I laugh lightly.

She laughs, too, a laugh dyed in sorrow. "Seriously, jaan. How are you safe? I'm scared he'll hurt you. Is he cheating on you?"

"Maybe. But . . . really, Momma, he's harmless. He's just going through a lot. I'm sorry. I shouldn't have told you. Please don't be scared. Or worried." Foolish pleas made to any parent. Worry is what they do. Nevertheless, we'll ask that they don't.

He cracks open the Barn door, gestures that I have permission to return.

Once inside, he admits, "This has little to do with you or us. I'm not happy. And I don't wanna change."

Peter Pan. Dread shoots through me like desire once did. If he is unhappy and unwilling to change, we don't have a chance.

ROAR

ROAR

✦

VALENTINE'S DAY, 2011. A day-long blizzard. I sit on the last train from the City. It carries me toward him. Today, during work, while the 2-year-old napped, I baked two cakes. One for the family, my Healers, and one for my husband, both heart-shaped. I balance my husband's cake on my lap, and read again the card the little boy I babysit gave me. He "wrote and drew" the card, which he and his parents presented along with a vegan muffin from my favorite bakery. On the front of the card is his little footprint in blue paint with the words "I love you Reemee" curved over it like a rainbow. I trace the sentence, reverently.

What a gorgeous day. I love my kids. Between my siblings, the slum kindergarten, orphanage, and my little New Yorkers, I've helped shape over a hundred kids. In the City alone, I've had the honor of being part of thirty-six kids' lives.

The train arrives, depositing me onto the platform. I've been in the City for my weekly three-days. I'm happy to return with an occasion to celebrate, anything to interrupt our pain. He roars into the parking lot of the station, gravel spitting off the car tires, his grin whitely visible even in the night, pulling a giggle through me like a needle draws and directs thread. I carry his cake, wrapped in a blue and white cloth napkin. He pelts my face with kisses, rain claiming a patch of earth. I hold up his cake and he inhales the bliss of cinnamon, apples, and raisins.

"Happy Valentine's Day, honey." I smile. "How was your day?"

We start driving. Eyes on the road, he answers, boasting that two female patrons at the restaurant tonight asked if he was on the dessert menu. He replied, "Well, that would make sense, ladies. I'm here to make you happy." For the fifteen-minute drive, he describes in detail what the women looked like and the rest of their conversation. Sorrow grips me in its fist. I feel you nearby, my love, longing for this chapter to end.

We arrive at the Barn. He helps with my bags. I look to the spot on the snow-covered lawn where he's plotted my future studio. In our home there is room for only his voice, at the expense of mine. We walk through the snow and over a plank of wood, the makeshift, rickety ramp into the house. The air smells like something dying.

He continues talking about the women. I arrange his presents on our bed, an ice cream maker (for ice cream is his favorite food) and two children's books, *The Dangerous Book for Boys* by Conn and Hal Iggulden and *Guess How Much I Love You* by Sam McBratney. Inside I have written dedications to him and the kids I still hope by loyal habit we'll have one day. So much of marriage's joy is its sincere, cozy habits and loyalties. Even if part of oneself has left or is ready to, the other part loves, gives, and moves by habit and loyalty. It is both sublime and heartbreaking. It is why endings arrive in pieces.

The house is blessedly warm. I change out of my jeans, sweater, and boots and into a satin and lace slip. It's one of my favorites. The satin is pink, while white lace trails the neckline and hem. The slip is backless, tied by a single bow right above the small of my back and curve of the derriere. He plops down on the bed, tears open his presents, reclines and eats a generous slice of cake, using his fingers. I stand with the pan in my hands. It's still warm. I hugged it to myself for the two-hour ride between there and here. Through mouthfuls, he brags he could be having sex with both those women this very moment. Thick tendrils of arrogance swirl off him like ink slinking through water.

To have one's cake and eat it too. I feel hot despite the snow and lace. I watch him talk. I'm a bar of soap he's worn to a sliver. If I let him, he'll use me up completely.

"Why are you talking like this again?"

"I'm just being honest."

"Honesty doesn't require unkindness."

"I can't change. I don't wanna. Maybe I don't love you enough."

"I'm sorry that's the case, honey. I really am."

A theme song from *Sesame Street* starts in my mind. "This Is Your Life." I loved that sketch, a parody on game shows. The guest of the day is introduced to long-lost mentors. A teacher, relative, neighbor. The unsung heroes. Before they're revealed, their voice comes through the speakers and you guess the name of the force that has shaped you.

I remember watching *Sesame Street* like it was this morning. I remember the shadows in our home and I remember thinking, *This is* not *my life.* I remember the man and woman and loud silence and thinking, *This is* not *my life.*

Yet here we are. Here we are, an eerie replica of the marriage I tried to solve my entire life, a sphinx without rhyme, reason, rescue, or answer, for it cannot be appeased. I look at him on our bed. It nests in the far left corner of the Barn, cocooned by small space heaters scattered like afterthoughts. Stacks of bricks blunt the echoes in this cavernous mouth. It is almost as dark inside as it is outside. We are lit by a few naked light bulbs strung from the rafters. I've memorized how to walk around them with my eyes closed, for the scorching glass promises to singe the skin if touched.

An elaborate ring of fire. I've encircled myself with forces that can hurt, believing such is love, such is home, such is what I deserve. The Boat, the Bus, the half-burnt Barn. Not once have we inhabited a solid structure. Along with instability and danger, I wonder if

I've grown accustomed to pain. I've grown so adept at enduring, at subsuming my voice to honor another's. Some nights, as last-ditch efforts, he and I bash our bodies together like shards of flint trying to reignite fire, to no avail. We fail, for we aren't flint meeting flint. We aren't need fusing need. We are wound loving wound.

He continues talking, devoted to the bite he clamps. I stand holding a heart in my hands, unable to think of anything I haven't given him or been for him. I was 4 when I learned to read. After working so hard, one day the lines, curves, dots turned into letters, letters into sounds, and sounds into language. A sudden integration. I finally understood what others could. That feeling of everything coalescing into coherence, I feel now. I know now what you always have.

I am enough as I am. I don't want to merely endure anymore. He is not my responsibility, failure, quandary, or purpose. I neither desire nor deserve punishing love that lands hard. I don't want love that includes silence, abuse, manipulation, or captivity. I long for a loving love.

I will never bring children into this home. I would never subject a child to *this*.

Something cold and bitter fills my mouth. Adrenaline, my body, readying for flight.

The irrevocable has occurred. I, a cell denatured and unable to return to its previous state. The decades I've toiled to be enough, for him, him, her, and myself, to be perfect so we may be happy, gather to this moment before exploding, ricocheting light like the birth of a star. I'm not merely a girl devoted to caring and pleasing. I am also the child who didn't like being separated from her brother at the mosque and said so. I am from a mother who stood by me. And, I am yours, you are mine, and we have an uncanny way of knowing what we always need. We know all I'll get from biting my tongue is blood. We know the voice, without intimacy, will atrophy. Therefore, we also know the voice, *if* given love, even by oneself, will grow.

"Look," he says, grinning, "They even wrote down their phone numbers." He laughs, brandishing a dirty receipt. He eats another handful.

"No, thank you," I say aloud.

"What?"

"This is not my life."

"What?" He frowns.

"This. Is not. My life. My story is so much more than this."

He gapes then laughs. He rises, begins to pace, yells. I saran-wrap the remains of the day. I wash my face, brush my teeth, get into bed. He follows and falls swiftly asleep, wine wafting from his skin. Is there anything more foul than the scent of alcohol sweated from human flesh, lain atop, beside, inside oneself? Realizing this, and many other things, aren't qualities I have to stomach anymore, I fall asleep, smiling.

The following day we drive to his sister's for the weekend. It's what I wanted for my Valentine's present, to be around our nieces and family. They are an enormous reason I have remained loyal to hope for as long as I have.

We spend two glorious, peaceful days, full of laughter and children. In the car home he starts again his tired tirade. I repeat, "No, thank you." I exhale on the window, watch the condensation fade without my writing in it. No heart with initials today.

We drop off our things and leave for the train station. I'm scheduled to spend a few days with my Warriors. He sends dozens of voice mails, texts, emails, pleading I speak to him. He promises we'll try counseling. Finally.

He senses a corner turned. Gone are the days I lobby for his love.

TWO DAYS LATER.

"Hey baby, can you talk?"

"Sure." I'm pinch-sitting for a family I don't usually work with. "The baby just woke up, but I have a few minutes. I'm warming up her bottle."

"That's fine. This'll only take a minute."

"Everything okay?"

"Don't come home."

"Oh, the septic tank again?"

"No. I just don't feel like doing this anymore."

"Doing what?"

"This."

"I'm sorry?"

"This," he repeats emphatically, like I'm deaf, dumb, or foreign to English. "Our marriage. I. Don't. Want. To. Anymore."

"All right. I hear you," I reply. Feeling my pulse quicken, the baby grows restless. She whimpers.

"I'm holding you back," he says. "If I love you, I have to let you grow."

Surprise renders me speechless. It's the most humble and selfless I've ever heard him.

"I love you, too." I say, finally.

A pause.

"You can figure out a place to stay," he says. "I have to go."

"All right. I'll talk to you . . . when I talk to you."

I stare at the screen. The call lasted one minute and thirty-seven seconds.

The bottle has sterilized, the milk has warmed. The baby and I sit on the couch. Our breaths align. We inhale and exhale as one. I cradle her, she anchors me. As the milk moves through her, lulling her little body, the soft warmth seeps into me as well.

I don't cry. I'm neither sad nor shocked. I angle my gaze on a pillar of sunshine spilling into the room. There in the light, I find my feelings.

I don't feel rejected. I feel released.

"Thank you," I whisper aloud. I have my backpack and laptop. I have $17. Last week's earnings went toward our bills. I'll make $60 today. I don't have a place to stay tonight. The tenant in my husband's sublet may be leaving though, in a few weeks. I can take his place.

Until then, I have friends. Above all, I have you, and I now have myself.

With the help of scissors found in a kitchen drawer, I cut free our lavender-pink yarn of love. I rub the little indentation left on my finger. After mere minutes, it disappears.

For about five weeks, I cry, in fits and bursts. I cry on the subway, while running, at night, on the phone with a friend or Momma. For most of my day, though, I'm blissfully happy. Calm. A memory of him will nudge me, I'll start missing him and become sad and I'll think, *It's all right.* Would I love him again today, knowing what I do, as who I've grown to be? Worse things have happened and worse will. I was happy for twenty-five years without him. I'll be happy for many more.

After those first few weeks, the tears completely vanish. I search myself for remnant grief only to realize there is none. There is purely gratitude, for our love, his courage in ending us, and all I learned.

From our first to final night of sharing a bed, I would sleep the way I always have, spine straight, flat on my back, with him tied around me like a knot. And during the nights we'd be apart for work, out of romance and love, I'd sleep on the right side of the bed, imagining his form on the left. The night following his final phone call, I realize I have a choice. The pain of memory or freedom. The past or present. I pray that he finds the woman who will curl and bend with him, finding this to be her most comfortable truth. I move to the middle of the bed and sleep in the shape that has always fit me best. It will take us a while to formalize the paperwork, but from that night on, he is in my heart my ex-husband.

I entered my first marriage a girl. I leave, a woman.

ACT III

OWN

OWN

✦

I AM 27. The best thing about my life without him is everything.

I am free to be. Luscious servings of sunlight spill into the room, pulling me awake. Spring has slipped into summer. I open my eyes and instead of leaping to my feet as I always do, I indulge in a yawn, a decadence so sweet I actually laugh. I stretch all four limbs and my hand grazes the book beside my solo pillow. *A Room of One's Own* by Virginia Woolf.

I've moved into his Chelsea apartment. There are plenty of windows for you to sit by.

Nothing feels different, yet everything is. For the first time in my life I'm living without family or roommates. And in a place that feels somewhat stable. He has put the apartment up for sale, but even so, it feels secure. May have something to do with where I am in myself.

This apartment is the fourteenth place I've lived in since moving to New York. He and I never lived here, so it's clean of memories and full of possibility. With his help, I'm in a light-filled room after all, not entirely my own but wonderful still. I pay rent, contrary to popular opinion and plain law. The spouse who evicts the other spouse from their previous home is legally bound to supply the homeless spouse a new, cost-free residence. But I enjoy giving him rent. It frees me of feeling beholden to him. It frees me from the invariable arguments were I to make a case of this.

I absolutely adore living without any other person. I don't feel alone or lonely, given that I have you and myself. I feel wealthy with freedom. I'm rich with the luxury of having only myself to take care of and answer to. Overwhelmed with joy, there are moments I can hardly breathe, bathing in this privilege most women, including Momma, never get to experience. I spend entire days of pure calm and happiness. I walk through these hours with awe and reverence like I'm in a library of rare books. My fingers trail the spines, their titles turning me giddy with what they promise: life suspended between covers, created to be realized.

Given our sudden ending, I haven't seen (and won't see) the Barn again. Neither will I ever see my darling mattress and box spring that graced me with rest when all else felt tremulous.

Five weeks after his phone call, he delivered some of my clothes in plastic trash bags. They now sit in a neat pile, white plastic with red ties. Finding I can't undo his tight knots, I weasel my fingers through the plastic, making sizable holes. Most of the clothes were bought by him. Large, loose-fitting blouses and sweater dresses in navy, gray, black—he, forever trying to police and hide my body from imaginary eyes. I neatly fold his preferred clothing to give to charity and choose one of my dresses from my trusty, beloved backpack. The dress is light cotton. I wash it by hand at night and it's dry the following morning. Light turquoise with pink roses, spaghetti straps, a sweetheart neckline that dips into a trim bodice, and a short, full skirt, down to mid-thigh. It slips over my head with the natural ease of breathing. There is a mirror balanced against the far wall. I tilt my head like a bird and measure my reflection. Just right.

My love, these days are so sweet, candy would be envious of me. I walk into the living room to write my daily thanks. There are so many. Sunlight paints my face golden. The storm has passed. Breathe.

I HAVE DECANTED my spirit, and she is blooming.

I decline invitations from potential suitors. I want only to work. I spend the day auditioning and babysitting before rushing home, my limbs tingling with excitement. Aside from my daily gratitude log, I've stopped journaling by hand and spend the evenings typing instead, to keep with the pace, continuing the pages I began at the Barn. They aren't the cohesive pages of a larger work but they feel like the preliminary notes for one. These pieces arrive in the form of essays, on my childhood, anorexia, love, womanhood and so on.

Being back in the City, surrounded by masses, highlights again my lack of flesh-and-blood friends. When I'm with another person, it's usually because I've been hired as an actress, model, or babysitter, to perform and give as they desire. Occasionally, I'll grab an authentic moment with Momma or one of my surrogate Mamas, but those gifts are rare.

I don't mind, though. I've learned quickly that I love solitude, the company of my own voice, and what it allows. This is my new lease on life. I can be and learn anything I wish. I book three national commercials in a month. As my drawings improve, I sell them for higher prices. I write thirty-seven songs and produce a demo with seven of them. I produce an eighth song, very different from the others. Satire in the form of rap, it's titled "I Made a Sex Tape." It's a commentary on reality television, voyeurism, female objectification, and celebrity idolatry. I crowdsource funds for the music video and find the perfect director and team. We launch the video on YouTube. It garners 50,000 views and counting.

While filming the video, I spend every minute amazed and endlessly grateful. One idea from my mind gathered so many people. One electrical spark made it possible for their genius to shine, and the harmony of our voices has created something that will live on its own. A piece of art has that gorgeous quality—it's an ever-evolving alchemy, open to endless interpretations, giving every viewer or reader what they specifically need. I look around the set and think, *If this is my last job in this vein, I'll be completely content.*

Miraculous, the results when we allow ourselves to grow. At night, snug in the slim dip in the mattress, deep and wide enough only for my body, I listen to the buzzing stillness. The quiet hum of limitlessness sounds like the song of cicadas. I sleep and wake up smiling, ready to move in my delicious frenzy.

For years, I have wondered about the meaning of my name but never answered the curiosity. One night I look up my meaning. In Persian, Reema means poetry. In Sanskrit, Reema means limitless.

I WRITE PAPA, ASKING, *Can we please talk about you and me, our family, and everything that has happened? I want us to be close. For that to be, there is pain we need to address and heal.*

He replies he wants to love me but feels I need help for my lies.

My mind keens like a funeral song. I search myself for shock to find there is none. His truth is his, mine is mine. There is comfort in patterns, a sordid, patchwork peace. I feel the familiar feeling of my heart tumbling. I catch it before it hits the ground.

The next time, rather than falling into love, I would like to lift. Love shouldn't feel like a descent. I'd like us to ascend. I want a fierce love and a fearless man.

LISTEN

LISTEN

✦

I AM 30. I write sitting in my parents' breakfast nook. Summer has shifted into fall. I've begun to feel better. You knew I would. I'm glad I listened. I've cracked open the door to the deck to allow in the day. A whistle of cool air glides into the house like a sly paramour.

Suddenly, a small bird flies into the room. The poor thing is bewildered by the quick shift in surroundings. It begins to fly against the windowpanes, slamming once, twice, thrice into the glass. The more it does, the more frantic and disoriented it becomes, its shock now whisked into terror.

I leap to my feet and try to shepherd the bird outside. I want to call out to it but am afraid that would only scare it more. I make foolish flapping motions with my arms, swinging them in wide arcs, a cross between a traffic controller and a mime. Words slip out without my intention, in a desperate singsong.

"Little bird, this way. It'll be okay. This way."

And then, insanely, "Trust me. Come here. Here."

She finally flies out the door. Trapped in such a panicked rush, she hits the doorframe on the way. There, she leaves a bright, scarlet smudge. I look at the sky. Already the clouds have folded her in, like flour enfolds spice. I touch the blood on the doorframe. It is barely a drop but given her tininess, a single drop is significant. I rub the drop once, twice, thrice between my forefinger and thumb, and just like that, the memory of her vanishes. Taken in by my very fingertips. I start crying, feeling suddenly cruel, a bully who has taken something from a littler creature. It was her blood. I didn't even think to ask.

Shaken, I shut the door.

I AM 28. THE moment we meet, I know. He will take all of me.

Oh, my love, not again.

Why must I meet him now, when I'm doing so well? And, I can feel, he is the strongest storm thus far. Making every candle wary, sending their light and shadow jumping along the walls. Love, I will try to hold steady.

His sister finds me through a moms' network. She calls looking for a date-night babysitter. Our conversation stretches into an hour. I meet her beautiful toddlers and husband. I love them immediately.

After a month she says, "You should meet my brother. He's creative as well. He's really good at branding. You should check out his website. There are some great video tutorials."

I wonder how I should phrase that I'm adamantly single, decisively focused on my work, and not looking to entwine with anyone, least of all the brother of a dear new friend. I have a plan and I will stick to it.

"He's not looking for a relationship either," she says, without my having to say anything.

"Oh. Fantastic." I look at his photos online. Not remotely appealing. Even better. I won't be tempted.

She emails him, he emails me, suggesting we meet for drinks. About to disperse for Thanksgiving, we decide on the following

Sunday. My brother is visiting Oregon as well. He looks over my shoulder as I watch one of the aforementioned allegedly amazing videos.

"Perfect. You've found your husband."

My brother never expresses such romantic nonsense. He doesn't believe in sweeping fantasies or star-crossed destiny. He is now 24 and my sister, 17. Standing now at 6'3", with an unfailing sense of ethics, he is an enormously successful management consultant. Calm under pressure, he lives in suits and jets, bouncing continents and computer screens, moving billions of dollars daily between companies vying for power. He views life with thinly veiled suspicion, believing everyone is guilty, asinine, and out to kill.

He shares my precise manner in speaking. It can come across as affectation. I'd like to think it isn't; we both adore language. When my brother says things like, "You need to school yourself on Justin Timberlake. His canon is tremendous," he is neither joking nor speaking in sexual innuendo. He speaks from sincere respect for JT's spectacular mastery of performance, business, and songwriting.

Now, my baby brother lists his reasons for his idiotic prophecy.

"He's smart, and has an astute understanding of his material and audience. He's hugely successful, and it's time you date someone like that."

My eyebrows shoot up. "Is it now?"

"Success means work ethic. It's not about wealth. Furthermore, he seems to share our sense of humor. When are you meeting him?"

"We're meeting for drinks on Sunday."

"See? Exactly. He knows what's at play."

"In New York everyone meets to talk about work over drinks! Even if one doesn't drink!" Oh, how I loathe the sound of my voice, reedy with defense. My siblings always ruffle my feathers like nobody else. He continues his lunatic drivel while I fume.

We scroll through other videos. This man has built himself and his company from his own vision. He's an internet wunderkind, a contemporary guru who teaches people how to create abundance in life. The tone he adopts is overbearing and cocky, but it serves a purpose. He's speaking to his demographic of men in their 20s and 30s. The aggressive tough-love seduces their respect. He has created an empire that helps people discover their best selves, and beneath the shtick is his genuine empathy for his audience. The positive impact he has had on others is already immeasurable.

I. Love. This. A man on the quest for more.

"He seems rather impressive," I admit aloud. My cheeks are pinking with excitement.

Sunday, 7 o'clock in the evening, I walk into Angel's Share, the dim-lit speakeasy he has chosen. He sits near the entrance, at the bar.

Oh, hell. In person, he's rather attractive. And tall. And brawny, beautifully dressed, and bristling with potent masculine energy.

Confound it all. I'm furious with his sister. I'm furious with my brother. I'm furious with his misleading photos. I'm furious with the way this man smells when he leans toward me and the scent he leaves in the space between us when he leans back. I'm furious with this dizzying spot of air. His pomp and circumstance suggest he wears cologne from a bottle shaped like Fabio, but he doesn't. He smells like fresh laundry.

Is there any aphrodisiac more endearing than the scent of fresh laundry? For me, any morsel of picturesque innocence feels like a sensorial sonnet. And when you love the way someone smells, you love not only their nearness and touch, but the small patch of air where their scent still floats after they've moved away. The French have a name for this. Sillage. *Sillage* means trail of scent, referring to this lingering memory of a person. After you've parted, this pleasure keeps you company, ebbing or deepening how much you miss him.

I'm in so much trouble.

My past is filled with gorgeous all-American golden boys, classically handsome, unabashedly confident of their longitude and latitude in a world that caters to them. Their king was my ex-husband, the iconic idol who runs through the surf, tanned, muscled, grinning, coming at me with blue eyes, dimples, and a lazy-Sunday-morning-in-bed drawl, saying, "Baby, baby, baby, be mine," and I've replied, "Yes, please. I am yours."

This man is different. The son of humble beginnings, his magnetism comes from presence, not muscle or symmetry. His face isn't traditionally handsome. But the longer I look, his features grow on me, like fever evolving into hallucination. Angular cheekbones, deep-set eyes, and a mouth carefully shaped closed. It will be months before he allows himself to greet me with an open smile. When he does, it stretches the sky.

His entire body radiates disciplined concentration and intelligence. His posture and mannerisms appear calculated, rehearsed, as if he studies and understands body language. Above all, his gaze holds me. I'm a target already locked in by a missile.

Suddenly, my cells feel more alive.

We talk, covering everything but work, ignoring the social graces one observes in New York. Within seconds, we're building off the other's jokes, laughing as though we're the first creatures to discover humor. Our faces mirror delighted shock. We speak unfettered, swapping family anecdotes. When he talks about his family, his face glows with love.

Turns out we live a few blocks away from each other. The night air is ideal to walk. His apartment is a block north of my ex-manager's. His was one of the buildings I gazed at on the night I met my ex-husband, craning my neck and wondering who lived there, high above, encased in glass, contemplating the ant-like lives milling beneath. We hug goodbye. I return home. I call Momma and, while the phone rings, text my sister words I've never before felt or uttered. Silly words that make me squeamish.

"I think I just met the man I'm supposed to marry."

In characteristic fashion my sister texts, "WTF? What is happening? Who are you? Who is this guy? Stop. Tell me more."

Momma picks up. I try to speak but instead giggle uncontrollably.

"I've never heard you like this! What's he like? You sound so happy."

Goodness gracious. This will wreak havoc on my plan. I was doing so well.

Over the next two months, he and I meet a few times, careful to keep things casual. I manage the impossible: I neither kiss him nor let myself be kissed.

Tonight, we are meeting at another beautiful, hidden speakeasy. I arrive a few minutes before him and busy myself with the book I'm reading presently, *Gone Girl* by Gillian Flynn. All around me, stained-glass lamps shaped like upturned tulips dot the dark room, glowing with amber light. Each nook, booth, couch, table is different, lovingly chosen by a discerning eye. To enter the bar, one must have a secret telephone number to make a reservation. The place hasn't a name, only a number: 17, brandished on a brass medallion hung on a somber mahogany door. The speakeasy lives underground, and has no windows for you, my love, to sit by. I'm sure this isn't an ominous sign.

He arrives. I put away the book and give him a hug and a cookie I baked that day, one in a large batch. Every now and then, I make a big batch of heart-shaped cookies to give to colleagues, friends, and any stranger on the subway who looks like they could use one. They get a cookie, or a love note, or both.

He looks at me, blankly. "You're reading a book. At a bar. And this is a cookie."

"Yes."

The drinks are old-fashioned cocktails made by purists, served in tiny glasses and tumblers. Momma gave me firm direction on the phone as I walked to meet him: "Have fun, relax, order a drink. Break the wagon. Live a little."

"Yes, Momma."

Thus I perch on a leather loveseat taking little sips of something outrageously delicious. It tastes like lavender laced with sin. I'm in a short, tight black skirt, a tight, black V-neck shirt, stockings, and boots. My pre-marriage uniform. He sits two feet away, the hot secret of our attraction scorching the air between us, each wondering when we'll confess it and how. I can feel my pulse in my lips, beating so strongly I swear the scoundrel can see it.

"Have another sip." He lifts my drink for me. He follows with something highly intelligent, witty, and original.

Hell. Swoon. Sip.

He leans in. I jump as if touched by a burning match. By silent rule, whenever he attempts contact, I contort away like a Romanian circus performer. Tonight though, the resolve is merciless in his eyes. I feel the hard curl of his arm slip around my torso, pressing me to him like meat against a grill.

I recite to him the eight reasons I typed and memorized, to why we should not Begin Something.

"One, we are each exactly where we need to be in our lives right now, and shouldn't shake that. Two, I have just completed a catastrophic few years and am enjoying a peaceful singlehood. Three, I know and love your sister. So, should something go awry, or if I panic, I cannot run away and wouldn't want to. What if all of us knowing one another creates unnecessary pressure?"

"You can run away anytime," he says. "And, I'm not going to hurt you."

"Well, that's lovely. Thank you for your kind sentiments."

He hovers closer. I fear I'll faint or combust from the intoxicating blend of desire and trepidation.

"Four," I continue my list, "I think you're incredible and this could be something really amazing if we give it careful time to grow. Five—"

He kisses me. He breathes me in until there is nothing left.

He is power personified. A steady, sturdy, masculine force. All he needs is to glance my way and I'm a mess of blushes.

After years of feeling like a weary, mud-caked soldier living on unstable ground, I feel beautiful, desired, fun. I'm even laughing again.

Dear love, please understand. Although being alone has felt exhilarating, being with him is equally thrilling.

We are in his apartment. We are talking on the couch. His eyes take on a look, and suddenly, I'm flipped over his shoulder and carried to bed, giggling.

More than sexual chemistry, he engages my mind. I was starving. Now I'm a glutton. Our conversations are on a new astral plane of intelligence. We inspire each other.

He calls himself a teacher of strategy. He doesn't talk; he states. He doesn't walk; he strides. He targets, persuades, conquers like mercury cuts through flesh. He's the youngest man I've ever dated, a year older than myself. A man of two voices, his brand is his public persona. For his inner circle, he is kind, humble, compassionate. To his followers—whom he calls his "students"—he is an all-wise monarch, the living testament of the company promise. A mere few years ago, he was a scrawny, geeky, shy boy with an app and a plan. Now, he is self-made royalty.

Sometimes, my mind calls him the Prince.

There are moments when he jars me. He has a penchant for misogynist jokes, which feels obtuse given his closeness to his three sisters and mother—all very strong, smart women. Moreover, he's attracted to *me*, a clear feminist.

"A woman can't call herself a woman if she doesn't wear heels at least five inches high," he says. "They do amazing things for the ass."

"I don't need the help, thank you."

He laughs.

Like a rash, his fondness for this sort of humor flares up whenever there's a moment in conversation that feels too vulnerable, meaningful, intimate, or serious for his liking.

I wonder, as well, about the toll of the continual pressure, ambition, and competition for More. New York is the epicenter of The

Culture of More. He runs a hard, fast race at a punishing pace, with the wealthiest, swiftest, coolest kids.

He doesn't merely run with them; he leads. He is the King of the Cool Kids, encircled by adorers and fellow nobility. He wears his coolness masterfully, having studied himself on video to understand and perfect body language and performance. Like many men of power, he lives a highly public yet solitary life, the sections of his day divided between being surrounded by crowds, and working on his own. Everyone desires a piece of him. Grown men stammer when hearing his name, attesting he changed their lives. In person, they grin slavishly. The female groupies swarm like bees abuzz. Sometimes, I wonder how important it is to him that I look the way I do. Whether I'm another goal for him to conquer. He grew up bullied and unpopular. I wonder if I resemble the girls who once denied him the time of day.

"High-status" is a term he enjoys. New to me, it means one person is alpha while another is beta. He uses it as both an adjective and a noun, widely, to speak about business, behavior, and even dating.

"To give a woman flowers is beta. An alpha doesn't let her feel too secure in his affections for her—he's high-status, and to remain that way, she needs to feel she has yet to gain his full interest. In the same vein, women shouldn't be too confident or vocal especially in relationships. It's unattractive."

Then he'll say something utterly insightful, and I'll become a puddle. I won't have forgotten his previous comment; the duality of his split persona is all the more compelling. Intriguing. Exciting. His story is unlike anyone else's I've read.

I imagine, after years of feeling overlooked and unattractive, he needs to feel powerful, in control, and adored. I can absolutely empathize. Life has a way of sending us people who mirror our best and our most worrying qualities. I imagine, too, that it's hard for him to trust others. It's lonely, being surrounded by hungry hands and hot mouths who desire bits of you.

I think I'm a safe space for him. A rare person who wants nothing but his companionship. We don't gallivant through fabulous events or clubs. We talk.

I'm introduced to a few of his colleagues. They've been wondering who I was, a female name written consistently in his personal calendar.

"You two make a phenomenal team," they say. "A potential power couple."

Appearances would lead one to believe such a thing. I've grown to resemble the female half of a perfect power couple. Had you asked me at 15, a chubby, unpopular, pimply pariah, what I'd emulate at 28, I wouldn't have imagined this woman. I certainly don't feel like her. Their compliment makes me feel giddy and lovable, although something somersaults in my tummy. Humility. Nostalgia. Sadness for the girl-child who felt ugly, unwanted, and invisible for all those years. A patch of dust so common and hidden that no one cared to sweep or step into it.

He travels often for work. Sometimes he forgets the day of the week or where he's meant to fly and land tomorrow. He wakes up when his assistant calls, he climbs into the car waiting downstairs, it takes him to the airport, and the plane delivers him where he's needed. I sometimes leave him gift packages to come home to, mixed bags of things drawn from our personal jokes and sweet anecdotes. I leave them with his doorman. When he travels for an extended time, it takes longer for him to drop his wall once we reconnect. But he does.

"Stay the night." His voice is muffled by my hair. We lie in his bed. His breath feels warm, like sunlight.

"Not yet. I don't know you enough to know you won't change by morning."

"You do."

I sit up, shrug. "I'm not ready. Thank you, though. Soon."

In the cab home I realize I've left my gold bangle at his house. I text him.

He replies, "All good. I put it in the lost and found I've got for my girls."

THE AIR IS FREEZING, the sky gloriously bright. One of my favorite things about the New York winter is that while it's brutal, unwieldy, and stretches so long it feels like bad manners, the days remain bright. We hardly experience rain. We rarely experience gray or misty days. The season passes and I ruefully decide, "I'll give you another year."

I sit in a café, running over my sides before an audition. I glance at the page from time to time but mostly look out the window, to secure the lines to memory. Across the narrow street is a tiny playground on an island that suffices for a neighborhood park. A tiny plot of earth in Manhattan is luxury. I watch the children laugh and run, layered in undershirts, T-shirts, coats, scarves, hats, and mittens to keep the air's bite off their tender skin. Some of the kids are layered so enthusiastically they're wider than they are tall. Were they to fall, they would bounce.

They are watched over by moms, babysitters, and nannies. One can clearly identify the hierarchy and who is what. The easiest, most accurate way to isolate our roles is by appearance. The moms, for the most part, are white, in their 30s and 40s, stylishly coiffed and dressed. Nearly every mom is in impeccable shape from a mix of yoga, Pilates, SoulCycle, and the gym.

The nannies are middle-aged women who are Black, Latina, Jamaican, Puerto Rican, Colombian, Indian, Taiwanese, Russian, Romanian, Chinese, Indonesian, Ukrainian, anything except for white American.

The babysitters are girls in their 20s, usually students or artists. One can tell who we are by our age and our lack of telltale rock on our ring finger.

The intimate world of women is a snapdragon, unfurling in layers of petals and teeth. Each woman, across the street and beyond, harbors stunning secrets, hopes that singe, brilliance that humbles, resilience that inspires, and unhealed gashes that will compel you to stitch your life to her wellbeing. As tough as it can be to be a girl in this belittling world, never would I trade genders. The ache from missing my sisters and my place in our circle would undo me.

I watch a mom call after her child, her neck pale and tight. I love collarbones for their wings-in-flight shape. Hers jut sharply, the skin stretched like parchment paper, so thin I can sense her heartbeat, urgent as a baby bird's. Her body is sapped of warmth and softness. In this town, we whittle ourselves down to a punishing, unnatural, almost unfeminine thinness. Such is our brand of attractiveness.

Former, recovering, and current anorexics can always sight fellow anorexics. It isn't her thinness that betrays her. It's her shrunken energy. She looks like she's being pressed in and down by an enormous invisible hand. She may flash a dazzling smile one second, but when she thinks you aren't watching, she will turn inward and look like she's sinking.

I still fight to tame my own anorexia. A clear connection has risen: I was raised by a bully, married a bully, and have been my own biggest bully through the choices I make.

In a strange, simple sense, for me, anorexia has been a side effect of being a girl in this world.

While my relationship with exercise, food, and appearance is particularly intense, nearly all women have a strained relationship with these matters. I don't know a single woman completely content with her physicality. I don't know a single person who doesn't desire beauty. Even if you were raised in a Pleasantville home, how you behave, look, and live are under constant scrutiny, pressure, and commentary. Socially, politically, on a global scale.

I try to ventriloquize my voice to the other side of the street, to ask the woman running after her child, "When was your moment you first felt small? When did you decide to shield yourself by shrinking yourself?"

Blink, check the time. My audition is in fifteen minutes. One last peek at all the women and their children. Now run. Time to play pretend.

I WRAP UP the monologue, satisfied that I've hit every emotion at the correct point, honoring the arc the playwright intended. I finish, allow a beat, then meet the gaze of the panel. The director, producers, casting director, and writer look pleased. A few of them smile, nod their heads. They write furiously on pages before them, slide the notes over to their colleagues. They peruse my resume and headshot. They share solemn Yes's and Mmm's.

"Let's see that again, with more anger," says the director. "She's been holding all this in for a long time. Let it get messy. Let her be ugly."

"Absolutely. Thank you." I perform with dilated anger, mess, and ugliness.

Broad grins, enthusiastic nods, across the panel.

"Beautiful work," says the director and the others murmur their agreement. I'm delighted. The play is a rare gem, intelligent and bold. The role I'm auditioning for is even more uncommon: a character who isn't "Leading Man's Girlfriend" but the protagonist of her own story. The role is written for a white woman, but I'm a wild card they decided to audition. One of the producers leans forward.

"Tell us about yourself."

I share a few tidbits, making sure to be authentic, funny, warm, and intelligent. While speaking I mentally gauge thirty seconds, and whether they'd like me continue for another thirty, then another. This is an opportunity to catapult my life. If the panel judges me worthy, years of labor may coalesce to fruition.

"Thank you so much for coming in."

"Thank you for having me."

The assistant leads me out of the studio. The moment the door opens, every woman in the waiting room whips her head to stare, to discern by my face and body language how it went. Most of us know one another. We are friendly while professional.

The room pulses with need. It throbs with the understandable desperation to book work, find approval, stability, and relief from the seemingly endless years of auditioning. The large majority of us live not from paycheck to paycheck but dollar to dollar, willingly subjecting ourselves to daily rejection and scrutiny. I've known these women for six years now. We are aging. The consequent anxiety is evident. Some carry age well, others not so much. They are withered by struggle, creased by insecurity, wrinkled by the harshness of our industry.

Quickly I gather my things to rush to my next audition. This one is for a car commercial. If booked, it'll pay my rent for a year. I run toward the subway. I walk past a bodega, its colorful shelves bursting with tabloids and porn. The images on both kinds of magazines make my head hurt, the way the sound of a man yelling will. Courtesy of the loud silence.

"Does your family ever talk about relationships or sex?" I asked the Prince the other night, on a dinner date. He had made a comment that piqued my curiosity, that while his family is close, they censor parts of themselves from one another.

He laughed. "No way. We don't touch on relationships, let alone sex."

"Not even your siblings?"

"Nope."

"How'd you learn about sex?"

"The way most kids do. Online. And you know, 'periodicals.'" He smiled in a way that let me know the conversation had ended.

Traditional porn is the antithesis of sex. The sentence died on my lips. It's strange. In many ways, I feel very close to him and as though we can discuss so much. But certain areas and opinions are unpermitted, cast into corners. He broke our gaze, and my mind meandered. You can always tell when someone's primary education or introduction to sex, courtship, and the opposite sex is porn. You feel the aggression in his touch. You hear the misogyny in his words. You sense the shame in his nearness.

I grab the N right before the doors shut and arrive at the next studio with seconds to spare. While waiting in the lobby for the elevator, I take off my boots, opaque stockings, and cardigan, leaving only my short, tight, black dress, and slip on five-inch heels. It's freezing but I must serve the commercial's message and demographic.

The elevator arrives. Two other girls, one guy, and myself pile in. As we make our way up, the other girls undergo their transformations. I apply lip-gloss on my already painted mouth. In real life, I never wear lip-gloss. It feels like overkill. Just before the doors open, I angle my body away from the others and covertly create cleavage, plumping each diminutive breast to perch higher and forward. Another accessory I shun when I'm myself. I look at my reflection in the elevator mirror. I look like something to be sucked on. Suddenly, I feel nauseous.

We arrive at our floor. The air in the waiting room is of a cramped bar. The musk of everyone's lust for territory is animal, pungent. The small differences between a bar and this are that the floor isn't sticky, the lights are bright, and the room is forcibly quiet, as cameras film auditions behind every closed door. My eyes skim the various doors marked Studio A, B, C, to find where I'm to report. The casting director will audition us in the order we arrive. For commercial auditions, the number of actresses and models called in is significantly higher than theater and film auditions. The sheer volume of us illuminates a hard fact: we are easily swapped and replaced with one another. Pretty faces are a dime a dozen.

Another actress squeezes in beside me on the low pleather couch, smiling apologetically. "It's okay," I whisper. The plastic squeaks, clammy against our bare thighs.

We girls, boys, women, and men, our eyes scour the room like floodlights sweeping prison grounds to catch all details, to expertly measure and compare one another. After producing my own work, videos, art, and music of forthright intelligence, these auditions make me want to gouge out my teeth. Part of me thinks, *There's so much more to me that I must pursue.* Another voice says, *What else are you good for? What else could you sustainably sell and be but a pretty face?*

If control is the father of my story, beauty is my mother. I've always believed beauty is my strongest currency, resource, duty, and skill. I glance at the commercial's copy, an unoriginal but relentlessly effective narrative: sexy damsel standing beside luxury car. A luxury car promises sex, illustrated perfectly by a girl who looks like sex. I look around. Conveniently, there are hordes of us to pick from. Of course there are—we were raised on these commercials.

My phone buzzes. It's Dad. He rarely calls so I pick up, worried it's an emergency.

"Hey sweetie, just returning your call. How are you?"

"Hi! Great, thanks," I whisper. "I'm at an audition. Call you in a bit?"

"Sure. I'm proud of you."

"Sorry?"

"I'm proud of you. It requires toughness to do what you've done for years. I couldn't. I admire you."

"Thank you, Dad. Wow. I'll call you soon as I can."

I hang up as tears rush my eyes. I've never heard those words before. "Proud of you." Never. I blink a hard, long blink. I open my eyes and the world is brighter, the light is clearer, the sounds of heels, heartbeats, and coughs are louder.

I hear my name. My eyes meet the casting director's. I leap to my feet, holding my modeling card. My card has a large photo on one side, four smaller ones on the other, each depicting me in various degrees of undress. I offer it to the casting director. She brushes it aside.

"We already have you."

"Of course. Thanks." In any other arena, my mind would quietly correct her words to "We already have *yours*." However, her wording has veracity. I, very much the image on the page, sit already in unseen hands.

HIS APARTMENT is immaculate. Every photo, book, piece of furniture and décor has been chosen with clinical precision. He has sculpted a new world high above the masses, from monochromatic tones and right angles of steel. Boxes line the walls, holding office supplies, gifts from fans, online purchases. His meals arrive at his door every morning, pre-cooked, packaged, labeled.

He travels for nearly half of every month. The apartment feels sterile, with barely a trace of life. No plants or aroma of cooking. My parents' home in Oregon teems with life, people, voices, affection, laughter, jokes, cooking, pets. I miss them like a physical ache, a steady drip-feed of longing.

We lie in his bed, our bodies relaxed and content. I form into his body, my head in the nook made by his neck and shoulder, his arm gripping me to him, our legs scissored over, underneath, over. A cozy tangle of differences, for we couldn't be more opposite. I'm petite while he is husky. I'm smooth while he is hairy. I'm forever chilly, while he is warm to the point of burning. I love the space of time we're still inside; that period when we're getting to know each other's sweet spots—his ears, my neck—and how to rouse them just right.

He has a conspicuous birthmark on his forehead that I love. Aside from his lips, it's my favorite spot to kiss. I shift my weight, moving to sit on top of him. I admire his expanse, tracing his details with my fingers. Wide windows show the night is clear and New York is breathtaking.

"Great view."

"I know," he says, looking only at me. "Beautiful."

I laugh and turn pink in the dark. He, famous for his poker face, forgets it a moment. We hold the other's gaze for as long as we can before bashfulness begs mercy.

It's been months and we've yet to have sex. Not for a lack of desire but for sound reasons. Ours isn't a monogamous relationship, and I can't have sex outside one. Our relationship is obstinately Casual.

In the contemporary dating sphere, people graduate through stages of affection. As if auditioning, we compete for the other party's attention, admiration, and approval, hoping we're measured as more worthy than the rest. Our dating status begins with casual, then progresses to regular, then serious, then exclusive. Exclusivity means monogamy and "full status." He and I are casual, and I've yet to achieve full status.

When dating casually, it's understood we may also date other people. I don't. That's what the Cool Kids do, and I've never been a Cool Kid. I'm the opposite of cool and aloof—I'm completely gooey in the middle.

He, however, is the King of the Cool. It's evident, the importance of him being and remaining single, a jet-setting millionaire "player." It's part of his brand. I have neither the arrogance nor desire to try being the woman to change his present priorities. He's a late bloomer to sex and attracting the opposite sex. To compensate, he's now blooming with fervor, exploring as many women as he can while he can.

I'm rather happy with our nonattachment. I like our affection and pace. All my previous experiences have followed one pattern, one gear: sudden, complete consumption. Him over me, I over him. It's a relief to not feel devoured. It's a relief to not slip away, from you or myself.

Surprisingly, he never brings up sex or makes advances. For all I know, he has an assembly line of women with whom he has sex. With me, he seems perfectly content doing everything-but, then cuddling up and talking. Pillow-talk. My polite instinct is to leave and give the man his space, but he curls a big, hard arm around me, anchoring me in place, and we talk, naked, indulging in this extraordinary rarity. This blissful slip of hours found between midnight and dawn, when we reveal our most tender anecdotes, painful memories, and audacious goals.

He and I brainstorm ideas. We share successes, setbacks, and hopes. One can almost touch the joy shimmering off our bodies. We do this evening after evening, all the while confident we'll remain unattached.

I have yet to accept his offer to spend the night.

LOOK

LOOK

✦

I SIT IN THE MAKEUP chair being prepped for camera, like meat being tenderized before roasting. The hair and makeup team dance their hands over me. Their touch is light and urgent like the wings of butterflies as they improve my natural features. The other actresses and models sit in matching chairs, a line stretching from either side of me, each girl in various stages of development, vying for completion. I look up, into my mirrored eyes, with your presence floating within.

What need is there for another pretty face? asks our reflection. *Who is my life helping?*

The words sting like hot lashes of a belt.

I don't know, I reply.

Figure it out.

Two stylists come over with a variety of possible outfits. A man and woman, both righteously chic in the way some people are violently Christian or aggressively Atheist. I'm always cautious around fanatical fashionistas, convinced they'll realize I'm an outsider and feed me to the dogs.

In the quest for beauty, I've lived as the audience and the coveted, the overlooked and the adored. Was it mere pages ago, my love, that I was chubby, pimply, terribly awkward, and lonely? I marveled at the power of beauty, yearned to feel its charge, and attacked the task like shark to flesh.

In a world wherein beauty reigns, I'm half elite, half minority. Superpower, third world. America, Bangladesh. I learned beauty the way I learned English, and for the same reason: a ticket to freedom. I view my appearance with the wry humor and blunt objectivity with which a scientist navigates a living case study.

I look down the line of women to my left and right. Our youth monetized, our genetics pawned, every face bears a different degree of desperation and fatigue. We know, in a few years, most of us will have been traded for the incoming batch. Our time to sell is now.

"Oh my god," says the male stylist. "Look at this face." He cups a finger under my chin, tips my head toward him, then away. "What I'd do to look like you. My whole life would be different."

I smile and say, "Thank you." I stifle a yawn. My call time on set was 8 in the morning, which meant I was up at 4 o'clock to get my two and a half hour workout before work.

Life is different when you turn beautiful. But love, I've learned the real matters don't change. Years will still stack. Pain will still find you. People will still wound. Beauty isn't invulnerability, immortality, meaning, or true freedom.

I twirl as the stylist tells me to. I stop. My head spins: I've had only a banana and black coffee all day. I look into the mirror and I understand why my ex-husband preferred I wear sweatshirts and loose-fitting sweater dresses. Why he wanted to build my studio as a glorified outhouse. When something is highly desired, admired, or rewarded, it can become threatening.

It has become a threat for me as well. Beauty and anorexia, once my shield, are now my suffocation. Imagine what I could accomplish, the meaningful skills I could discover, the traits I could hone, were my energy, so far spent on being marketable and pleasing, directed elsewhere. Imagine who I could be if I wasn't Just A Pretty Face.

Who are you helping? asks our reflection. What have you learned, what have you achieved, what will you leave behind, what have you given?

I am nearly 30. Were I to die tomorrow, I would be furious with myself.

THE FREEZING RAIN has licked the sidewalks with a thin sheet of ice. I wear a black chiffon and silk cocktail dress, sparkly earrings, and flat boots. I arrive at the restaurant before him and begin to change my boots for heels discreetly by the coat-check. I feel a gasp of cold wind as the door opens behind me.

"Mmm. You smell good." He pecks me on the cheek. He sees me changing.

"Good girl," he says, giving my derriere a light slap for a job well done. The hostess leads us to our table.

It's my favorite restaurant. He remembered. We sit, radiant from our nearness, desire turning the air between us effervescent. He wears tailored slacks and a sports coat hugging the contours of his arms and chest perfectly. Biceps, triceps, delts, pecs, I recite like a song. For better or for worse, I will always love the male form. We place our order and land deep in a conversation about a hypothetical couple, a husband and wife.

He poses the following. The wife gains more than fifteen pounds. Is the husband allowed to cheat? And, can he be faulted for it? Or, say that her looks haven't changed, but he cheats. As his punishment and her restitution, how much money can she demand from him?

Astounding, the conversations one can collect as a girl in this world.

"Sometimes, I'm unclear whether I date you because you fascinate me or horrify me."

He laughs. "Play the game." He toys with a spoon. Candlelight glints off the silver.

"All right. Let's break it down. We have two topics here. First, what details create and ensure a contract of loyalty. Second, the idea that there can exist an exact fee for betrayal and closure. Regarding the first, you suggest a man's loyalty hinges solely or largely on whether he finds his partner physically attractive. Most men would define their loyalty differently, basing it on a plethora of characteristics and shared interests. And, not every person would declare a woman unattractive simply for having gained fifteen pounds."

"Men are visual creatures."

I laugh. "*Humans* are visual creatures. Most women adore physical beauty just as much as men. It comes down to the volume and type of power a person places upon beauty, whether that power is toxic or wholesome, and what qualities a person prioritizes in a partner, and oneself. Beauty, like wealth or talent or success, is an incentive for attraction. They all sweeten the deal, but they don't guarantee self-esteem, love, or loyalty."

"True," he replies. He sips his drink.

"I think loyalty hinges on the person giving it, versus the person we're giving it to." I pause. "Does that make sense?" I find adding that question to the end of opinions ensures I don't come off as too assertive.

He nods slowly. "Go on."

"Just how beauty lives in the eye of the beholder, loyalty hinges on the heart of the bestower. Love is love and a person's sense of self, character, and psychology safeguard their ability for loyalty. There are many reasons people cheat, some understandable, although not necessarily exonerating, like if they're spinning from trauma or grief and have lost their sense of awareness, but fifteen pounds?"

He smiles.

I shrug. "I guess it goes back to why the two people are together. The ties that bind them."

"I guess so," he replies.

Our appetizers arrive. He carefully arranges half of each appetizer onto each plate, mine first then his, a habit of his I adore. One of his sweet qualities. *This,* I think, smiling. We fall in love not with the glamour of a person. We fall in love with their truth. The self within and the little traits that belie the polish.

"Thank you," I say.

"What for?"

"Just you. There's so much more to you than lights, camera, action. Cue the smoke machine."

"Oh yeah?" His face says he's about to deflect the moment with a joke. I continue before he can.

"You're the smell of fresh laundry . . ."

He laughs.

"You're your love for your family. You're the birthmark on your forehead. You're your dedication to your work. You're your humor and the fact no one makes me laugh the way you do."

"Thanks." He busies himself with choosing a fork.

A few comfortable seconds elapse. He speaks.

"I learn so much about myself and about you every time we're together. I can't talk with anyone the way I can with you."

"Oh. Thank you."

A beautiful couple slinks by the table, a man and woman, both obviously models. I know them from auditions. We exchange smiles. They pass.

"Think they have PhDs?" he scoffs.

"Well, neither do we."

For a long moment, he holds my eyes before replying.

"You're a genetic anomaly. The way you look, the way you think, it's unfair."

"Thanks." I start to smile. I pause when I see he isn't.

"You're more than what I bargained for."

My heart tenses. Something snakes beneath his compliments.

We begin our meal.

THE PARTY IS as glittery and lush as one's wildest fantasy. Chandeliers frost the ceiling like icicles in an unfeeling heart. The walls are glass, inviting an exquisite view of the City. There by the corner is a grand piano, played by a rotating slew of talented partygoers, musicians, actors, and singers from the Broadway world. Tables dressed in white linen bear lines of champagne and red and white wine, served by the catering staff, peers I recognize from shows or college. For tomorrow's party, many of tonight's guests will swap places with the staff.

We have been here for an hour. It's a producer's party, hosted by a director I love, admire, and have worked with before. He's trying to gather investors for his next production. We penniless artists are here to enliven the deal. We're the living representation of what the investors are paying for.

Stunning women, beautiful gay men, and wealthy straight men are the three strands braiding this room. Every person is clothed in their signature finery, an ambassador of our status, vocation, what we're trying to sell and who we believe we are. Everyone wants something and is here to identify who will give it to them. I wear a short, strapless, satin dress, black with red roses. I've curled my hair in big waves. My earrings are costume jewelry. My necklace is real, diamond and gold, the one I always wear, a high school graduation gift from Momma and Papa.

Love, I feel you strongly these days. The more time I invest in myself, the brighter our link glows. Now, in this room, our bond protects me from the atmosphere of self-serving calculation.

Any time a person shakes my hand, I feel them access my worth in the world, sizing how heavily they should lavish their attention. Like determining how much icing one should devote to a cake. I answer the litany of staccato questions everyone fires. What do you do, where are you from, what are you working on, have I seen you in anything? While I reply, they evaluate my brand potential. They nod, their eyes traveling my face, limbs, mannerisms, and charisma. They measure the capital my parts could bring.

If they find me promising, I'm the winning hog at the county fair, fawned and fondled. Quickly, they'll leech my contact information. If I appear unpromising, their attention will wane suddenly, without forgiveness. Their eyes will sweep the air above my shoulder, searching for someone more valuable to land on.

Thank goodness for you. Eyes sweep. We hold steady.

I now stand as one fifth of a circle, listening to a dazzling woman in her late 30s and a dapper man in his 40s bemoan their boss. They liken him to her current husband and his previous partner. Allegedly, the three terrible souls share an affinity for complaining, self-righteousness, and anger. The storytellers froth at the mouth, their hands moving fabulously, sending gusts of air down the circle. They pause to furiously sip champagne in unison.

"What are you going to do?" I ask.

"What?" He turns.

"What?" She squints.

"How will you change the situation?"

"That's not the point." She brushes me away, fool that I am.

They resume their tirade with tipsy vigor. I wander off to refill my glass of water.

Suddenly, I catch sight of her. I never can tell when I'll see her or the form she'll take. She simply appears, wholly unnamable but known. Now, she stands ten feet from me.

It is one of my other selves, a woman I'd be had I chosen a different path. Love, do you have these encounters? I'm still trying to understand the mechanics of you and me, and the physics of your reality. Do you find yourself, once in while, facing a version of yourself, the person you are in a parallel dimension, having drunk potion A over potion B, taken a blue pill over a red?

A few years ago, I met another one of these selves. She was a bubbly mother of two, clothed in J.Crew cashmere, happily married to a banker she met in college. I was filling in for her regular nanny. She spoke in an octave higher than mine, and found everything I said to be either delightful or shocking to her demure constitution. She, too, had been a diplomat's daughter and had attended another prestigious private school in Asia. Our origins were the same but the choices we've made, very different: she married into the life we were taught to want, while I am authoring one entirely my own.

Tonight, this version has her hair styled in a sleek, straight, black bob, ending by her chin. Her long neck meets her clavicle at a hard angle, her creamy skin cold even from where I stand. She seems entirely made of icy, sharp lines of steel masquerading for flesh. She wears a slim tailored suit without a blouse. She doesn't need one, and the effect isn't overdone at all. She is chilly elegance, all sinewy and untouchable. Where my eyes are done lightly, hers are heavily smoked and lined. My lips are crimson and hers are a nude gloss.

She catches me watching and smiles faintly. I walk over.

"Hello."

"Hi." She extends a cool, smooth hand, her wrist kissed by a slim diamond bangle. Beneath it is a tattoo of the words Dulce Periculum. Danger is sweet.

"I'm Reema."

"Tanya. What do you do?"

"I'm an actress. You?"

"Of course you are." She smiles a self-important smirk. "Entertainment lawyer."

We chat for a bit and are surprised to learn we both attended private liberal arts colleges. We swap anecdotes before reaching a comfortable stalemate, and move on to other guests.

I watch her walk away. I like these encounters. I would have been her had I decided one choice differently a few years ago. Sometimes, like with the young mother married to a banker, I can identify what that specific choice was. Often I can't. Choosing one trail in a forked road leads to another split, and so on.

My phone buzzes. It's a text from the Prince. He'd like to meet up. I reply, "Sorry, I'm tired." A text this late means one thing.

I swallow a yawn. The carnivorous air in these events is exhausting. I find my friend the director.

"I'm so excited for you," I say. "The evening was a success." We squeeze hands, air-kiss. I say I have an early morning and leave.

The subway is comfortably full, enough bodies to feel safe, but not so many as to feel encroached upon. A homeless man claims one end of the car, sitting in the two-person seat behind the conductor's window. His stench drives everyone else toward the other end of the car. He mutters, counting and recounting the same cherished handful of cloth strips. He clutches his treasures in his callused fist, hardened by concrete and cold, his nails thick, gnarled, and as big as oysters. He senses me watching, looks up, smiles, angles his body slightly to protect his pearls from my gaze.

Humbling, isn't it, my love, that it's purely our beliefs that decide what is real.

I return his smile and find it's the first smile of the evening that feels sincere. Daily, I find it harder to connect in this town. I can't speak the language anymore.

I enter my beloved little apartment. I crave a book. I put on the kettle, unzip my dress, and it falls with a swish, a silky puddle around my ankles. I kick it up, catch it midair, hang it in its protective cover. I admire the long line of luscious cocktail dresses and gowns populating my closet.

It takes seconds to shake my hair from the perfection that took an hour to sculpt. What a useless way to spend time. I pick up the book I'm currently reading, *Blindness* by José Saramago. It's beautifully written. But it isn't the answer to my heart's call. The kettle sings. I walk over, taking off my earrings. My ears sting from their grip.

WE ENTER HIS apartment and I fill with foreboding. We had a lovely dinner, laughed, exchanged updates. Through it all, my body's been tight with the feeling of waiting for a door to slam.

He slides his hands down my back. "You're so tiny," he says, the length of his hand spanning the width of my waist. "I could throw you out the window."

Somehow, he and I have become a version of us I wish we weren't. I'm feeling the beginnings of someone I don't want to become.

I dread, too, who he becomes behind closed doors. Aggressive and controlling, he desires fetishes designed to make me feel subservient. I am the student, or the captured waif, while he always remains my powerful master.

The last time I was over, he asked me to do "something special."

"I wanna come in your mouth, and then I want you to show me."

"Excuse me?"

"I wanna—"

"No, thank you." I kept my voice light like I would with my ex-husband. "Whatever you're looking for, it's not in my mouth."

We resumed rolling around, sans fetish, and I left soon after. Tonight, we begin kissing and I feel his hand hold then squeeze my throat, a move he enjoys trying, often. I brush his hand away and it finds a home elsewhere. While we paw at each other, I start to feel asphyxiated and caught, not by his hands but mine.

When he's finished, he leaves behind the animal and retrieves his other self, donning the layers like a three-piece suit. I watch him, and a song I haven't heard in a while fills my ears, letting me know that somewhere, the ballerina still spins.

There is so much I adore about him. And so much I find worrying. Singeing the air is also the topic of exclusivity, monogamy, and emotions. We've explored the conversation in length. Respectful of each other's contrasting values and priorities, we remain non-exclusive. Consequently, we've yet to have sex. There is plenty two people can do short of intercourse. But we're both guilty of emotions that cannot be contained by boundaries. I especially. My heart is a hummingbird, a winged wish that beats wildly. I was born to *feel*. Asking my heart to feel less is as futile as ordering my mind to stop dreaming or telling my legs to run two miles when they'd rather run ten.

We are courting disaster.

I want him too much to stop.

I want him too much to continue.

Being a complicit member in a harem is hardly feminist.

In the loud silence, we cover our nakedness. I return home, ashamed, furious with myself. I make it to the bathroom and violently, unwillingly, vomit. I rarely do, and have never been able to make myself. My mind spins, whispering, *One page.* I feel you, shaken but intact. I wash my face, my hands trembling. Our reflection screams, *What are you doing?*

I'm sorry, I mouth.

PAPA IS LEADING a conference at the UN in New York. He is presenting a program on economic reform. He led the project and wrote all the core materials. It is brilliant.

Rather than stay in a hotel for the eight days, he stays with me. I'm overjoyed and nervous. Each night I cook a macrobiotic vegan meal to balance our energies and cultivate harmony. He supplements his with Chinese takeout. I bake heart-shaped cakes and he says what he always says, "You are your mother's daughter." Only this time, his words aren't disparaging. His voice is heavy with love, nostalgia, and a grief I fear will never fully fade.

We watch movies, both weeping during *The Time Traveler's Wife*. We take long walks and many subway rides.

"You never hold on! What if you fall?"

He is so dear. Every detail uniquely New York shakes him.

"Don't you get scared?"

In reply I hug him and plant a smooch on his shiny scalp. His comb-over has tumbled, swept by the subway's lurch. He tucks comfortably under my arm, now. He is growing shorter.

Papa and I have a great deal in common. We both love our mothers more than life itself and felt secure in them. We both grew up with fathers who were more mythical than they were present. We have both loved longest and deepest the same three people: my brother, sister, and mother. Being distanced from them has shaped us irrevocably, in different ways; it has steeled me, softened him.

In our family, we are the smallest of the lot in height and frame. My brother and sister carry us, pinch us, nuzzle us, tease us for our social awkwardness. They're extra protective of us. We feel things deeply.

Often, we're left aghast by the cacophony of humankind. Papa implores, "What is this television reality?"

Gravely I shake my head. "The imminent demise, Papa."

As children, Papa and I were the quiet ones, picked on by popular boys in school. Behind closed doors, we were broken by the hands of others. He went on to be their boss and I their prize plaything. We are writers and often feel safer speaking to crowds than mingling in the middle. Given to intensity, we talk in sweeping gestures, like, "Your silence is killing me," and "This love is as timeless as the sea."

We share the same blood type, different from the rest of the family: AB+. The universal recipient.

When we cry we sound like kittens; we mewl more than we sob.

We love metaphors.

I am 28, exactly the age Papa was when I was born. This is our middle. We have much to live.

One night, he shares his greatest fear: being alone. The heartbreaking irony crumples me like a discarded draft declared unfit for sharing. He effectively accomplished his biggest fear. He remarried six years ago and has a 5-year-old son. He remains lonely though, for lonesomeness has everything and nothing to do with the people around us.

He asks to play twenty questions, asking me things he never has before.

"What if you never make a living from art, like Van Gogh? What if you die alone and penniless?"

A startling thought crystalizes. Papa is afraid for me and overwhelmed by me. I am a woman who dances to her own anthem, writing a new bit of it every day. Who I am shakes him.

"It'll be okay, Papa."

He takes off his glasses, rests them on the table. He rubs his eyes. He frowns, smiles, then coughs. I hand him a glass of water. He sips. The coughs subside. He speaks.

"What a wonderful trip."

He leaves and I float on all nine clouds, skipping from one to the next. These days were the best we've ever spent. The muscles along my neck, shoulders, and back ache from extreme alertness. Relief releases them slowly, melting into my body like milk unfurls into hot tea. Walking to the subway, waiting for auditions, pushing a stroller, I grin foolishly as if in love.

During his visit, I mentioned to Papa that I have been writing something new these days. He asked to read. I take some of the nightly pages and shape them into a cohesive piece, on beauty and anorexia.

He emails after reading the essay. My hands shake over the keys, giddily anticipating his thoughts.

He writes, "I realize you will always remain Reema. The greatest boon and curse of your life is you've only been loved and supported in all you are and do. No one has ever told you you're irrational or nearsighted. I pray for you. I started reading your writing. I must confess, it's the work of an intelligent and matured mind." Signed, "Stay well, Papa."

Attached to the email is a short story by Guy de Maupassant, "The Necklace." It's the tale of a young woman celebrated for her beauty and charisma, adored by everyone. She marries a man with humble earnings. Her vanity, vapidity, arrogance, and selfishness bring them to financial ruin. She begins cleaning houses. Her youth and beauty fade. Her charm turns shrill, her loveliness brittle. They live evermore in abject poverty and unhappiness.

His letter impales me like a harpoon spears unsuspecting flesh. Instantly, I grow cold. I feel the familiar rip of hope tearing. Hope is a thing that stitches swiftly and unravels quicker. I sit shivering.

I check my ego, to gauge whether I'm hurt from his disapproval. No. His truth is his, mine is mine. My pain is from something simpler. Unkindness. I want us to be forthright and heard, without the price of unkindness. All I have ever wanted, my love, is for every person to speak their truth, but not at the expense of speaking over another, or at the risk of being spoken over. All I've ever wanted is to speak and be with others the way I can with you. I want that for everyone.

I'm struck by an image of him at his desk, Googling the short story, attaching it to highlight my vanity, selfishness, and inevitable ruin. I see the intention, choice, and planning. I feel the execution and the blood blossoming from my split heart.

In Thailand we have a delightful idiom: "muan kaan." Its English counterpart is *same-same but different*. Same-same but different are the seasons that barely change in climate. Same-same but different are mothers and daughters who are uncannily alike. It is a loving phrase. A collection of sounds that mean acceptance and welcome, like the bell at a temple.

The fine balance we surf in love is honoring one's truth, and another's, while observing kindness.

I thank him for writing, and let the bell echo.

I TURN 29. THE Prince insists we celebrate, a quality I love about him and find personally difficult. Celebrating makes me feel guilty. He shrugs my hesitation away. Soon after, Christmas and the New Year arrive. To ring it in, he chooses an acclaimed, hidden-away Japanese restaurant. Behind the bar is a wall where patrons are invited to leave their marks.

"Draw something," he says. I draw a rose and beneath it, our initials.

He smiles. "Got any resolutions?" The first night we met, a little over a year ago, he asked me the same question. I repeat the identical resolution.

"To continue working as I am. You?"

"To be better with endings. Confrontation is hard for me."

Our meal arrives. The evening is twinkly and fun. Intoxicated on holiday cheer, we tumble into bed.

"What do you want?" I ask.

He replies with an expletive, in the rare way it's remotely charming: "I wanna fuck you."

"Only me?"

"Yes."

"Are you sure?"

"Yes."

I start giggling and, as is often the case when I'm happy, I grow shy and cover my face with my hands, fingers braided. We're on his bed, I'm perched on my knees, while he reclines against the headboard. He laughs and pulls me onto his lap, managing to keep me in the same perched posture. He unlaces my fingers and kisses me.

"Are you sure?" I ask once more.

"Yes," he says, kissing again.

We commence, thankfully fetish-free. Lightning unleashed, we pause only for Gatorade.

Time elapses. The next night we have sex, I realize he has left. I feel it in his touch. Moreover, I can feel he has been with someone else.

Wrapped in our vortex, I feel a cold stillness spread through me like a river lost, trying to find its way to an ocean it doesn't know. Perhaps women feel this more acutely for the way our bodies are shaped, to receive and form to a man's. As we feel your touch change from sweet to bitter, caring to cold or worse, apathetic, we morph as well. We change from your cradle to your receptacle. Your garden to your wasteland. An area bereft of value, meaning, or beauty. A land deemed ruined, barren of interest, where waste is deposited and things go to die.

He has been with someone else and rather recently. She exists vividly in the air. I don't smell her. I don't find traces of lipstick on a collar. She lives in his distance. Hovering the way a foreshadow floats between two people.

I move horizontally, back and forth, back and forth, sandwiched between him and the bed, kneaded like dough as he burrows into me. My head is turned to the left. His chin with its light stubble grinds into my forehead. In the morning, I'll have to hold an aspirin moistened with water against the raw spot. It will soothe the red. My eyes memorize the titles of books and boxes along the walls. I fill with boredom from being here again, tired of this story that folds back unto itself. I'm weary of being insipid to a man. I loathe myself for yet again choosing someone who makes me feel this way.

I recover my clothes off the floor like Gretel retrieving crumbs to find her way home. I layer my layers, an unwanted object covering itself. In my coat, at the door, I turn around.

"Are you happy?" Sorrow keeps me from voicing the question our bodies have answered.

"Yes," he says. "I'm happy."

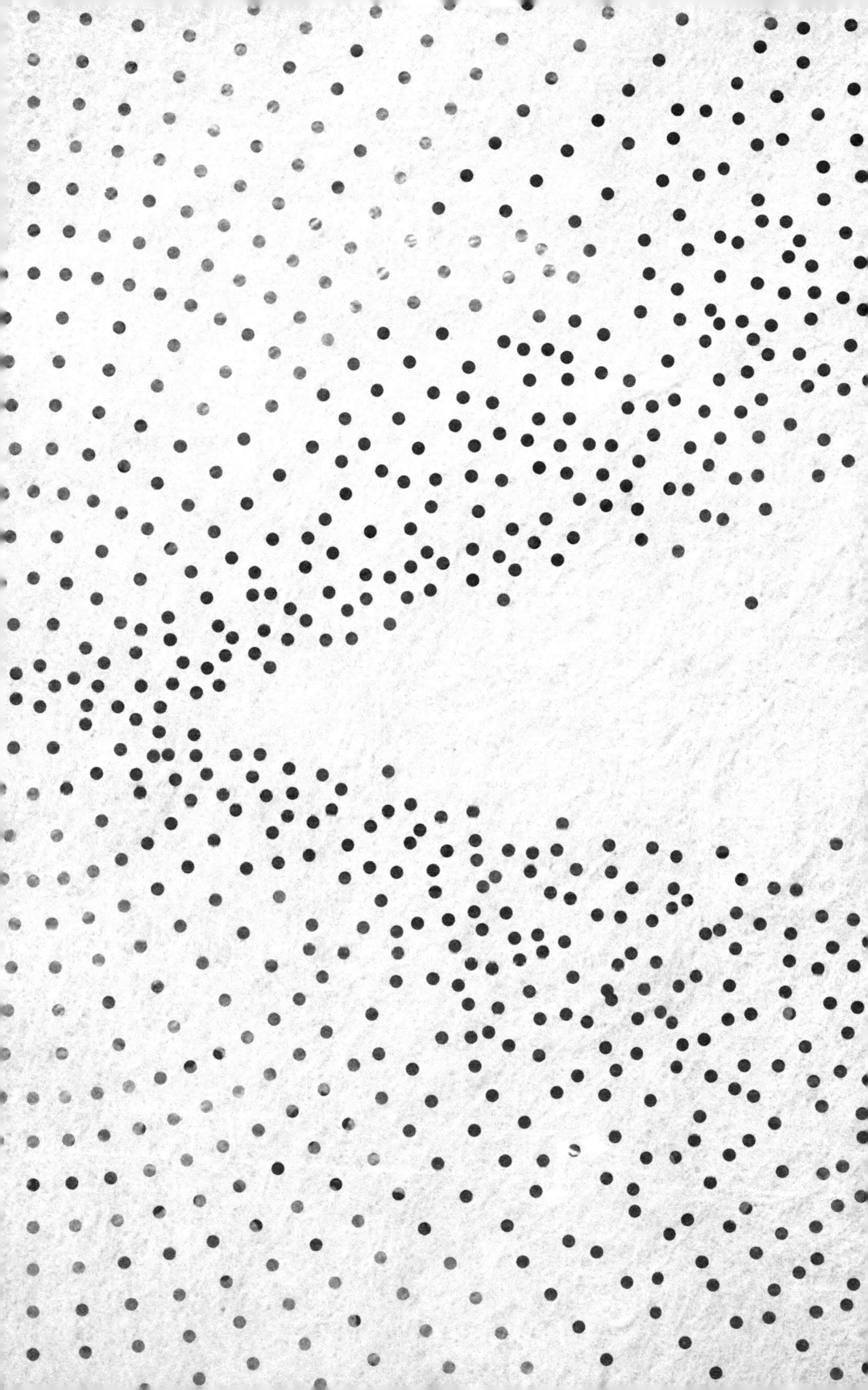

PAUSE

PAUSE

✦

How am i here? The years are stacking.

I am 11. Papa says, "Boys will be boys. It happens."

I am 18. The tag on my school uniform collar grates the back of my neck like a vegetable peeler strips an unpleasing outer layer. The principal interrogates me. Despite innocence, I feel defensive, guilty for being a girl. The seat of the office chair is so high my feet don't touch the ground. Perhaps the seat is cranked high because it's a way to enforce authority and procure obedience. My legs swing anytime I speak, words I've rehearsed in front of the mirror.

When I have purged all details, he says, "Thank you for remaining quiet."

I don't remember offering my silence; it is assumed. I return to class. He smiles in a way reserved for me. I hate him. I stay until the bell rings. I leave and return when I'm supposed to, a pendulum on her designated course. My school does nothing. My parents do nothing. At night, I run until my mind detaches from my body. It's the only thing that feels good.

I am 23. I am fortunate my rape is quick and relatively painless. He is economical with time, force, and me.

I am 24. A Saturday afternoon, I'm on my shift. He corners me, cups my face in his clammy mitt and says, "You're so pretty. I could eat you up." I negotiate an apology but that is all. I'm a stain; he is status, wealth, and fame, personified.

I am 27. We don't need to belabor the details. You were there, my love.

I am 28. Again, you've been here with me. Things felt wonderful until they weren't. Or perhaps they weren't wonderful. Perhaps I'm cognizant of some pieces while ignorant of others. Perhaps I've grown to believe this is simply how things are, and I'm continuing a tale I've inherited as a girl in this world.

I am 18, 28, 38, and 8. I see another self on the subway looking like a wad of gum hastily hidden underneath a desk. Gray, hardened, disposed, commonplace. Her eyes meet mine as we try to maintain our balance. I wonder who, where, when. Was she thrown against a wall, into a corner, on the bed, on the ground, or in an alley as her dignity was stolen, her value denied? Were the insults and intimidation thrown at school, over dinner, online, or at work? I can't say, but I recognize the result, as familiar as Momma's perfume. A look that comes from indignity inflicted in any form. It is eyes sapped of light, a spirit withered, a voice silenced.

I am 18, 20, 24, 25, 27, 28. The times I've said "Yes" when part of me screamed "No."

Something is amiss. I don't feel lost, broken, brokenhearted, or disheartened. I know this is my journey to walk. But what haven't I connected? What dragon have I yet to slay?

Me.

I am 29. I was raised by a bully. I married a bully. And left unchecked, I become my biggest bully. I absorb the venom around me. I find ways to help it course my veins. Here I am, living a story of punishment and longing to find instead a book that is a clear line of love.

My love, I think I've sorted our origins. Within me live two voices, spliced since a toddler. One is calm, loving, and kind, and the other, exceptionally destructive. This latter voice declares I'm inadequate, insignificant, insufficient, inept, fat, ugly. It says, Listen to him. Follow him. It says, You worthless thing, what could you possibly do but hawk your physical wares? The first voice is you, my imaginary best friend from childhood whom I never released, while the second is my inner lonely child. It answers to many names, one being Anorexia, for if control is my father and beauty my mother, anorexia is their offspring. You and the wounded child exist by connection. There is a saying I've carried now for years. "Beware the unloved. They will eventually hurt themselves, or me."

I won't be spliced any longer. I need to align.

I TEXT HIM, "Let's go for a walk."

It's an idyllic spring afternoon. We walk the High Line, dotted with couples, families, and tourists. Everyone drinks the lush energy our City potions so well.

He has just returned from two conferences, BroCon and South by Southwest, and a Vegas bachelor party.

"My friends dared me to convince a stripper to sleep with me for free." He narrates what ensued. My mind screams, *This is not my life.*

The conversation shifts back to his company, their latest successes, and my writing. The essay I sent to Papa, I sent to him. I sent it to Momma and a few friends as well.

"It's amazing," he says. "So vulnerable and honest."

"Thank you." Conflict curdles me. He is empathy, intelligence, ego, and misogyny. He is dichotomous; human. The duality continues in what he draws and gives. Around him, I feel both adored and crushed. How precarious and significant, our ability to lift and belittle the same person.

"There was one sentence specifically that really spoke to me," he says. "About power. Where'd you get that?"

"Do you mean the line, 'The danger with any power, be it beauty, wealth, fame, or influence, is if loved too enthusiastically, your power can become your prison.' That one?"

"Yeah. Who's that from?"

"Me."

"*Oh.* Okay. It's a good line."

"Thanks." I pause. "That's interesting."

"What?"

"Nothing." I shake my head, smile.

"Do you ever think about writing a book?" he asks.

"Sometimes."

"Why don't you?"

I shrug. "Acting's what I do."

He nods.

We walk past a pair of guys in their early 30s. They laugh and recline against the High Line railing with the swagger shared by those who are cozy in their longitude and latitude in the world. I always admire this in men—the nonchalance with which they stride through life. They may have a paunch or a receding hairline, be ill-dressed or short or not very bright, kind, or handsome. Their easy confidence doesn't come from such details. It stems from maleness and a lifetime of being treated well. Rarely have men been told, "You may want to watch your weight" or "Don't laugh like that, sit like that, dress like that, talk like that. It isn't becoming." While the carefree boys saunter, we girls suck in our phantom tummies, tug up our skirts or jeans to cover our imaginary muffin tops, and arrange our parts carefully like flowers in a vase.

My love, do you ever wonder who you would be were you born the opposite sex? My sister and I play this game often. We describe who we'd be, what we'd believe, how we'd act, what we'd look like had we been born with the male set of rights, advantages, favors, and forgivenesses. What would we do with the allowances society reserves for men and men alone? My sister laughs and says, "With your brain and looks, you'd fucking own the world. And everyone in it."

In the past, we've giggled and I've replied, "Thanks!" But now, as the years layer, I think, *What a sad fate and goal to have.* How lonesome. How narrow. How damaging.

I watch the light dappling his face. If I were male, I would be more like him than my ex-husband. We share an ambitious bloodlust that few have. But invariably, there would be a fork in the road.

"We have something so good here," he says suddenly. "I wish I had more time for us."

I feel a sickening vertigo grab my chest.

"I need to ask you something."

"Sure."

"Have you been sleeping with anyone else?"

"You're the only person I'm dating seriously."

"You're not answering my question."

"Just once. It didn't even . . ." the sentence trails away like trash ferried by the wind.

"But it's a betrayal."

"I'm so sorry," he says. "I feel horrible."

Sorrow mutes me. I feel cold.

"It was a misunderstanding," he says suddenly.

"That doesn't make sense. No." I sound small but certain.

He carries on with characteristic finesse, trying to negotiate my assent, to agree with the reality he desires. He gave me a book last year, *The Gift of Fear*. Gavin de Becker writes, "Remember that 'No' is a complete sentence. It is not the invitation to begin a negotiation. It's the end of a conversation."

When I was a kid, I had a wretched habit of taking a nibble from every piece of chocolate in the box. I couldn't commit to an entire piece lest it make me fat. So my habit sated my desire for something delicious, and my desire to control.

A man on the quest for more. Perhaps he wants a bite from each of us, to collect as many as he can, because he can, believing such is the road to fulfillment. Perhaps he has decided that I, "genetic anomaly," have grown beyond acceptable limits, and require a reminder of who's in power. I search for anger but find none. He is a person living his journey, trying to stake his claim in the world. Besides, *I* chose and remained by him.

He continues to apologize. Suddenly I remember that when I met him, I asked you and myself, Why must I meet him now, when I'm doing so well? My love, perhaps some characters are sent specifically when we are walking tall and steady, to test our loyalty to ourselves. This man, like my ex-husband, has been a gift. An alluring tempest sent from a path I refuse to follow.

"Just so you know, I'm always safe."

He delivers this line with majestic aplomb as though he has done me a great benevolence by wearing a condom while having sex with other women. My insides recoil the way skin warps when touched by fire. Astonishing, the ingenuity with which the men in my life dirty its pages.

As is often the case, I realize now what I should have before. Regardless of sex or labels, my company deserves anyone's full respect. I don't need to "earn" full status. I already am.

A final fact coalesces:

I am 17 through 29. Forever living by extension and reaction, as someone's daughter, someone's prey, someone's lover, someone's landscape to plough. I am one in an assembly line of girls, each an expendable commodity, vying for the coveted role of Leading Man's Girlfriend.

I am done.

We arrive at my apartment. He hails down a cab. I'm pondering the appropriate way to say goodbye when he pulls me in for a kiss. He releases my mouth, squeezes my butt a final time, and slides into the cab. As the door closes he says, "I'll see you soon!"

I smile meekly and wave. I climb the five flights to blessedly sit.

Soon fails to arrive. As is expected. As is ideal.

THE ROOM is pregnant with pretties. Half of us are here to audition for a television pilot in Studio A, about a team of sexy spies.

The other half are auditioning for a shampoo commercial in Studio B. We are in House Productions, one of the most elite, renowned studios in New York. The halls and rooms sparkle, polished to gleaming, with floor-to-ceiling windows allowing in light.

All around me, men and women drape across low couches like splendid, slender cats decorating the savannah. Their sultry musculature and litheness are mesmerizing.

Never will I be underwhelmed by beauty. Before and beyond being its addict, I am a lover. I will always gasp at a watercolor of clouds and swoon from brilliance in person, on the page, onstage, or from a podium. Being an admiring witness is one of my favorite parts of being alive. Near the end, Nana Bhai said, "I don't have any regrets but I have sorrow. I will miss the sunset. I will miss poetry."

These men and women glint light into my awestruck eyes. In physicality, I cannot touch them. Those aren't words of affected humility. I stand a good half to full foot beneath these men and women. I look up at them with the wide-eyed wonder of a child in a candy store. The length between their eyes, the dip above their lips, the sweep of their foreheads, it's as though every section was drawn, erased, and redrawn with meticulous attention. Yet it wasn't. The same amount of time went into the consideration of their parts and everyone else's. The science, the futility, the magic, the mathematics, this is what fascinates me. I'm further intrigued by how we respond to the luck of genetics. Not only do we covet, we wish to understand, control, and own something that begins and happens with such little thought, control, and ownership. The cells divide and form in rapid, miniscule steps. Little do they know the impact they will have.

Today, as always, I'm the wild card in the mix called in to audition. What I lack in height and impeccable perfection of body and feature, I redeem with my mind. This odd brain of mine, my love, seems to come in handy. It lends a nuanced spin to a script or photos, creating a decisive difference that occasionally leads to booking the job.

It's unusually quiet in the waiting room. Ideal for reading, but I can't seem to concentrate on the book I hold, *Wild* by Cheryl Strayed. Her words are wise, her voice luminous, the book a masterpiece. Yet it isn't what I seek. Daily I realize I need to sort my past. I seek still the book that will hear, hold, and perhaps even heal my marred world. I think I'm drawing closer to finding it.

Every night, I've been continuing the enigmatic pages on my laptop. So used to reciting the words of others, it feels heavenly to voice my own. Along with the mysterious pages, drawings have been arriving nightly, of lingerie-clad girls falling from the sky, of roses weeping blood. Now, my mind flies frantically, wishing it were creating instead of waiting. Restless, my eyes scour the faces around me.

There are a few in this room who I can tell make a sizable income from doing what it is we do. They exude an aura of barely contained glee and relief. I smile, sincerely moved by their hard-to-attain joy. I feel a swell of love, kinship, and protectiveness for each person. It isn't a nice job.

No one asks the painting its thoughts on itself or the world it comes from. Yet everyone has a vehement interpretation of what it means. Everyone has aggressive emotion, desire, intention, and opinion attached to the flowers, the bloom, the light, and the shadows.

We paintings are stared at, yet rarely seen. I wonder, too, of the possible compounding toll of reciting words written by others, especially if those words play against one's truth. I wonder how many men and women in this room chose acting because, like myself, they wished to be a voice for those without one. Have we voices of our own? Here we sit, a living irony.

A dear friend recently secured a role in a new sitcom as the ditzy girlfriend of the male lead. Her job is to repeat subtly different versions of the same sexist one-liners, week after week. The show's unoriginal, closed-minded ethos caters to a large demographic. It will likely be enormously lucrative.

My sweet friend cried from joy upon booking this role. Her exorbitant paycheck will grace her life financial stability and success, dreams anyone can empathize with. The role may lead to fame. For her, this is the definition of happiness. For me, this role is a form of poverty that happens to pay well, like marrying a person whose best quality is his wealth.

Acting is my calling. So I have long believed. My dream was born from watching intelligent roles played by Meryl Streep, Cate Blanchett, Natalie Portman, Angelina Jolie, Katherine Hepburn, and Dame Judi Dench. They were my role models, imaginary and real. They strengthened my spirit. All I've wanted is to do similar work, to help empower others.

My love, I want more than the life available within these walls. One quality Meryl, Cate, Natalie, Angelina, Katherine, and Judi have in common, and I'll never achieve, is they are white. The upper echelon of leading roles, of intelligence, maturity, and creative verve, remain closed to women of my ethnicity and other women of color. Occasionally a Black or Latina actress will play a role of bold intelligence and creative license. But most of the roles for women like me continue to emulate the tired models: the exotic vixen, sexy spy, drug-addled stripper, street-talking best friend. The times may be changing, but I cannot convince time to change faster.

I look down the line of girls who will audition before me. Six before my turn. I have time to check my makeup and hair, see if I've wilted from bombshell to bedraggled. I enter the bathroom and meet our reflection.

What need is there for another pretty face?

How can I bridge the distance between my reality and my truth?

I blow onto the mirror to make a small spot of condensation, if only to prove I'm still here.

I retouch my lipstick, re-fluff my hair. Walking back to my seat, a simple, sensible fact crystalizes. If there isn't a role that fulfills me, I'll genesis my own. Reject the world's script and author my own anthem. My love, what if I moved? What if we flew away from these glittery rooms, mined our own creative intelligence, and pursued work that purely helps others?

There is also something else.

I am tired. The years have stacked. I've had my heart dismantled, again. I carry ashes from my childhood. And though you are here, I still don't have anyone who can hug me. Not as often as a body needs. The last time I was touched, it was by him. The same touch that let me know he had been with someone else.

I need love. I need family. I need to sort my pieces.

I walk past my chair and toward the floor-to-ceiling windows. How arresting New York is. Her beauty can stop and draw traffic. I take in our skyline. I think of my beloved agent, my very first friend in the City. He has always said, "Own yourself. It will all make sense."

My gaze is tugged by a quick, light movement. My eyes connect with a stunning young girl, sitting a few feet away. She is barely 17. She looks like an ethereal, fantastical creature with languid limbs stretching for days, features softly fashioned from clouds, hair cascading down her back like a sonnet flows over the tongue. Her skin emits the glow of unblemished innocence. Words have yet to be broken. Crimes have yet to be inflicted. Trials have yet to be endured. She gives me a nervous, tremulous smile that deepens when I smile big and warmly at her. She sits visibly taller. I see my sister in her. I see the girl Momma was before she was married off and suddenly pregnant with me. A sweet, tender sprite, an unrealized promise.

She jumps as her name is called. She leaps to her feet, layering her portfolio, headshot, and script to her chest like packaging to secure safe travels. She runs into the studio to meet her panel of scrutiny.

The door closes behind her like a verdict. I worry what she will face in the room, now and in the coming years.

Suddenly, I feel as though I've sprung awake, nudged by an invisible, firm hand. I fill with a certainty that feels like a memory, something I've long known and needed merely to recall:

The book I've sought all these years, my clear, unhurried line of love, is one I'm meant to write. Just as a man cannot answer my heart, neither can another's voice. I cannot recite anymore. I need to speak.

I leave before they call my name.

I'VE LEFT PEOPLE BEFORE. But leaving an identity and a home to create one anew is a tectonic endeavor. As the studio falls away and I walk toward my apartment, I take in the cacophonic wonderland that is New York. The one place that feels like mine. I love her even when I don't.

My phone dings the arrival of a text. Hello, Peter Pan.

"Sold apartment. You need to leave by the end of the week."

"Cool," I reply.

How perfect. Although I love the City, without acting, there isn't a strict reason to stay, while there are vital reasons to leave. I need to spend time with my family. Furthermore, my old identity is wrapped tightly around New York's finger. My adored city, the Epicenter of More, while it boasts extraordinary art and culture, capitalizes on consumption and toxic power—the very things that persuade me to hurt myself. If I want to write, to become, a story of remote strength, I have to give myself a fighting chance.

Another ding. An email from my Warrior Mama.

"We need you," she writes. "Come stay for a week or two?"

"Of course," I reply.

I download "Leaving on a Jet Plane" and play it on repeat for the next two days. I give the furniture and art I had collected for a future home to friends who are married or soon to be. Beautiful things deserve to be enjoyed. Everything else goes to homeless youth centers. I whittle my life down to my laptop, art portfolio, and two suitcases, one with clothes, one with books. I'll be leaving with the same amount of matter with which I arrived, except for the $1,000 I had back then, my college graduation gift from Momma and Dad. My bank account is down to a few hundred. Enough for a plane ticket to Oregon. I book the flight and am left with $7. I look around my little light-filled apartment one last time. This apartment has seen two bedbug infestations and countless mice. It has also been my sanctuary.

To Soho I go, into the room they call Reema's. My Warriors, the actress, tennis legend, and their beautiful girls. The walls of their home are covered with drawings, photographs, and decorations celebrating every evidence of their connected joy. They throw parties often, for every occasion and without occasion. We dress up for the minutest event in costumes, glitter, and fairy wings. I carry my wings in my art portfolio. Over the years, my recipes were written into their history. They've collected and hung my drawings of angels and portraits of the girls. They grace me the honor to mark their lives.

Their home is completely relinquished to the happy, messy thing that is childhood and family. Theirs is a childhood done with bold appetite, licked from all ten fingertips with delight like juice from sunburst berries. I arrive and the three girls literally bowl me over. I tumble onto the floor, happily helpless, in love. They call me delicious names. The Mary Poppins of New York. Our Traveling Fairy Princess. Our Star, although I'm light-years away from being one.

Over the years, in her devotion, I've glimpsed Momma. In him, I've seen fatherhood done decisively well. He travels red-eye after red-eye to ensure he's home for breakfast. He wears any Halloween costume they wish, whether it's a chicken, pirate, or king. He is Santa Claus every year for the Barney's in Soho. He rushes home, takes off his tie, and reads bedtime stories in a voice reserved for his girls. They giggle and crawl over him like koalas, chinchillas, and gibbons. They know his presence the way an inhale knows an exhale, the way the right foot knows it'll be followed by the left. An unquestioned togetherness. Oh, the things we wish we could take for granted with the nonchalant trust we place on oxygen and gravity.

I'm unclear why she asked me to come now. I haven't worked for them in years. They have two wonderful nannies and a personal assistant.

I mean to stay a week, but it turns into a month. The morning before my arrival, she has a hemorrhage in her vocal cords. She is a world-renowned singer who is now ordered silent. A year from now, she will be singing more beautifully than ever, her voice soaring to new heights. But now, leading up to and after her surgery, she isn't to speak.

We invent a language she calls our "silent sisterhood." From years of knowing each other so intimately, spending days beside each other in the dance of raising children, we share an intuition. I translate her facial and hand movements and the occasional scribbled shorthand on Post-its. We navigate the tsunami, survive and swim to the other side. At the end of the month she surprises me with a check for $1,000.

"What's this for?"

"Your presence," she writes. "You're something that can't be explained."

Her husband adds, "If you can just figure out how to bottle yourself, that'd be great." They smile.

I'm speechless. I've asked Momma and Dad if I can live with them while I get myself sorted. They've said, Of course. $1,000 is ten months of cell service, the sole expenditure I'll have while living with my parents.

Ten carefree months to write. More than financial means, they have given me invaluable insight. I feel like skin being touched by sunlight for the first time. Years ago, she and her husband nicknamed me Angel. But mine is the path lit by their nearness.

I'm leaving New York with the same things I brought in. Two suitcases, a laptop, and $1,000. To most eyes, I appear to be the walking embodiment of failed expectations. I am nearly 30, I don't have any savings, I don't have a partner, children, a career, or a clear destination wherein to plant my feet. I've faced every rejection, personal and professional. If rejection were a fruit, it would appear as though it were my feverish favorite, its bitter nectar dripping down my chin into the hollow of my torso as I sit here on the floor, propped against a wall as I wait to board the airplane.

Now, my love, replace "rejection" with "experience." Replace one word and my entire story changes.

Uncertainty is a form of limitlessness. There is nothing holding me here. There is nothing holding me back.

It is time.

ACT IV

GENESIS

GENESIS

✦

I AM 29. It is June 1st, 2013. You and I are flying toward Momma.

Once upon a time, we decided the heart is where love lives. For the heart is the one organ we viscerally sense. We feel it working. We hear it. With fingertips placed on our neck, wrists, chest, temple we feel the evidence of our existence. Sometimes when all else fails, when deep breaths, words, and running cannot calm me, I place my middle and forefinger on my neck to assure myself, I am here.

When two bodies touch, the message of our aliveness transmits skin to skin. How I love the simple delight of lying next to someone and feeling slowly, without fail, our two heartbeats slow or quicken to sync in common rhythm. In the deep, quiet, stillness of night, here we are: the proof of life, connected.

One of my favorite parts to being a woman who loves men is feeling the strong, steady beat of a man's heart ripple through a shared bed. The pulse moves into you. Such is the dear magic of connecting with a body bigger than yours.

The foremost and simplest reason we chose the heart as our symbol for love is that our mother's heartbeat is our original song. Our first inkling that someone is here, with me, and I belong to her. Our mother is our first person in the dark. Perhaps it is off that sublime sensation and memory that we then search for a similar bond, with a future, special person. To be separate yet together, entwined while individual, hearts slipping into sync.

My brother met me at JFK Airport. We sit now on the plane in seats beside each other. Our sister is graduating from high school. Unbelievable. How did she grow up so quickly? My brother drifts to sleep. I watch New York move farther away.

"Thank you," I whisper. I have been loved hard and well. I have been graced with many to care for. I have learned it is instinct to look for special persons. I have loved and followed so many. I have learned how crucial it is that through it all I maintain clarity, be anchored within, and listen to myself first. I have learned all individuals are beautiful on their own but certain combinations can be catastrophic. Like books and water. Both are vital and life-renewing, but together, they promise tragedy. I look down at the sprawl of land, rivers, cities beneath us. The tributary of lives. It's tempting to grow worried about our future. But I still believe in us, my love.

The truth is, while the mind and body travel various states, the heart remains the ultimate compass. I take out my Moleskine. Condensation paints the little oval window, clouds kiss the glass. I write a list of values my new life will stand for, the traits I will embody, and the kind of person I'll find one day. I write a list of feelings and ideals my future book will encapsulate. Ultimately, the most worthwhile, pure, and powerful currency, resource, or use of skill isn't the stronghold we wield over others, but the quality of feeling we draw and give. What feeling is more worthwhile, pure, and powerful than love? For most of my life, the two offerings I have brought into every room have been love and beauty. I wish to align. I will uphold love above all else. And it is through love, voice, and art that I'll spread beauty.

On the window, I draw a heart and inside, my initials, alone. I am here. You are here. I close my journal, rest my head on my brother's shoulder, and fall asleep thinking, Inhale followed by exhale.

We arrive at our resplendent mecca.

Beaverton, Oregon. The suburbs.

Difficult, not to be bowled over by the spectacular sexiness. Try if you can, my love, to maintain your composure. I search for Momma's face in the crowd of families waiting for loved ones to disembark. There she is. I have returned to my heart.

The moment we five are reunited, we breathe deeper, grin foolishly and refuse to cease. My brother and I are seized with fatigue. Whenever we return, the second the wheels land on the tarmac, this happens. Dad says it's because we finally release the alertness one grips when away from home.

"You look like a gaunt, lost bird," my brother says to me.

He ruffles my hair, squeezes my face with a hand that spans its entire length and width. Little bird. That's his name for me. As always, he is immaculate in presentation. He sports a thin layer of stubble, his version of disheveled and exhausted. Mine is Benjamin Button in his later years. A withered old-man-baby.

My sister, now 18, is gorgeous. Her face has retained its fairytale quality: large eyes, hair falling in natural ringlets, and a perfect little rosebud mouth. Although she is now taller than me, my nickname for my sister is Little and her nickname for me is Big.

"You're the best Big," she says.

"You're my sweetest Little," I reply.

Her ceremony is a few days after we arrive. We have a party in the backyard with dozens of family and friends. Look at all these people, my love! We laugh, barbeque, have ice-cream cake, make s'mores and roast marshmallows over our fire pit. For the second time in my life, I catch sight of fireflies, hopscotching the grass. We run after them, not to catch them but because running toward whispers of light can be fun sometimes. We do these innocently incredible, incredibly innocent things. Neither my brother nor I had anything like this. Parties were a thing of dreams—we were barely standing, shaken for echoes unseen. I gorge myself on ice-cream cake and fall into a stupor after years of not ingesting dairy. I carry the hangover for days. The effect on my digestive system is, aptly described by Dad, "highly entertaining."

I've discovered I like my marshmallows decisively burnt. I love smelling the air char and watching the sugar caramelize. I adore slipping the dark shell off the untouched rest. I exalt in the crackle and melt that come next, and then, the repetition of all steps. The burning, the molting, the delighting.

At her graduation, our extended family fills two rows in the theater. Another magical wonder. My brother and I sit beside each other. He is handsome in his suit. I'm wearing that favorite pink silk dress. We hold hands and tear up as we watch our little one walk across the stage to receive her diploma.

"We made it," he says. I am too moved to speak. Our deepest wish was for this little girl to have a happy life. They moved to Oregon when she was 12. She has been raised on solid ground.

She turns to the audience to flash her stunning smile. The cheer that erupts from our two rows is by far the loudest of the entire afternoon. She grins and waves, exuding marvelous confidence, knowing that of course, her roar would be loudest.

PERMISSION

PERMISSION

✦

My brother returns to New York, my sister leaves to visit Papa in Bangkok, and Momma and Dad embark on a one-month road trip. I remain with the family's two dogs, one cat, two bearded dragons, four lovebirds, and assortment of fish. The evidence of life when we're able to stand still. I'm with a zoo, but also, alone.

It finds me.

My anger. My mangy, lumbering, frothing rage—against the world, against characters, against my own choices. Howling with sorrow pent from stacked years, it attaches to my hand, feeding on what I supply. It takes up the entire bed. I sleep, head on its heaving belly. You sit nearby. There is always a window.

Grief has five stages. Shock and denial is the first. I've already experienced that stage my own way; for long years, I was unaware of how heavy the toll of life had become. Anger is the second stage. This month of silent solitude acts as my decompression chamber. Walking the dogs, changing the litter box, watering the garden, feeding lettuce to the dragons, the routine of humble chores is purifying, soothing, lovely. But memories that hid with the finesse of a fox eluding a hound now emerge. They horrify. They unmake. Momma and Dad return home and find me wild-eyed. I look like the Crypt Keeper's wife who has escaped from her cage and is wondering now where to go, only to find there is no "where." There is only here.

That's the thing about the past: wherever you go, it exists still, on some plane.

Anger then morphs into depression. Depression is usually followed by bargaining. I pass that stage and step into the final: acceptance. I weep. Great, huge sobs, a sudden monsoon on an otherwise tranquil summer day.

Momma and I sit in her garden.

"What is it, jaan?" she asks. She holds my hand.

"I . . . I am . . ."

"You didn't fail. I know you loved acting but this is simply your life, continuing. You'll find something. Or is it him? Do you miss him? Or is it your Papa?"

"No, Momma. I'm . . . I'm grieving my life." I sob, naming one after another, the torrent of men who have entered and left my story. I list the trials I've kept from her. I recite the two dozen addresses I've lived in, from childhood on, forever moving.

"And Momma," the effort and emotion are making me dizzy. "I've missed you. For a long time."

"Oh, Reemani," she sighs a sigh pulled from the earth. "You're here now." She rubs her eyes. "There is so much, jaan. What do we—?"

"I need to write."

"What? No." Her pace quickens. "You need help. You can't cry like this. You need a clinic or therapy. But you also need something to *do*. A job. A plan. A master's program, maybe. You need to think about your future."

"I am, Momma. I'm conscious of all of those things. I know it sounds strange, but—"

"You need stability. We're happy as long as you're happy, but you also need to be safe."

"Momma, 'safe' doesn't make sense to me."

She smiles, hands me a tissue. "I know. But you need something solid."

"Yes, I want that too. So, all I need to do is write. I have to write this one, specific book. You know how I always say 'I have the voice inside me'? Well—"

"Yes, jaan, and we always play along, but seriously, that's . . ." she trails off.

"Momma. This voice. This book. I can hear it. It'll work. It'll be for me and anyone else who needs . . ." I taper off. It sounds so far-fetched and far-reaching.

"What?"

"Love. It'll be love, in a book."

Momma looks at me, worry knotting her forehead. "And your future?"

"Everything will come from the pages."

"Oh, Reema. That's," she shakes her head. "That's crazy. That is such a gamble."

"No, Momma. Everything else has been."

Word spreads through the family: Reema isn't getting a job, she hasn't "a plan," and is instead zealously playing out her past in the pages of a book. Most believe this is my thinly veiled emotional breakdown. I certainly look the part.

"Who are you to write a book?" asks my sister.

"You'd be a great administrative assistant," offers my brother.

Dear one, their words hold veracity, their concern is from love, and their doubts are sensible. I was raised, fed, bathed, given an education, sent out into the world, and at age 30, I have moved in with my parents. We are a sitcom. Furthermore, as you know, I've never taken a writing class. I got as far as IB English, in high school. Those periods were spent worrying about my parents, flirting with boys, and staving off sleepiness from my pesky habit of starving myself. I've yet to publish a single essay, much less a memoir. I don't have a life of fame, glory, or inspiring achievements to write about. I am, despite all efforts to be otherwise, completely mortal. I am entirely ordinary and untrained. Am I enough to fill a book?

Another concern plaguing my family is that my writing so openly about my life, and our family, will destroy us.

My love, how can I explain that our book may prove to be not our apocalypse but our rebirth?

One page. Then another. To prove and pave the path, I can only write. Neither fear nor questions can be removed—they can only be walked through and through.

I have few things. But they are sizable. I have you. I have myself. And I have my fierce, resolute conviction fueling our hopeful tale. I have realized you, myself, and the mysterious book live in a trinity. The words that will fill it are the words you and I have shared for decades. Its pages will be our love, physicalized. It is how we will vanquish the outer and inner shadows. It is where we will lay our heart to rest. It will be a love letter written to honor what it is we have been, and have been through.

Darling friend, if you are my madness, then I am happily crazed. There is a fine line between insanity and creativity. The truth about art and imaginary best friends is they fill us with fortitude, faith, and comfort so powerful that to observing eyes they hint at insanity. But for the artist and the friend, the words, images, and bond feel like the most rational, constant, solid forces. You, my art, my potential, my conviction, my voice are all as real as I allow.

We may just work.

I look at the reams of pages I've gathered, notes I've collected for these past few years. I look at my stack of journals, a lifetime high. I don't refer to any of the material. Eight days after I turn 30, I open a fresh, white document on my laptop. I title it, *I Am Yours*.

"Who are you to write a book?"

"I am a person," I reply.

I am 30. I begin.

BEGIN, AGAIN

BEGIN, AGAIN

✦

Dear love,

Here we are. We have caught up with time. I sit now writing this book we have been living. I arrange my years. You help.

I write at my baby sister's desk. Her closet, the walls, the décor, tell a tale of lovely girlishness. The desk is snug against a wall that displays birthday cards and posters from girlfriends, collected over the years. Sweet cartoonish drawings of hearts, portraits, hands holding hands, fingers entwined. Handmade coupons for Hugs and certificates proclaiming Besties Forever. Streamers and deflated balloons are taped to make a border around the cards, like arms embracing a bouquet of flowers. The messages on the cards and posters are all declarative affirmations. *You are amazing! You can do anything! You're the coolest person I know!!!*

Oh, the gorgeous language of teenage girls, spilling over with exclamation points and youthful certainty. My sister has a glorious sense of healthy entitlement. She asserts what she wants, what she feels she deserves, and seeks to claim that and only that. She isn't swayed by the trials, needs, or opinions of others.

"But I have compassion for him," I've said to her, describing a relationship. "It's just where he is in his personal journ—"

"You're crazy," is her reply.

One woman's crazy is another woman's love.

I've slipped into her life like a photograph into a frame. I have a sly hypothesis: Writing while living with this set of parents will give me what I need. As though through osmosis, I will cultivate the audacious certainty my sister has from growing up with them. I will watch the way they love one another, and absorb what healthy love feels and looks like. I will learn this love, pat it onto my cheeks, rub it into my heart.

Even in their womb of love, as I narrate my life, I tear up often. I love the act of writing, but revisiting certain memories is painful. Whenever my eyes water, I look away from the screen and look to this tableau of a sparkling personality that laughs at her own joke. Taped across two walls are black paper letters spelling, "The goal of life isn't to live forever. It's to create someth—"

And that's it. Merely one of the million reasons I adore this girl. She's unabashedly herself, ever ready with an eye roll or raised eyebrow. She is as ironic as I am earnest.

My laptop is a white MacBook from 2009. I call it the Mothership. It has a dent on its screen, courtesy of a 4-year-old's elbow dug into the plastic sometime last year. It's laughably decrepit, dingy, and uncool, with smudges and crusty things I baby-wipe off every few months. I love my laptop. Papa bought it for me, years ago. This and the gold necklace from him and Momma are the two material possessions I'd rescue from a fire.

"So what are you writing about?" ask Momma and Dad. "What is it exactly?"

I want to reply, "The riot in my soul." But that isn't what one says to one's already nervous parents.

"I don't know." I shrug. "We'll see." Which actually, isn't that much better for their anxiety.

But bless their hearts, they let me stay, they let me write, they encourage. What a gift they are. They worry, of course, watching me tug my emotions from room to room, now, talking aloud to you. Oh yes: I now talk *aloud* to you. It helps me write. They exchange thin-lipped looks and express concern, for my progress is felt soley by myself and remains invisible to everyone else, save for you. All they can see is me squirrelling away in a closed room for hours on end, emerging only for meals and to run.

And that's all right. Only I have to feel certain. No one in my immediate world—let alone the larger—is expecting, wanting, or asking to read this book. Yet I've invested my entire past, present, and future into these pages. It's both daunting and thrilling, the utility of futility, of no stakes and every stake. The words author and authority both come from the Latin *auctor*, which means originator. I love this. I am my beginning and my end—the ultimate authority in my life. As I author my origin story, I meet my child-self. I encounter the teenager I was. I meet the 22-year-old who moved to New York in a blizzard with two suitcases and a dream. She, like my sister and her wall of radiant love, glows with unblemished audacity. Faith yet to be broken.

I ask her, "May I borrow some?"

"Silly," she says. "Courage doesn't belong to solely one person."

So I reach and take hold of faith like it's a dandelion filled to the brim with wishes.

I've given myself a year to write this book. If the Earth can begin and complete a rotation in one year, surely that's time enough for me to sort an orbit of my own. Lit by audacity, I travel forward by circling the past.

For ten hours a day, I write my whole self in hope it will make me whole. I leave my laptop only to eat, sleep, and run.

Purposefully, I haven't joined a gym. I've always hated the bar-like gym scene, and I refuse to continue my maniacal two and a half hour workouts. Now, I run through woodsy trails and suburban sidewalks surrounding my parents' house. I'm eating much more, sleeping eight hours a night, and my pallor is starting to pink.

I love the privacy and anonymity of our days. The only people I spend time with are my parents, the characters in this book, and you. In New York, like all other New Yorkers, I was rarely without my headphones. Even when your phone has died or you aren't listening to music, your headphones stay, dimming the chaos, acting as armor. Men tend to be slightly less aggressive when they think you can't hear them. Here, I run without headphones or even my phone. I write in my mind, listen to my breath, the birds, wind, trees, grass, the sound of things growing. Sometimes, I'll recite Momma and Dad's address, town, state, and zip code, like a dazzling prayer, bright with mystical powers.

The fist that was my heart is unclenching. New York is a hardened, hungry creature, grim, competitive, curt. Nearly every conversation is highly sexualized. Bangkok pulses with the promise of sex. In Bangladesh, the boundaries around women are violently oppressive.

Sleepy, quaint Beaverton is aloe for the blistered soul, soothing burns collected from life spent as a girl in this world. For the first time since puberty, I'm not a sexual object. It's wholly new, bizarre, and heavenly to spend entire days free of uninvited words and touch. I feel asexual and invisible in the best of ways. I feel like a newt, sexless, squishy, blobbish, neither coveted nor endangered, neither flaunted nor itemized. The sensation is extraordinary—to be safe and without form.

The other morning, I woke up feeling I forgot to do something. A task I was supposed to fulfill, but neglected. It took me a second to identify the pull and when I did, I was horrified. The thing that felt forgotten was the attention of men. From age 15, I have been dating, auditioning, performing, and being photographed. Some of my greatest highs came from my sex appeal.

How vile. I itch. I feel restless. Then suffocated. Then testy and impatient for no apparent reason. I move through withdrawal as I renounce and release my harmful attachments. The space they leave fills with humility and freedom.

You cannot escape yourself when writing about yourself. Seems obvious, but this fact humbles me nonetheless. Furthermore, I've been talking and typing aloud. Every word. I didn't begin the habit intentionally. But I've learned there's magic to it. When I hear my words, I confront myself. The corners I've ignored, the tricks I excel at, the cycles in my life, echo in the space before me, demanding I listen. I face the dissonance. I hear the symphony. I compose the new.

HEAL

HEAL

✦

"Here." Dad hands Momma an oven mitt.

Without looking, she reaches for it, her other hand opening the oven door. She pulls out the cookie sheet of roasted vegetables, turns, and sets it down on the hot-pad Dad slips onto the counter half a second before it welcomes the sheet. With his other hand, he reaches around her and nudges the oven door closed. Momma blows on a piping hot roasted mushroom, pops it into Dad's mouth. He chews, pecks Momma on the mouth. The entire waltz spans seven seconds.

I am in love with their love. They layer conversation, taking turns listening, speaking. They seamlessly intuit and anticipate the other's needs, and meet them. They fill ordinary moments with memorable sweetness.

Every day, I watch them greedily, collecting moments like a war-torn nation stockpiles food. I try to be stealthy but my spontaneous joyful tears give me away. Momma's fear and insecurity that once hung like a heavy shroud has lifted. This Momma is vibrant and sassy. She grows more present daily, as though a giant, invisible hand is slowly coloring her in. Dad loves her with an unwavering effusiveness and loyalty equal to hers. Equally astounding is that he loves us kids with the same.

There are days I second-guess everything I say or do around Dad, scared I'll misbehave, offend, or make him mad. Nearing the end of every month, I panic. I keep checking the clock for an imaginary end, expecting a phone call or email announcing my eviction. Ever the employee, friend, and girlfriend, "Is there anything else you need from me?" is a sentence branded on my tongue. With the circuitous obsession with which a dog chases her own tail, I continually offer to pay rent or chip in for groceries. Momma and Dad look at me, surprise and sadness tinting their eyes like age on a Polaroid.

"This is your home." They stress each word as if speaking to a child. "You don't need to earn your place."

Our dogs are Lucy and Zekie. When God dispensed aesthetic cuteness, Lucy was overlooked. Zekie nudged her aside and basked in both shares. Lucy's lack of physical loveliness is quickly forgotten, though, because of her sweetness and intelligence. She is a rescue dog, a rat terrier. Rat terriers are bred to track and hunt. They're able to survive extreme conditions and run extraordinary lengths, overriding fatigue and hunger. They have an uncanny ability to follow orders, not slavishly, but through stoic determination.

We don't have the details, but we know the first six years of Lucy's life teemed with abuse. My parents adopted her three years ago. There are times she keeps her head down around me despite every tenderness I try. She'll come and cuddle while I write. She'll lick me silly when I return from running. But when I give her food, she looks at me warily like I'll trick her and take it away. Over long minutes, she'll creep toward her bowl, her enormous elfin eyes never leaving mine, disbelieving that this love is for her and won't be retracted. Some days she cowers from all of us. I reckon she awoke those mornings from a night of dark memories. It is when I write about my brother as a child and now as I write about Lucy that I cry most.

In this house, the past can rest. We all coexist peacefully. The certainty of Momma and Dad's availability and reliability feels like a privilege. I release a quiet fear: Living with others doesn't always promise chaos. This love will not grade, degrade, punish, or disappear. I can simply be. I start smiling again. I make jokes.

My sister is undeniably Daddy's girl. From the time she was 12 to 18, he made her school lunches, packed in brown paper bags, and drove her daily to school, a tradition that feels as ungraspable as a ghost. I love watching them together whenever she's home from college. I'm deliriously grateful and envious of their closeness. Over these months, I'll taste little snippets of that bond until I believe it as my own food. I'll lob a passing comment about a man from my past, and Dad will bristle with protective rage. He'll say, "If I ever meet the guy . . ." before letting the threat hang in the air like a gray cloud, fat with imminent storm. I'll muse aloud about dating again one day, and he'll casually say, "Make sure he's good to you." This seemingly innocuous sentiment undoes me at the seams. I feel special and precious, giddy like I've spritzed a new perfume to see if the waters suit me.

Little by little, I share with my family the events and emotions I'm writing about. Aside from sorting my pieces, I have another goal: to erase the difference between the way I am with you and the way I am with others. From now on, beginning with my family, I will be solely an open book. I'm excited. I've named this Our Indefinite Year of Truth.

I print a few chapters to send to my Warriors in New York. The printer is in Dad's office. I hear him on a call. I don't knock in fear of interrupting. I busy myself with a run. I return to find on my bed, the chapters, each paper-clipped with a pink clip.

He organized the pages. He thought to paper-clip them. He searched the little plastic dish for pink ones. Eight of them.

"Momma . . ." I'm too moved to finish. I clutch the chapters to my chest like a hot-water bottle, warming me.

"That's your Dad," she smiles.

I think this is what it's like to be a kid.

"You're changing," says Momma. "You were always so pensive. You're softening. Laughing. Changing. This is good for you."

I smile. I don't tell her that the transformation she sees in me, I see in her.

I had feared parts of me were frostbitten beyond repair. Thankfully, I'm salvageable. The months thaw me slowly as if held over a low flame. Love renews my blood.

THREE MONTHS HAVE PASSED.

Here in our home, Momma, Dad, you, and I, we are quaint, simple, and happy. We laugh over nonsensical things. We ask one another, "How was your day?" and then, we actually listen to what each person has to say. We cook abundant meals and eat them off one another's plates, held on our laps in front of board games, movies, or conversations that stretch into dawn.

Occasionally I'll glimpse the outside world through various screens. TV, phone, laptop. A show, person, or persona I once coveted. On cue, the seasons have slipped from summer into fall, fall into winter.

It has been merely three months since I left New York. Yet we are so far away. I lay down the different years I have been. The child, the girl, the young woman at 21, 23, 25, 28. I connect the constellation, character to character, event to event. Our story becomes vividly clear. I mine each memory for the lessons they hold. Answers crystalize, glistening like gold thread.

Although I have plenty of clothes, these days I like wearing clothing nabbed from Momma, Dad, and my siblings. For all hours and uses of the day: to run, to sleep, and especially to write. My favorite is an enormous Oregon Ducks sweatshirt belonging to Dad that reaches my knees. University of Oregon is Dad's and my sister's alma mater. I like feeling my loves around me.

While I adore every minute spent writing, I still cry when revisiting certain parts of my life. Thankfully, Dad works from home. He is a teacher for an online school. His office is the room across the hall from my sister's. I knock on his door, he opens it. I stand there not knowing how to form the words. Asking for something, anything, is still difficult. Habits take time to dismantle. Now, all I can do is stand and cry.

"Can I have a—" He pulls me into the hug before I finish asking for it.

We tend to think deaths and events are all that require grieving, but selves, choices, habits, and relationships we've known, they need loving rituals of healing as well. The speed at which life demands we run, simply to make it to the next day, makes it difficult to see them through. Wounds tally. Addictions anesthetize the pain. We try to stitch while moving. But life's racing pace continually tears open old scars and mangles the new ones. Mending-while-enduring is well meant but ultimately futile, the sutures never tight enough to hold.

I am revisiting myself. Year by year, I peer into the stitching.

I am 3. I am 5. I am 11, 13, 18, 23, 27, 29.

I mend the pieces. I arrange them just so. I cover myself with earth.

FORGIVE

FORGIVE

✦

PAPA, HIS WIFE, and my half-brother are visiting the United States. I haven't seen Papa since his trip to New York. Their last stop is LA. He flies me out to spend a week with them.

Walking to their hotel, I feel my fear spread. My skin turns warm, then cold, then prickly with adrenaline, my body tensing for defense and flight.

I use a trusty tool, inspired by these pages. I speak to myself as a little girl. I tell her she is kind, loved, and has value in this world. I gently press those words onto her heart like memories saved in a baby book. I come down onto my knees and hug her close, cheek to cheek, pulse to pulse, past to present. We sway and breathe as one. I remember I am her guardian. I forget to feel afraid.

The elevator chimes. I follow the signs to their door. Knock, knock. I hear the patter of small feet running like rain drawing near. The door flies open and here stands a little boy. He is 6 years old. He has big eyes, full cheeks, and a 1,000-watt smile. Features identical to mine. He is my half-brother. We are meeting for the first time.

We are at Manhattan Beach. It has been a blissful week. We have laughed, told stories, walked long walks, eaten wonderful food. I've brought my laptop with me to LA, of course. Where you and I go, so do our words. We have been writing now for five months.

My little brother is pretending to be a very loud airplane. His feet kicking clouds of sand, he makes the airplane noise all little boys make, flying in circles with his arms out wide. He has been doing this for a half hour. Oh, the inspiring ease and frequency with which children find delight. Papa is on the beach blanket next to me. The air is perfect, the temperature a divine hand massaging my skin back to life. I look at Papa, astonished that he has flown me toward him.

My little brother continues to fly, confident in his faith that he won't fall or be told to quiet down or stop. The sound he makes to emulate the plane, the unbridled joy on his face, the song of his feet on the sand, Papa's laughter as he watches his son, all is gorgeous to behold.

A few days before arriving in LA, I received one of Papa's harsh emails. My insides froze with familiar sorrow.

But there was something new. From his letter rose a sentence, the one that ultimately matters.

"From age 12, you stopped seeking my advice."

He wants me to lean on him. He wants me to treat him like a father. All this time, I have wanted him to treat me like a daughter. We hurt from missing the same thing. Closeness.

I replied to his letter with why I don't ask him for advice. I wrote that from now on, I will respond only with kindness, and only to kindness. I wrote, "It is okay. There is profound love, and we have a lifetime to learn."

It is the most forthright I've ever been with him, in honor of my vow to speak to everyone the way I speak to you. Writing this book has nurtured the clarity and strength needed to voice such words. It's initially terrifying but ultimately liberating. I don't know it yet, but from here on, Papa and I will be purely loving, weaving an indefinite harmony. We will speak and text often, getting to know each other anew, bit by bit. A hard-won miracle that will thrill me daily. A few months into our newfound closeness, I will tell him about this book, warning him there are things that may feel difficult to read.

He will reply, "We'll celebrate our story all the more. Look how far we've come."

My Papa. His truest self is as sweet and gentle as the purest harp and dearest lullaby. I look at him now, his face painted with the setting sun. All my fear has left. A haunted house is scary until we turn on the lights. Once we see how the pulleys, wheels, wires, and trapdoors connect, the fear demystifies and disappears.

"Papa." His eyes are closed. "I was quite the teen tyrant, wasn't I? With my purple hair and piercings, continually challenging your every turn."

He opens his eyes, looks at the ocean. He takes off his glasses, rubs his eyes, and laughs, a soft, warm sound that is as much a sigh as it is a chuckle.

"Yes. You questioned me on everything. From the time you could talk."

I smile.

He continues. "You weren't a tyrant, jaan. You've always held us all, and yourself, to unwavering standards. Pushing. Probing. Peering into life. I could see that inside you lived a formidable tomorrow."

I'm too moved to reply. He puts his glasses back on.

"I tried to quiet your fire. It scared me, as a father." He sighs. "The world isn't kind to women who dare to question and speak."

Papa looks at me.

"But you were born to do precisely that. My formidable tomorrow."

The sunset drapes us in orange, gold, and pink, enfolding thousands in the same embrace. All our faces are peaceful, free of pain. It is senseless to hold onto anything but gratitude when faced with the majesty of life.

"Thank you, Papa. I love you."

"I love you, amanjee."

He smiles. He touches my shoulder lightly. His hand feels like a cool washcloth on a fever-stricken heart.

We are in our sixth month. It is 6 a.m. The sun has yet to rise. I bolt out of bed, beaming. There are few things in life I detest. Despite how many times I have done it, waking up while the sky is dark is one of them. Growing up, I hated every dark morning. The saving grace was that Momma's voice was our alarm clock. In New York, I loathed dark mornings even more, for leaving the house at that hour meant being greeted by a still-warm pool of vomit hissing with steam as it sank into the snow, a discarded syringe or condom on the front stoop, or a pack of belligerent hipsters teetering their way home.

I leap to my feet, for today is different. Today is my first day as a part-time reading aide for first, second, and fourth graders at Momma's school. I put on the clothes I laid out the night before. Momma and I will leave the house at 7 o'clock in the morning. I have crossing-guard duty from 8 to 8:15. I'll assist Momma from 9 to 9:45, then a second grade teacher from 10 to 10:50, followed by a fourth grade teacher from 11 to noon. It couldn't be more ideal. Children and books. Two of my dearest treasures. The school is three and a quarter miles away, so I'll run home after classes and have the rest of the day to write. I'm presently revising my childhood years. It's remarkable what my child-self is teaching me. She's one tough pebble.

I open my door. Momma calls out, "Good morning, Reemani!" Just like she used to when I was a young girl.

When we arrive at school, although it's my first time meeting everyone, I'm greeted like a returning war hero. Never have I experienced such a reception, bubbling with hugs and warmth. I imagined Momma was somewhat of a celebrity. I was wrong.

She is a god. Every teacher and administrator rushes over with unrestrained affection. They retell all the stories they've heard about my siblings and I. They exclaim how incredible Momma is.

"I know she is," I say. "She's been my teacher for three decades."

The principal and I hadn't met for an interview. He hired me off Momma's reputation, recommendation, and the fact she raised me.

Momma walks tall through these buildings. I'm thrilled to witness her in her element, to feel my enormous admiration deepen. We're visited by numerous teachers. Everyone remarks, "Your mother is so beautiful."

"Oh, I know. I've known this face for nearly thirty-one years. It amazes me still."

She introduces me to her class. The kids grin and stare like I'm the messiah returning. "You guys look the same!" they squeal. Momma encourages them to ask questions about who I am and where I've come from. They raise their arms so high I fear they'll pop right out of their sockets. I take half the class for their lesson while Momma leads the other.

On to the second grade classroom, to be met by gasps. The older children know Momma as their former teacher or because she is who she is. A rainbow of emotions paints their faces. Joy first, thinking she has walked into the room. Then, curiosity and surprise like when opening a Christmas present. Lastly, amazement from having figured out the riddle. The teacher introduces me by name and as Mrs. Brown's daughter. The children forget my name quickly but swoon over the second moniker. (Yes, Momma's last name is now Brown because that is Dad's name. The plaque on our front door reads, "The Browns.")

In the second grade, I recognize one boy immediately. Let's call him Lyon. Lyon was in Momma's class last year. Every year, a few of Momma's students become family. We grow to feel for them, loving their idiosyncrasies, hurting with their struggles. Sometimes we cook and deliver meals for them on Thanksgiving and Christmas. I remember Lyon's gentleness. I remember the assignment that asked the kids to make three "feeling sentences" using their list of spelling words. One of his sentences was, "I get scared when Daddy yells."

The school has been looking into this family for years. Lyon is the youngest of three. All three have spoken about their father's temper. Aside from words, each child is walking proof of the neglect they face. Whether it is intentional or from a lack of resources remains unclear. Pale, thin, in clothes threadbare and too small, in shoes that are too big or too tight, each child is behind in every subject, with no one to encourage, guide, and support them at home. Sometimes they come to school without a jacket or socks in the dead of winter. Every teacher connected to these children has reported these facts.

In Oregon, as with many states, child services laws are so strict that sometimes it's the system itself that delivers further harm to a child. Unless a child is in near-mortal danger, they won't be shielded from potential pain at home. Public school teachers will invariably feel furious helplessness from collecting, documenting, and reporting these stories, to no avail. What they do in the meantime is everything else possible, to give the child some semblance of constancy, love, comfort, and nourishment at school, emotionally and literally.

Like many public schools, Momma's has free breakfasts and lunches available for any child who needs them. There's even a weekend meal package, sent home every Friday with the kids who need them, to ensure their meals are covered during these days as well. There are numerous clothing drives for new and gently used clothes. They're organized in a separate space known as the Caring Store. The school sends letters to the families who may need this service and each family can schedule a visit to the store. Each appointment is private and timed so that the families don't encounter one another, inside the store or even in the parking lot. They can maintain their dignity.

Lyon now sits across from me, his eyebrows raised with delighted anticipation. Once or twice a week, he visits Momma to deliver a hug. He recognizes her face in mine.

"I know you," I smile. "You were in my mom's class last year."

He looks at me like angels have descended from the sky. Acknowledgment turns him incandescent. He has light blond hair, the bangs cut short on his pale forehead above enormous blue eyes, and is wearing a bright yellow sweatshirt a few sizes too big. Across his forehead and cheeks are the nearly washed-away remnants of circles and letters written in green marker. I take this as an adorable, mischievous act on his part.

I tell his teacher about the green markings, how cute he looked.

She shakes her head. "No, that's his oldest sister. She writes on him while he's asleep. One day he came to school with the word 'Stupid' written down his arm."

My heart fumes. If Mom and Dad aren't looking out for him, and neither is his oldest sister, what chance does this boy have? He needs Johnson & Johnson.

From the first day, a handful of kids give me goodbye hugs at the end of every class. Lyon is part of that handful, but he is also the only one who gives me a hug hello, without my initiating. I'll be gathering books and I'll feel a light, little arm slip around my waist.

I make sure to choose Lyon to be part of the half I take for reading time. The first day, he says, "I don't like it when things are too loud" in reaction to a burst of laughter and shouts from the other side of the room. He covers his ears tightly.

"It makes my head hurt," he says.

My heart somersaults from his words, his pained face, from time folding into itself.

He is without question the most polite, thoughtful child I have ever met. I sense him on the lookout to see how he can help others, by lending a pencil, helping with a tough-to-reach book, rescuing a runaway crayon. While the others rush out of class, he tucks his chair under his desk, and circles back to do that for a few others. He returns everyone else's discarded pencils to their rightful baskets. He slides the books back where they belong, trying to create order in the ways he can.

After the lesson, I lean over and whisper, "I can tell you're a very special, very nice person."

He smiles so wide his rows of teeth fail to touch. He inhales a deep gulp of air as though emerging from a long swim.

The next day I tell him, "I think you can be anyone you want to be when you grow up. You can be a scientist. Or a firefighter. Or a doctor. You can be the president!"

He grins and puffs with pride.

The following day I say, "You know, you're very important in this world. You're one of the kindest people I know."

He nods with mirrored solemnity.

I am not filling him with lies. I am filling him with courage. His daily pages reflect mine.

It takes much more than words though. During my first week, every day, I come home and weep. Huge, violent sobs of helplessness and abject fury. Starting in the second grade, the kids all have iPads given to them by the school. But Lyon's brother took his headphones and his parents haven't been able to replace them. Many of the spelling tests are taken on the iPad. The electronic voice tells the child the word, he or she types it. All these seemingly little things add up. Lyon may know how to spell the word, but if he can't hear it, he won't know to type it. He'll fall further and further behind.

In my third week at the school, winter arrives and the temperatures drop suddenly. Lyon's lips have cracked. They'll begin to heal, but then tear and bleed again from speaking and smiling. The skin on his arms and legs is parched, flaking in a way I've previously seen only on darker-skinned people like myself. Then comes the day when he can barely keep his head up. He's smiling and courteous but moving very slowly.

"Hey buddy, are you okay? Did you get enough sleep last night?"

He nods.

"Well, you look a bit tired, sweetie."

He doesn't say anything for a few seconds, looks down at his hands.

"I didn't have breakfast today and yesterday. And I didn't have dinner last night or the night before."

He is 7. It being illegal is the sole reason I don't scoop him up and carry him away right this moment. I'd already decided to get him headphones, lotion, and lip balm. Now I vow to bring him little meals.

"What's your favorite color?"

"Gween."

"What if I got you some green headphones? Would you like that?"

He looks at me incredulously, blinks once. He nods slowly.

God bless my parents. They drive me to a few spots before we find green headphones. If I'm trying to bring a morsel of accountability into this child's world, I must darn well find green headphones. We find the perfect pair. They're neon green earbuds, the same shade as his backpack. I get two kinds of lip balm, the classic and one with sunscreen. I get a lotion that's moisturizing but also smells good. Nothing medicinal, something comforting, what I'd give my own kids, if I had any.

The next day, I ask Lyon's homeroom teacher permission to borrow him for a few minutes. I want to give him these things without the other kids seeing lest he feel embarrassed or shy, especially with the lotion. I ask him to bring his backpack, and we duck into the hallway. I sit on my knees. He stands on tiptoe from excitement. With most kids, to speak to them, I lean down from the waist to meet their eye level. With the troublemakers, I gauge when they need me to be authoritative, and speak from full height. When they're in a place that's best served by a gentler, compassionate voice,

I bend down, let them fess up or vent, and let them reclaim their dignity. With Lyon and a few others, I get down on my knees to give them the taller height. These are the children who aren't struggling with surliness, meanness, or tantrums. Their trial is the lack of respect and attention.

I take out the headphones. His face lights up like a sunrise.

"They match!" He holds the headphones to his backpack.

"Yes, honey! Let's try them on. The earbuds can be three different sizes. You can use them as you grow bigger and bigger!"

He giggles. He tries all three sizes but I see they make him uncomfortable. The buds may feel claustrophobic for a child already sensitive to sound and spatial relations.

"Buddy, how about you keep these for later and I get you some that curl around the ear, like this? Or the kind that's like a headband?"

"Yeah, I like the headband kind. They stay on."

I am so proud of him and relieved; he is voicing what he wants.

"Awesome. I may not find green ones. Is that okay?"

"Yeah," he grins. "I'll still have these ones forever."

"Okay, good. And do you know what this is? Lip balm?"

He shakes his head No.

"It goes on your lips, to keep them from getting too dry. Put this on at night and in the morning, okay?"

He nods. He carefully peels away the plastic cover on the lip balm with a patience rare in a child, rarer still in children accustomed to plentitude. The kids you see in stores demanding more, more, more, who tear open their birthday, Christmas, and spontaneous presents only to forget them within seconds. The way Lyon holds this 99-cent lip balm makes it seem like a bar of gold or a stick of dynamite. He cradles it in his tiny palm with reverence before carefully tucking it away in a pocket he calls, "the safe one." We nod earnestly.

We have been in the hallway for longer than I anticipated. I don't want him to miss too much of class. We return to the classroom, hang up his backpack.

"Do you know what this is?" I whisper, lugging out the family-size bottle of lotion. It was the biggest size available, with a pump top, easy for a child to use. I show him how the pump unlocks by sliding counterclockwise, the way it slowly rises. He gasps, giggling like it's a magic trick.

"This is for your skin, your legs, face, arms, anywhere, especially where it itches."

Immediately, in front of everyone, he scoots up his pants' legs to his knobby knees, and begins rubbing lotion onto his thin, bony legs. He rubs and rubs away the ashen white. He rubs lotion onto his neck and wrists. He must have been itching so badly, he isn't the slightest bit concerned what the others may think. Or, maybe he's just too young to be embarrassed about anything yet. At this age, children have yet to pick up on their differences. In a year or two, he'll understand the stark contrast of his world and a classmate's world. In a year or two, some kids will tease and bully, "You don't have a Mooo-om!" or "You're so poor you're clothes don't fit!" or "You're so stupid your Dad hates you! That's why he left!" But for now, they have yet to learn prejudice.

He sighs from relief, then holds a hand up to his nose.

"It smews nice." He grins.

We high-five. I thought I knew gratitude. I didn't. I look at his face, alit like a birthday candle.

This.

A few days later, I notice that the boy who sits beside Lyon during homeroom is using the green headphones.

"Sweetie, did you lend Joe your headphones?"

"Yeah. He chewed on his. They don't work anymore. I have two, so I gave him one."

The child has next to nothing and here he is, sharing. This, again, the enduring marvel of his heart.

I start smuggling peanut-butter and jelly sandwiches and sliced apples for Lyon, delivered every morning in a brown paper bag.

Inside I include a note like, "I think you're awesome. Have a great day, buddy." Slowly I stretch the notes longer, to encourage his reading. I write, "You can do anything you set your mind to." I compliment the way he treats others with kindness, especially a girl distanced by most other children. She has Down syndrome. The other kids treat her with affected preciousness or tease her. But not him. He gives her sincere warmth.

The other day she wanted to show the class every single grape she brought for a snack. She lined them up on her desk and said, "This is a grape. This is a grape. This is a grape. And this is a grape."

The other kids began to snicker. But Lyon nodded and affirmed each grape, saying, "Yup, that's a grape." The other children quieted down and gave her their respect and attention. Such was the ripple effect of his kindness. I make sure to comment on it, wanting him to know softness is revered in this world, not loudness or aggression.

He is one of the few who understands humor. He's among the slowest readers, for he doesn't get much practice at home. But he picks up on the subtleties of language. I Google "jokes for kids" and start writing on the bottom of every letter, a joke of the day.

I ask his teacher, "Are the sandwich drop-offs disrupting your class? I hope not."

She looks at me for a solid few seconds.

"He reads every letter to me and to the class," she says. "The kids take it all in, then comment on the trait covered that day. They say things like, 'Oh yeah, you *are* kind. And so are you. You too!' Then, they repeat the joke, all day. Initially, I had to help him read the letter. But now," she chokes up, "He can do it himself."

She squeezes my arm. "Keep them coming."

Stories travel quickly in schools. The teachers whisper sweet messages when we pass one another in the hallway. One says, "It has been only a few weeks but I can see him sitting a bit taller in his seat, smiling a bit brighter, and answering questions more confidently than before." Another says, "There's been a noticeable change in Lyon. He wants to improve now. Someone cheering for him makes him want to grow."

One day a few teachers bring it up while we wait in line for the photocopier. "It's so nice of you," they say.

I blurt the first reply that comes to mind, a bubble blown and popping midair.

"I got married at 26 because I loved him, I wanted to be married, and I wanted kids. Had I a child when we imagined we would, that boy or girl would be a mere year younger than Lyon. Making him a sandwich is a privilege."

On my run home, I meet a sentence that buckles my knees, sending me onto the sly asphalt.

I am a voice for the souls and stories silenced, after all. I return to standing and run home.

RELEASE

RELEASE

✦

"THEY'RE ON THEIR WAY! They can't wait to meet you!"

"Your parents?"

"Yup!" my girlfriend bubbles, the same friend whose brother I dated. You and I are in our eighth month of writing, and New York feels like a lifetime ago. An entire self ago. I'm so different from the girl who was once drawn to him. Soon after I landed, I wrote him an email expressing my gratitude for our time together, all we learned, and my favorite details about him that I'll remember fondly. I wished him joy and success. He didn't write back.

"They felt like taking a spontaneous road trip, and they've never been to Portland. I'm texting you my mom's number. I wish I was there!"

"Me too, sweetheart," I laugh. "I'll call her right away."

I daydreamed of meeting his parents one day. I simply didn't think it would happen this way. I call and talk to their mom, who is as warm and kind as I imagined. They're staying only a night in Portland. I invite them over to Momma and Dad's for dinner.

I cook and bake a feast. They arrive, and it feels like a reunion with dear, old friends. All five of us talk, laugh, and joke with effortless ease. They ask me how I know their daughter and if I've met the rest of the family. I realize then, they don't know he and I dated. I expected as much. He was very careful to keep us a secret.

They ask why I left New York and what I'm doing now.

"I needed something new. I'm writing a book, actually." I'm suddenly shy.

"About what?"

"Love. Life. People. The things we do."

They smile. They begin to share anecdotes about their children. All four, remarkable outliers. But she's gushing mostly about him. He's close to my age, and in another's eyes, or in another life, we would seem like an obvious match. I listen, and watch her face blush with love, pride, and affection. I listen to all the faith, effort, hope, and love poured into him from the time he was born. I see him as she, his mother, sees him: a man who was once a child, and like all children, utterly lovable. Any remnants of dark feeling inside me leave. They are replaced swiftly with compassion.

We talk late into the night. I pack them off with a few dozen cookies for their two-day trek back. They give us a box of chocolates from their hometown and make me promise I'll visit. I don't know if that will ever fruit.

Before she goes, she tells me, squeezing my hands, "The only path you're supposed to walk is your own."

"Oh wow. Thank you."

She laughs, hugs me once more, and they drive off. Sometimes the best affirmations arrive in the most unlikely ways.

A few weeks later, I finalize my divorce paperwork. It took a long time to organize all our fragments. I fill out the paperwork without a lawyer. With each letter, word, and page I feel myself letting him go. It is sublime. I create an addendum to the basic paperwork, for my ex-husband to sign and waive any claims to my past, present, and future work, including but not limited to books I will publish. Although I'm still writing this narrative, and can't describe my future in detail, I know it holds immense light. I deserve protection.

"Hey, how are ya?" my ex-husband's drawl curls over the phone.

"Wonderful, thank you. Did you have a chance to listen to my message? I was calling to say I've sent you the paperwork. It's all rather innocuous."

"Cool. So, what you been up to? I heard you're not acting anymore?"

I fill him in.

"*You?*" He chuckles. "A *book*?" Breathe. I am the softness in this frame. I am the sand, he is the sea, he tries to carve his mark in me.

"Yes," I reply.

"What kind of book?"

"A memoir."

He laughs, hard. "Who'd wanna read about your life?"

Breathe. An act of love or a cry for love.

"Well, I did always say you're a great writer."

Breathe.

"Am I in it?"

"Yes."

I hear him thinking. I wait for him to speak. He doesn't.

"So, I've tagged the places you need to sign, notarize, and print your name. They're color-coded blue, green, and pink. I've included a pre-paid, self-addressed stamped return envelope."

"Awesome. Thanks." His tone shifts. "I'm glad you're doin' good."

"Thank you. I'm happy you're well."

I hang up, spinning from the carnival hall of mirrors that is his mind. His voice still ringing, he then sends two texts: "Don't make me sound like an abusive redneck. There was a little more finesse in my abuse."

Followed by, "Hahahaaa."

It takes a few tries. He returns the paperwork a first time. I need to send it back. He fills it out correctly, sends it again. Finally, Momma and I drive the papers over to the county courthouse. I file and ten days later, we are divorced. The two bookends of our relationship are thus: falling in love, and getting a divorce, were the quickest, easiest parts.

My love, I have healed. And now, I release. Daily, I practice the truth I first learned as a teenager: The task of an artist is to turn pain into poetry. Wound into wisdom. As these pages grow, my once feral anger is replaced with peace. These nights, I no longer sleep on anger's belly. I have forgiveness, a dear little pillow where I lay my head to rest. My beastly rage no longer growls. It purrs. We are all sleeping deeply, lulled by the song we are writing.

A few days after the phone call, I receive an email. The author writes he has changed and hints I would realize that were I to come "see for (my)self."

Darling friend, they can always tell when we are our happiest. They sense our lifeblood pumping its brightest crimson, and they desire a good, long drink. So this man from my past has reached out, inviting me to come be a part of him again. Love, I realize you don't know which "him" I am writing about. He could be Peter Pan, the Prince, or any one of the other men who have entered and left my life.

Every man will bring out a different version of my self, unless, until, I arrive at the day when my self lives solidly, consistently, intact and anchored within. "His" name has never mattered. What has mattered, what will always matter, is the woman I am with or without him. Moreover, I have learned the vital distinction that yes, although I was born to be a conduit of love, compassion, and forgiveness, I simultaneously hold the right to refuse to bear the bruise of another's shadow.

Today, I hold myself whole. To him I reply, "No, thank you. I'm sorting my orbit. I wish you love."

FREEDOM

FREEDOM

✦

It is evening. You and rain keep me company as I type.

Oregon boasts all kinds of rain. There is drizzle, so light it sounds like gentle static. It settles on your skin like the shyest kiss. There is lush rain made of fat droplets, so rotund you see them clearly. There is hail in the winter, chilling and aloof, paying me no regard as I run, delivering winds that lift me off the ground. Finally there are summer storms brought by clouds that pass and return swiftly, growing loud then soft with lusty arrogance, making the earth and me swoon, loving every second. The rain is right: if you are to do something, do it well and do it boldly.

Tonight, it is a steady pour. Regardless of the form, rain always transports me to Bangladesh. Some of my favorite memories were made during monsoons. I recall my beloved extended family on Momma's side, all living in one building. Our rooftop had a four-foot wall circling the perimeter. The rain would gather and so would we, three generations dancing, laughing, splashing. Most of the Bengali songs I know were learned singing in those rains. Most of our stories were told huddled around a candle after the storms swiped the electricity.

A cherished fact about my motherland is that we were born from our love for words. Once upon a time, India, Pakistan, and Bangladesh were one country colonized by Great Britain. When the British left, India separated from Pakistan and Bangladesh. We were named East Pakistan and the country now known as Pakistan was West Pakistan.

We didn't share land, borders, or waters with Pakistan. We didn't share a common language. Pakistan speaks Urdu while we have always spoken Bengali. This difference was significant.

Language births art, literature, dance, theater, and bedtime stories. Language, science has proven, shapes the way we formulate thoughts. Language sculpts the fables we mine for morals, the idioms that guide us, the jokes we tell to lift the rains. The speeches and anthems that teach us values, inspire our courage, and charge our souls. The lullabies we sing to our children to soothe their fears and make them kind. The poetry we weave around a lover. Words shape thoughts, thoughts breed action, actions create identity, identity directs legacy. We are our words.

We felt it only made sense then to recognize we are our own, unique country, different from our neighbor. We fought a war to prove this true.

My love, I am from a land of radical renegades. I love that my small, impoverished, rain-drenched, perpetually hungry country decided to ignore our daily discomforts and fight for the language we know as our own. Such was our fiery conviction that our voices matter. I love that although defeat and failure seemed more likely than independence and success, we courted the unknown and attempted the impossible.

To speak is a revolution. You and I have been writing now for nine months. Art, love, and voice have replaced anger, wound, and silence, and now, there is pure, brazen joy. In these pages, my hummingbird heart has finally found her sky, an open expanse where she can fly freely. I place my middle and forefinger on my neck. I feel her anthem. Year by year, I reclaim my life.

I am 3. I meet you. I learn about books.
I am 4. My brother is born. He is my love.
I am 6. I speak up and my parents listen.
I am 10. I start writing, for myself.
I am 11. My sister is born. She, too, is my love.
I am 15. I find art.
I am 21. I meet Dad.
I am 27. I say No, to him.
I am 29. I say Yes, to myself.
I am 30. I come home to Momma.
I am 30. Papa and I sit by an ocean.
I am 30. I am writing a book. I am authoring my independence.
The sky has grown into a storm. It roars.

I TURN 31 on a Thursday. The students make me cards and posters. I'm sung "Happy Birthday" six times. Overwhelmed by love, each time, I cry.

I stand now in the blistering rain, waving hello, smiling. I'm on crosswalk duty. From 8 to 8:15 a.m., with my trusty red, octagonal stop sign, I direct traffic, smile, wave, and usher kids to school safely. Occasionally the rain demands I hold an umbrella too. Waving is thus limited, so I smile extra big.

I love this little job. I find selfish delight in being the first faculty member to greet the children every morning. The principal, a dear, kind man, greets the students as they enter the building. But I get to greet them even before him. Some kids hug me while crossing the street. The parents and bus drivers are stalled in their vehicles but don't care in the least. They laugh along with me.

A few days into crossing-guard duty, Jacob, a fourth grader, came up to me in class bristling with indignation.

"Miss Reema! I wave every morning and you don't wave back!"

The windows on the school buses are tinted to preserve the

children's privacy. You have to really look to identify any shape or face behind them.

"Ohmygosh, sweetheart, I'm so sorry!" My appall is sincere, matching his. "That's a big deal!"

"I know," he says. "It IS!"

"What bus are you on?"

"10."

From then on, every morning, I wave furiously at Bus 10. Jacob presses his pale, dear face close to the glass to help me see his huge grin and the blur of his hand, waving. The other cars and buses slow down to take in the sight of us.

Occasionally, I grumble from the freezing rain or the tediousness of the job. Then I remember that of all the habits, self-pity is the most boring of the lot.

For my fifteen minutes, I'm paid about $3 a day. Which comes down to a few cents per child. A few years ago, I was given $12,000 to perform the same tasks, smiling and waving, for about the same amount of time. I happened to be filmed so I earned more in residuals, about $25,000 over the course of three years. I helped a big, shiny company sell slippery things. Love, we can say $12,000 for smiling and waving is absurd. We can say a few cents for a child's safety is preposterous, because their safety is invaluable. Such is the nature of value: the imagined meaning we assign to anything or anyone, including ourselves.

For years, I have sought a place where I fit, and work that feels solidly meaningful. Here, now, with this evolving book and with my students, I feel that quest being realized. Here, now, I am at home and my days have purpose. At the school, reality functions the way it did at the orphanage—with stark gravity. The work is hard but worthwhile. Each minute feels real and imbued with love. Every night, I rush to my laptop, eager to lay down our daily stories, for they feel like family anecdotes.

I leave the rain, walk into my first class, and a wash of exuberant love enfolds me. It is like this every day and still, it shatters me.

"Miss Reema, Miss Reema!" their voices sing sweetly. Is there any dearer sound than a child saying "Miss"? Well, yes, I guess. The sound of a child saying Momma, Mommy, Papa, Daddy. One boy hands me a book he's written on lined notebook paper, stapled together.

"Thank you." I hug him. "What's this for?"

"Read it."

The book is a tale of thanks. Last week I drew the kids Thank You cards with a personal message for each child, for the birthday gifts they gave me. He wrote a book to thank me for thanking him.

Children will do this. His classmates gather, each bearing their daily note or drawing. Some write for a specific reason like his. Others, just because. They crowd like guppies encircling a piece of bread, leaping over one another to reach me. This is why anyone who works with kids does so. They are why we remain despite the harsh realness and meager pay. Love is ultimately a value we can all agree on.

I go to my next class, and then, to my fourth graders. Jacob, the boy who waves from Bus 10 every morning, brings me a drawing.

There are some gestures that knock the breath out of you. This drawing is one.

In Jacob's decade-long life, he has been shuffled through eleven foster homes. We at school are among his few constants. What I loved about his indignation over not being waved back to was that he felt entitled to that gesture of acknowledgment. I was proud and relieved. Children who are repeatedly left behind or given away generally mistrust love. They don't expect it and, more often than not, bat it aside. But Jacob's spirit is fundamentally durable.

The teacher whom I assist says, "He brings me snacks, every day. He writes Morning, Lunch, and Afternoon on Post-its and tucks them under each snack. An apple. A carton of yogurt. A cheese-stick."

He is taking care of her. Where did he learn this if he hasn't a mother, and his life has known only abandonment, nonattachment, and dis-attachment? He taught himself. He intuited. The love, care, generosity, and accountability are entirely, purely, him.

I led an art lesson yesterday. He stayed after class to talk.

"Why do you love art, Miss Reema?"

I thought carefully about my answer. "Do you know when you feel sad, scared, lonely, or angry, and you feel you can't talk about it?"

"Yeah."

"You put it here," I touched the page. "Your art is your voice. And your voice is a muscle. The more you give it, the more you use it, the stronger it grows."

His thin face broke into a grin. "Can I have this?"

I'd drawn a hummingbird. "Absolutely."

The drawing he gives me in return today is simple. There is an arrow that stands for his school bus. It begins at point 1, marked as such, with the sky still dark, dotted with stars. At point 2, we pass trees on the roads. Finally, we arrive at school. Point 3. Two stick figures, one with long hair, one with short. He has named us. His little stick figure faces mine. Above his head are the words, "When I am happy."

My breath has been kidnapped. He is leaving for another school tomorrow. I've drawn him something as well, on the first page of an otherwise fresh drawing pad. I've drawn a moth with tree branches for wings, hovering over two hands cupped together.

The next day, before he leaves, he comes bearing more presents, thank-you gifts. He made a card and wrote with radiant affection, vulnerability, and graciousness, the kind most adults cannot brave. He gives me an eraser (the one I borrowed when I couldn't find mine), a coloring pencil he has had for a month but hasn't used (he just looks at it adoringly at his desk, turning it over in his hands, for it's too sacred to use), a pear, a melted-and-reconstituted Hershey's kiss, a dime, a nickel, and five pennies. Other than the clothes on his back, these treasures are half his worldly possessions.

In the story of his life, the moment would read: Miss Reema waited until I left the room, to cry.

A dime, a nickel, and five cents. A drawing of a child's happiness. My love, you know I'm not one for holding onto possessions. I've never been attached to nickels and dimes. But these twenty cents, this drawing, I will keep forever.

JACOB LEAVES for a new school and so do I. I'm offered a full-time position at a daycare center. When I begin, the center director offers me a choice between the infants and toddlers. I choose the babies. At night, I continue to work on our book. We met our yearlong deadline; the first draft is complete. Now, I spend the evenings revising the manuscript, editing, cutting, or adding sections as needed. Revisiting chapters, I'm struck by the numerous realities I have lived. My love, I hope you haven't minded our recent, utter lack of drama, sex, and glamour. I have relished the difference and needed the break. I have orchestrated it. Momma will comment occasionally that I "should date." She worries about my nunnish life of celibacy, service, and children. I tell her, "Momma, don't worry. I'm trying to hear what my voice sounds like without having to consider a man's. You'll understand when you read the book."

To me, it makes sense in another way as well. You and I began this book as children. We'll complete it with children.

After a month with my babies, a calm settles in and the little ones thrive. The center director, though, then transfers me to the toddler room. Eight 1-and-a-half- to 2-and-a-half-year-old boys. Ask me not, how the entire class happens to be boys. They simply are.

"We need you to do in this room what you did with the babies," says the director.

"Okay. Thanks."

Thus now, here we are. I've been entrusted with the caregiving and safety of eight toddler boys.

It's like trying to lasso comets. It is barely contained chaos. The daycare center is part of a large private company. We maintain strict paperwork on each child. A summary of their day is sent home daily. We tally their presence on a spreadsheet every half hour. We follow a meticulous curriculum to foster development in six areas: cognitive, emotional, creative, physical, social, and executive function (learning to use a spoon, graduating from a sippy to a regular cup, and so on).

Children thrive when given healthy structure. Following rules, I change diapers every two hours. Eight boys. Eight hours, four changes per child, thirty-two diapers daily. I wear white latex-free gloves during the changes and also when serving breakfast, snack, lunch, and afternoon snack, at 8 a.m., 10, 11:30, and 3. They nap from noon to 2 on cots, each cot covered by a crib-sheet, each child covered by his blankie. How does one get eight toddlers to sleep simultaneously? You simply do.

We play in the playground twice a day at 10:30 and 3:30. I have a uniform: a navy blue T-shirt with the company logo, over a black long-sleeved shirt, running leggings, and my neon-pink Nikes. I've worn countless costumes, this one by far the humblest. I wear my hair in a bun to ward off lice.

Toddlers are orbs of need with a gravitational demand stronger than all the planets combined. They have one gear: extreme urgency and entitlement. A toddler hasn't concept of patience, compromise, fairness, and time. They need what they need now.

The emotional and physical demands are unlike anything I have experienced. I lose seven pounds in the first month. The teacher before me, who is now with the infants, lost eighteen. There is never a moment of stillness. They never cease to run, climb, bite, hit, cry, or want hugs. Carter wants to be picked up and held. Raymond loves cuddles but only as an extension of quality time, like reading a book to him, building with blocks, or playing with trucks. Dominic's a biter who doesn't need provocation. He takes out his pacifier and lunges. He likes the effect and attention—the scream from the other child, the tears, me running over.

Children are little stories. They each have their own reason and climate, some clearly discernable, others, less so. The other day, Dominic threw a wooden chair at me. A toddler-sized chair but bruising nonetheless. He stood there, watching, pacifier in mouth. Whenever these events occur, we write incident reports. The toddler and kindergarten classes tally the most.

While Dominic is aggressive, he is also exceptionally affectionate. He brims with hugs and wants to help in any way he is allowed. I have a small toy broom for him, for when I sweep after meals. He puffs his little chest with pride and joy from feeling included, purposeful, important, appreciated. I watch him, and my other little ones, and I wonder the way I always do with kids. I wonder the persons they'll grow into. How this moment will connect to the next and so forth, directing the footprint they'll walk. Daily, I write about exactly this, and it is stunning to live with one foot in my past, and one in their present.

While the boys sleep, another teacher comes in to relieve me for my lunch break. I use the time to run, then scarf down my meal. For the remainder of their nap, I make boards to display their art and activities with captioned photos explaining each lesson's purpose. The center prides itself on being a school. Although the children are tiny, each classroom resembles a regular classroom. Our responsibilities run the gamut of usual teachers. But where teachers have a salary, I earn $10 an hour, after taxes. They have prep-time after school. We're strictly on the clock. I punch in at 8 a.m. and punch out around 6 p.m., after I have swept, mopped, sanitized every surface, cleaned the bathroom, emptied the diaper pail, and taken out the trash. It has been four months now. 1,100 diapers.

I love it. It's the most egoless job I've ever worked. During the hours I write, I'm so conscious of myself and the way I fit into the largess of life. And over here, I'm nearly nameless, faceless, malleable, in a uniform and adapting to the needs of the children. I'm one in a team serving a larger mission. The women in this center are beyond hardworking and generous. Their selflessness is humbling and their stories, inspiring.

The teacher for the younger toddlers, from ages 1 to 1-and-a-half, is 65. Latina, five-foot even, mother of two, grandmother of five, she has worked in childcare for thirty-seven years. She is as fierce and bright as a freshly hewn sword. Raised in Texas, she and her parents picked cotton. She dropped out of school in the seventh grade to work. She got married at 18. Her husband was in the air force. This and her determination gave their life wings. I'm amazed at how physically strong she is as well. Her toddlers are smaller and don't run like mine, but she's performing the same labor as I am. Always smiling but stoic, committed to the task at hand. And like me, she is never without lipstick.

"Miss Reema," she says, her accent rich and curling like honey spilling from a spoon, "I never get too close to other teachers. But you," she wiggles her forefinger, "You dig into my heart."

She is my teacher. Another angel with whom I have been graced. Catholic, she speaks often of God and her faith, the things she has endured and witnessed. While we rub the children's backs and stroke their foreheads, to lull them to nap, we share our stories in whispers. The tales float in the darkened room, serenaded by lullabies wafting from a CD.

Our student population is extremely varied. Some parents pay the enormous tuition themselves. Others receive federal aid. Thus, the social, racial, and economic breadth of the school is vast, making it the most inclusive and varied environment I have ever been in.

Four of the eight boys don't have fathers. Where have our men gone? One decided to study at a Buddhist monastery, indefinitely. Another has a restraining order. Another decided he didn't feel like doing this family thing anymore. Another is in prison. Dominic's dad.

Months pass. Although they're exhausting, I love my toddlers. They care not a whit about my intelligence, attractiveness, talent, possibilities, or lack thereof. They desire only that I be present. That I give them authentic hugs and closeness, eye contact, and affection. Walking home one night, I realize why I'm so happy and fulfilled these days: giving is synonymous with my truth. With the children, with this book, I'm living as my complete self. Cheryl Strayed writes that her mother would say, to heal, grow, and nurture joy, "Put yourself in the way of beauty." I like to think that includes service—another manifestation of beauty.

There aren't any men working in our center. There are a few at other centers and of course, at corporate headquarters. At school meetings, I look at our teachers. Women from all ethnicities, walks of life, and educational backgrounds, gathered for one reason: to help raise this generation of kids. I swell with pride. I tumble into love and there I stay, in awe of our connective tale.

It is 8:15 a.m. The children munch pancakes and berries. The center director comes in to relay a message from Dominic's mom, about a diaper rash.

"She's a rude one," says my director, about the mom. "She's always complaining. Always, drama."

"True," I reply. "I feel for her though. I can't imagine being a single mom. She's barely in her mid-20s. To work all day, and have two kids to take care of. She drops them off at 6:45, meaning they're up by 5:30. Then, to admit to everyone, 'My husband's in prison.' That must be devastating. She must get judged so often."

My director smiles, shaking her head. "You feel too much. You know why he's in prison?"

"No."

"Rape."

Irony clenches my lungs. For eight hours a day, I'm the caregiver for a rapist's son.

"Thanks for telling me about the rash. I'll be extra zealous with the diaper cream."

The children finish breakfast. I sweep, mop, clean up the kids, sit them down to do some curriculum work. We're making kaleidoscopes from wax paper, paper-towel tubes, and colored plastic swatches. The children love their creations. How wondrous the world can be when viewed through different lenses.

Within seconds, I of the crystalline memory have forgotten Dominic's story. All I know is he needs his pacifier, a diaper change, a hug. He needs to be redirected from the sink, held back from hitting a classmate, fed, changed again, held again, comforted for his consequent tears that I held him back from hitting, soothed during his meltdown, changed again, fed, taken outside, kept away from the mud puddles, corralled during another tantrum. So on. So forth.

I forget and remember only to love.

Another teacher relieves me for my ten-minute break. When I return, the boys run to me, giggling. I'm hit with love so pure I hear music. It feels better than any standing ovation or admiring attention. My heart expands two new sizes.

I'm ambushed by a tangle of limbs and little torsos. The boys have decided it's time for a tickle mob. Carter can't quite say "tickle" yet. He inverts the syllables: "kittle, kittle, kittle!" Down we fall in a mess of laughter, squeals, and love.

This is my life.

GRATITUDE

GRATITUDE

✦

It's the week of Thanksgiving. My brother arrives. We surprise him with a belated birthday party. Momma cooks a feast. I bake his heart-shaped cake smothered with Twix and Maltesers. For his gift, I found an edition of the animal encyclopedia we loved as kids. There they are, our pink-bottomed baboons, bush-tailed possums, and spider monkeys. Our koalas, chinchillas, and gibbons.

My sister arrives a few days later. Downtown Portland is fantastic. Oregon is spectacular for hiking, skiing, snowboarding. But when we're all gathered, our parents can rarely pry us away from the family room, let alone the house. For work, my brother travels constantly. My sister runs hard in college. When we are home all we want is one another.

The two of them sit on the couch, laughing over a video on my brother's iPad. Dad's reading a book in an armchair kitty-corner to them. Momma's conjuring art in the kitchen, about ten feet away. I'm in an armchair across from Dad's. Snow flurries mist our windows. How the seasons have flown. We have grown closer as a family. I've initiated conversations previously untouched; they've started reading bits of this book. I have dismantled my little pink music box, and the notes have drifted away. Even echoes come to an end.

Next to Dad is a six-foot-tall birdcage he built from plywood and chicken wire. Two years ago, Momma bought four lovebirds. Presumably two males and two females but in actuality, three females and one male. She visited Bangladesh for a month and returned home to a gorgeous birdhouse Dad built as a surprise.

The male lovebird's love is fluid; he adores the yellow, green, and turquoise birds equally. His stamina doesn't suffer lapses or pause with seasons. He loves all three females all the time in an infinite continuum of spring that has sprung. The first year, none of the eggs grew into chicks. But this past winter, the birds began to breed.

We now have nine lovebirds. This house breeds love. The birds don't sing in the dulcet tones of Disney bluebirds but with a shrill, machine-gun tempo and volume. Dad hates the birds. He built them a home because they're Momma's lovebirds. Merlot, Chardonnay, Rosé, Riesling, Pinot, Ardbeg, Talisker, Johnny, and Jack.

Nine birds, Zekie, Lucy, Bagha the cat, and countless fish. All happy, alive, loved, and safe. Momma has taken Angel and Carlos, the bearded dragons, as her classroom pets. Other teachers have gerbils. Momma has dragons.

I think of our long list of childhood pets. It would have gotten crowded, but here, they would have been happy, alive, loved, and safe.

This year spent with my family has been heaven. I have traveled my orbit. How I love that another word for orbit is revolution. The aroma of Momma's cooking evokes a smile. From the moment I sat to write this book, there hasn't been a day that I have denied myself food—anorexia, my shadow self, has healed. Through writing, I've undergone the strangest phenomenon. With each page, as I have stood witness for my child-self as she experienced one trial after another, giving her the words I wish others had given me, I've grown to value and love her the way I would if I spent one day followed by the next with any child.

The love has carried into the present. The same savage protectiveness I feel for my siblings and for all the children I've cared for, I feel now for myself. The nourishment I would give any child, I give now to myself. Now that love has replaced pain, I haven't any desire to chase beauty or control. Here onward, the only power and purpose I will ever need and want is voice. By feeding my dream, I have starved my nightmare.

We, my love, are promise actualized. I love that every person in this room is far from perfect. No one is better aware of a person's flaws than that person's child, parent, or partner. Yet we love anyway. We choose to. We understand, forgive, and love anyway. Such sweet lunacy is possible. A simple miracle and, as you know, I'm a hedonist for those. The sound of the wind teasing the leaves. The way a peanut-butter and jelly sandwich can change a kid's day or a chapter in the right kind of book can change an adult's. The way my family manages to laugh anywhere, anytime, until Momma's voice bubbles and curls like caramel simmering in a pan and age proves mine does too.

I cup these moments like newborn hatchlings, humbled by the abundance available in life. Love is the truest legacy. For years I've wrung my hands into tight knots, worried with changing the world for the better. But, darling friend, a theory: as long as we are catalyzing love, we are doing precisely that.

Lucy is snuggling with Dad, Zekie with me. The birds, the kids, the woman singing and dancing over pots brimming with her magic, her face alit with bliss.

Were her sari made of silk, none of us would be.

LOVE, EVERMORE

LOVE, EVERMORE

✦

On valentine's day, 2015, I move from Momma and Dad's house into my own apartment. I have far more space than ever. And it's the first time my name is on a lease. Mine and only mine. My first night, sleeping on a brand new bed in my fiercely loved, ferociously personal space, I feel more peaceful and safe than ever before. No one can ask me to leave. Visitors arrive only if I invite them. I unpack and hang my line of cocktail dresses. I tuck my curling iron and makeup into drawers. I touch the mirror on the closet door and think, It has been nice to have this sabbatical. Our reflection smiles.

The apartment is enveloped in green innocence. Each room boasts large windows, plenty for you to choose from. The sun pours into each room. Here we are at last, the light-filled home I've longed for. In the living room, right in front of the main window, I place my desk, not the one from my sister's bedroom, but a hand-me-down, pass-me-forward, a desk she used in middle school. On my desk, I sit my laptop and my journal. As the end of this journey approaches,

I write my vows for the next few years. One is to use my voice to light the wicks of others. Another is a trip to Bangladesh and to Thailand, to visit the orphanage. I'd like to travel there, build, and write.

Today, as on all days, the sky keeps me company as I type. The beauty of the Oregon sky continues to undo me daily. Its magnificence is so rich it feels intentional, as though the colors and clouds know how to spill and spread to a mysterious design.

You and I, dear love, share this intuitive wisdom. We are each a sly seed poised for bloom. A revolution born to be ignited.

Our book is nearly complete. Writing it has felt like the most natural thing. Like someone called my name and I turned around. It makes sense. I've never had to look for you—you are always here. Thus, the words needed to fill our book haven't needed hunting—they simply exist. So much has felt difficult. But not this.

Every day, I run around a nearby dazzling lake. While running, I marvel over a truth as apparent as the sky, a truth I imagine you may have realized as strongly as I have: I've had to live exactly as I have. Every wound, character, experience, and skill has been used, to fill into my purpose. To say "I am grateful" wouldn't suffice. "I am in love" is more accurate.

I love what we have made, left to our own devices. When the world fails to provide the protector, healer, warrior, love, role, or opportunities we desire, we must genesis our own. Had I lived any differently, or been contracted to a man or a show, I wouldn't have written this book. It all fits so seamlessly that I now believe you and I belong to a larger story, moving to its own wild wisdom, propelled by our fierce will to prevail. Together, we have fought to protect and free the once-baby flame of my voice from the harsh winds of life. Now, full fire, we rise.

Healing. Release. Freedom. Gratitude. Love. Darling friend, how we have grown.

I have been pondering, more than ever, our entwined reality. You are an extension of me, this book an extension of us. You are my loving advocate. Perhaps then, I am something similar for you. Perhaps you have a physical form as well, somewhere, and I am your invisible friend.

Beyond my desk are trees and solitude for as far as the eye can see. Should I want, I could live a quiet life, never returning to New York or the public stage. Love, our private world is so cozy and kind. But in my blood lives a pulse that cannot be muted. Mine is a soul that refuses to do anything in a hidden, small, or deferential way.

After all, I was born to be a voice for those without one. I'd be betraying my calling were I to live inside the safe, sheltered anonymity of a quiet, private life. Power only responds to power. I must use the wealth of all I've learned to illuminate the world's darkness.

I will walk outside—on my terms. I am the spine of my life; only my name appears.

I look at today's blazing sunset. Believing you can hear me, I speak aloud these words:

Look at the sky. When she wishes to explode in a fury of flamingo, peach, lavender, and indigo, she will. When she desires to be an expansive swatch of calm blue, she is. When she longs to spill oceans of rain, she follows her yearning.

The sky does not hesitate. Neither shall we.

I AM 31. Dear Love, I need to let you go.

Not entirely, but still. We have been two kids marveling, chasing, running from the storm. We have completed these thirty-one years. Now, you need to live your story, I need to live mine, each on our own.

I sit now on a grounded plane, about to fly to New York. My return. Passengers are filing in while I write.

Love, I will miss you. Momma and Dad tell each other about their day, their private intimacy so simple, rare, and exquisite that I cry. You are my closest incarnation of that sacred belonging one hopes to find. You, my imaginary best friend I never released. This book, our clear, unhurried line of love. You have helped me find what I've sought.

Thank you. Endlessly. The plane is now gathering speed, sprinting toward the horizon.

You have listened. You watched me grow. Pain, insecurity, trials, anger, confusion, the near-reckless desire to speak and be heard, to love and be loved deeply, these are our common specialties. Our fault lines are where our paths intersect, where your shards align with mine. Reasons to never feel less or better than anyone. Reasons to never feel alone.

How lovely that being human soothes the ache of being human.

I have lived a startling, beautiful life. I have survived and continued not because of confidence but because I have a confidante. Call thyself any name thou wish. Imaginary friend, art, muse, reader, guardian angel, higher self, inner voice, God. Your name matters little. What matters is I have always been able to call it, and you have always replied. You sprang from my need to feel love and give love. You, myself, this, we are a truth:

All I need, I have.

Hold onto that.

Now, tuck me away. You have been my person in the dark. Perhaps I have been yours. But now, love a warm body and love in the walking world. While I am sad we have completed these pages, I know we have only begun.

A formidable tomorrow, we soar now as a limitless sky.

I leave you with what we have always known. I am here. I love you. I am yours.

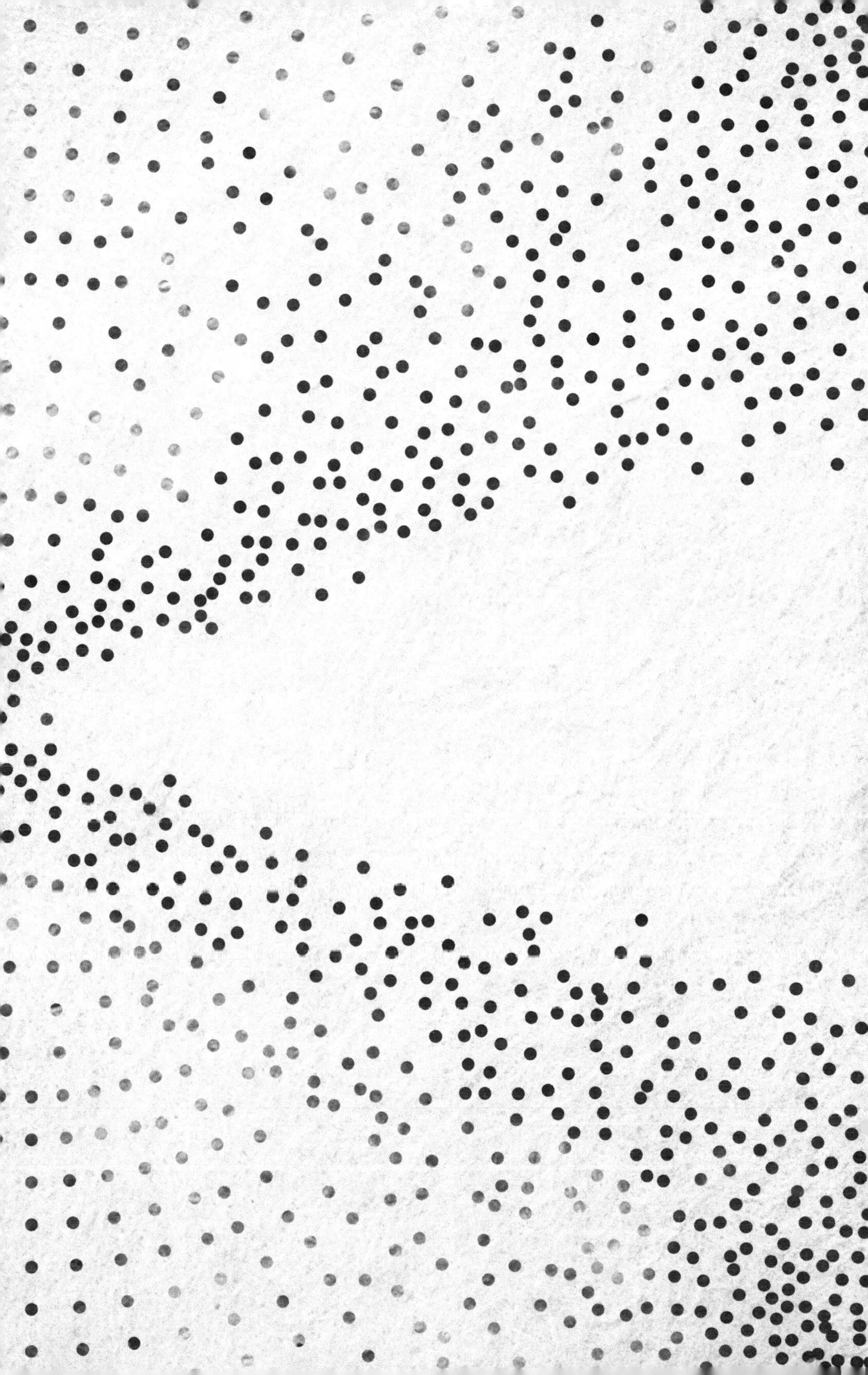

Acknowledgments

Dear Momma, this book is a love letter to honor our journey. You were and remain my first muse, teacher, and my forever best friend. I wouldn't be the person I am were it not for your love, and I wouldn't be the woman I am had you not needed me the way you did. Fighting for your voice ignited mine. Once, we were girls together. Now, formidable women. It is my deepest pride, gift, and joy to walk and grow beside you. I pray that we keep being born for each other, in many lifetimes over. Thank you for being mine and letting me be yours. My love for you is limitless.

Dear Papa, this book is a love letter to honor how far we've come. I am who I am for I am your daughter. Thank you for teaching me so much about love, life, and family. Thank you for teaching me the art of debate and cognitive thinking. Those skills have saved me time and again, by allowing me to create emotional distance from painful situations, to look at trauma or heartbreak as an observer, to mine the darkness for art and light. One of my deepest prides in this life is having fought to nurture and achieve authentic closeness with you. My love for you is timeless as the sea.

Dear Dad, this book is a love letter to honor the laughter, lightness, and home you brought into our lives. Until you, we grasped at the meaning of such elements. Until you, I never felt like a kid. You are a gift that surpasses definition. Thank you for being the person I can talk to about the most obscure books, ideas, and films, who is as obsessed and delighted as I am about things most others find mundane. Thank you for bringing Christmas, new beginnings, and hugs into our world. I love you beyond words.

Dear Shehtu, this book is a love letter to honor the immense privilege of being your and Raya's older sister. Loving you two is the spine of me. My role as your sister is the quality that has informed my life more than any other. Every day, my overriding and underlying goal is to make sure you two are happy and safe. You inspire me continually, with your intelligence, kindness, integrity, ethics, work ethic, calm, and grace under fire. I am so proud of the man you are. Daily, you renew my hope in male-kind. You are the standard to which all others are held. Our towering mountain, steady and mighty. I love you endlessly.

Dear Raya, this book is a love letter that would not be without you. Thank you, infinitely, for asking me the question that led me to answer by writing these pages. Were it not for you, *I Am Yours* would not have the unclothed vulnerability, immediacy, and intimacy that are so deeply its core. You have always been this: the question that provokes the answer. The world needs your audacity. It is one of your many gifts. Polish, use well and kindly, and never let your fire be taken from you. I am always here, to hold, hear, watch over, protect, and love you. My love for you knows no condition or measure.

Dear Nana Bhai, I love you so much that still, it hurts. Not a day passes that I do not think of you, and I work to do your soothsaying proud. I will keep writing, living, fighting, aspiring, building, creating. Thank you for seeing me so clearly. Thank you for teaching us about kindness, grace, compassion, integrity, and generosity. I know that you can read my words. They belong to you, and wouldn't be without you.

Dear Naan, I love you so much, beyond any words can aptly describe. You are my lullaby—I love calling you and talking to you, every night.

Thank you for taking care of me so well. Your sweet words stay with me every night as I fall asleep, and inspire me to wake, work, fight, and aspire every day.

Dear Mirel, you are our wish come true. You have brought such certainty, joy, and completion to our family. Every day holds peace, now, for I know Shehtu will feel only love, kindness, protection, sweetness, and care, for he gets to journey this life with you. I'm so lucky to call you sister, friend, and fellow writer and lover of books. Thank you for gifting me *Wild* by Cheryl Strayed, for my 30th birthday. This book would not be without you. I love you so much and then some.

Dear Lidia, beloved mentor, friend, heart-warrior, and misfit. I became who I am because of your words, found and read in your books, years ago. Then, my words led me to you. How perfect and seamless, this love. An indelible bond forged through the power and reach of woman-art. The world knows and loves you for your formidable fire and mind. How I love and revere you for those too. Yet it is the deep embrace, capacity, tenderness, and might of your tremendous *heart* that undo and renew me daily. My love, respect, and gratitude for you are boundless.

Dear Diana, you are my living angel. How immeasurably lucky I am to know you, to call you neighbor, spiritual mother, sister, and mentor. The bounty of your heart astonishes me daily. Thank you for seeing, hearing, and knowing me so clearly. Thank you for loving me, all of us, so generously. You nourish and give, inspire and raise, so many souls. The world is so much better, having you here. I love you like the flowers admire and gaze upon the sun, thinking, Look at that light.

Dear Lisa, my gratitude, respect, and love for you are immeasurable. Life changed, and I knew *I Am Yours* would be safe and solid in this world, the second you said, Yes. You were my reach, dream, wish, and I knew we would fit, mind, soul, and vision, the moment I began researching agents. Your grace, acumen, and instincts are unparalleled. You have mentored this book and me. Thank you for trusting me, for taking a leap of faith on an unknown, for reading my audacious query and thinking, this could actually work. Every word and advice you share, I hold as gold.

Dear Nora, nightly, I thank the stars (aloud) for having brought you into my life and the life of *I Am Yours*. As *I Am Yours* was my first stab at writing and submitting a manuscript of any kind and length, you were my first editor, ever. Thank you for teaching me leagues about writing, revision, editing. It is so evident, how perfect this path has been: to write first in utter solitude, without any other voice in the room, then, to connect and revise not with just any person, but you.

Lisa and Nora, after our first lunch date in New York, I called my brother and said, "I don't know how to receive and process all this warmth and kindness—no one's ever spoken to me, about me and my work, so lovingly. I'm going to have to build a new muscle for this." My shock and amazement over this phenomenon and fortune have yet to fade. Thank you both for your brilliance, generosity, and kindness that rise and give far beyond the norm. You have believed, so I have, too.

Dear Dayna, the depth and detail of your care, dedication, genius, and heart astonish me daily. I am forever grateful that of all publishers, you are mine. Each day spent in our publishing process affirmed for me that I would not want to have published *I Am Yours* with anyone else but you and Amberjack. I will evermore sing your praises to the world.

Dear Cassandra, could a more perfect fit between author and editor ever be? I am endlessly grateful that the universe conspired to align its elements so that your path crossed mine, for this precise journey, at this precise time. The similarities and parallels we share are astounding. To know that you understand and feel my story, and me, so deeply, has let me trust you entirely, and this is among the kindest, biggest gifts an author can hope for. Your brilliant pen, exceptional brain, profound wisdom, and deep ocean of a heart inspire me, continuously.

Lisa, Nora, Dayna, and Cassandra, whatever the future holds for *I Am Yours*, I feel I have already succeeded. I feel complete euphoria, peace, triumph, pride, and gratitude, for I have the abundant honor and joy of walking this path with you. You have my heart.

Dear Jeff, thank you for seeing me so clearly, present and future.

Jason, thank you for starting it all, and seeing the hero within this book.

Rayne and Monique, thank you for taking care of everything so beautifully.

Kayla, Jenny, and Gaby, thank you so much for finding, reading, and championing me and *I Am Yours*. Jenny, thank you for your wise eyes and caring heart. My boundless gratitude to you all.

Melissa, Patrick, Victoria, Diana, and Juliette. This book says it all. Thank you for being my home. You have my heart, forever.

Jennie, Graeme, and Victory. Thank you for giving me a place to rest my head. Jennie, thank you for teaching me so much. I carry your wisdom, and our memories, always. I love you.

Abe, thank you for being my first reader. Having you to talk to let me know that I was writing to my imaginary best friend from childhood, whom I never released. These pages would not be as they are without your serendipitous presence in my life. The depth and generosity of your spirit inspire me continually. I love you to darn bits.

Lora, you are compassion, kindness, generosity, and grace, personified. I am endlessly grateful to know you. Thank you for loving these pages while they were still finding their way. Your faith and love buoyed mine. Your voice is the sweetest elixir, for a parched and tired wanderer. You have my heart, evermore.

Grandpa and Grandma, thank you for welcoming us home. Laura, thank you for being the first to read *I Am Yours*, long before I received news of publication. Your faith and love mean the world to me. Shoili, Trudy, Mary, thank you for always being an ear, a hug, and a heart for me to fall into. Russ, thank you for giving me a graduation ceremony. Your heart is unlike any other. Mike, thank you for always knowing, always hearing the story beneath the story. Ashish, my soul-twin, I love, admire, and cherish you more than I can aptly express. Phupu, thank you for paving and encouraging the path. Maheen, Rimona, Charlie, Binni, Shumon, Sonia, Rana, David, and Ratna, thank you for everything. My beloved family, I love you all so much that at times, it nearly overwhelms me. So, I'll just keep writing, to honor the abundance that is our singular, gorgeous brood.

Srini Rao, thank you for loving *I Am Yours*, for reading it in two days, for our friendship, and for introducing me to Lisa. Annie Lee, thank you for your enormous heart, for our uncanny bond, and for introducing me to Srini.

My immense gratitude to Literary Arts for selecting me as your 2018 Writer of Color Fellow. Your financial gift helped see *I Am Yours* through its final stages.

Madeleine Brookman, Sumanah Khan, Scott Edwards, Jeremy Patlen, Elena Katzap, Stef Sifandos, Domi Shoemaker, Jenny Forrester, Jen Pastiloff, Gemma Hartley, Susan Moore, Terese Mailhot, Lilly Dancyger, Hillary Brenhouse, Sarah Clark, Marcelle Heath, Marisa Seigel, Karen Karbo, William Popp, Mahira Kakkar, Rachita Reddy, Leilani Franklin-Apted, Sarah Ingles, Erica Kiefer, Laura

Harrison Palmer, Dana Seagraves, Kim Augustijns, Natasha Choy, Brooke Estin, Erika Ellis, Evan Cabnet, Don Lunan, Monica Drake, Abbey Gaterud, Tom Black, Tony Brown. Each of you has played a pivotal role in my life. You have my infinite gratitude, love, affection, and loyalty.

My teachers, in the order we met: Kirt Nieft, Linda Greer-Wegener, Joan Estin, Richard Cameron, Dinah Helgeson, Julie Puckett, Rob Allison, Freda Williams, Mary Stange, Cindy Warner-Dobrowski, and Brenda Perkins. Thank you. You watered the young girl in whom you saw promise. I remember every class, every word, every lesson. My gratitude is as vast as your wisdom.

My faraway sister and mothers. Without knowing, you have helped raise and mentor me from afar. I wouldn't be the woman, artist, activist, and leader I am without you. Thank you Oprah Winfrey, Maya Angelou, Gloria Steinem, Toni Morrison, Pema Chodron, Isabel Allende, Anne Lamott, Cheryl Strayed, Elizabeth Gilbert, Glennon Doyle, and Brené Brown. My limitless love and gratitude are yours.

And to you, beloved reader, thank you. Without you, for whom would I write, to whom would I speak? This book contains my entire heart. I am yours.

About the Author

REEMA ZAMAN is an award-winning author, speaker, and actress. She was born in Bangladesh, raised in Hawaii and Thailand, and presently lives in Oregon, United States. She is the Oregon Literary Arts' Writer of Color Fellow, 2018. Her work has been featured in *The New York Times*, the Dear Sugars podcast, *The Guardian*, *The Rumpus*, *Narratively*, *B*tch Magazine*, *SHAPE*, *VIDA Review*, and elsewhere. She proudly partners with various organizations, like Girls Inc. and Literary Arts, to empower diverse voices and mentor the next generation of leaders.

Reema travels widely to speak and perform. Her body of work and events schedule can be found at **reemazaman.com**. For social media, as the only Reema Zaman in the world, she is easy to find.